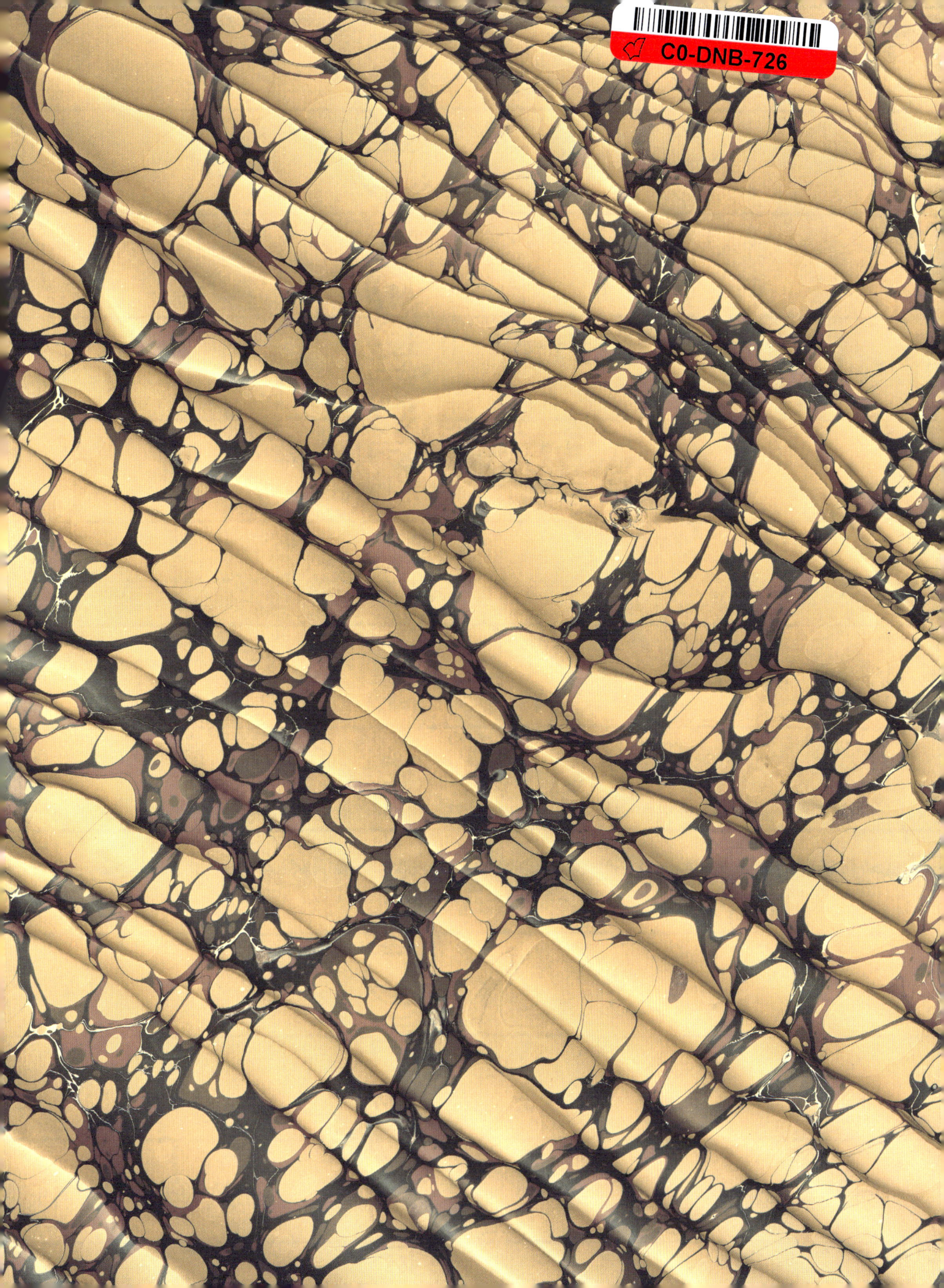

THE VOLKSDEUTSCHEN IN THE
WEHRMACHT · WAFFEN-SS · ORDNUNGSPOLIZEI
IN WORLD WAR II

Rolf Michaelis

Schiffer Military History
Atglen, PA

Translation from the German by Dr. Edward Force.

Book Design by Stephanie Daugherty.

Copyright © 2012 by Schiffer Publishing.
Library of Congress Control Number: 2012942401

All rights reserved. No part of this work may be reproduced or used in any forms or by any means – graphic, electronic or mechanical, including photocopying or information storage and retrieval systems – without written permission from the copyright holder.
  The scanning, uploading and distribution of this book or any part thereof via the Internet or via any other means without the permission of the publisher is illegal and punishable by law. Please purchase only authorized editions and do not participate in or encourage the electronic piracy of copyrighted materials.
  "Schiffer," "Schiffer Publishing, Ltd. & Design," and the "Design of pen and inkwell" are registered trademarks of Schiffer Publishing, Ltd.

Printed in China.
ISBN: 978-0-7643-4261-5

This book was originally published in German under the title,
Die Volksdeutschen in Wehrmacht – Waffen – SS Ordnungspolizei
by Michaelis-Verlag.

We are interested in hearing from authors with book ideas on related topics.

Published by Schiffer Publishing Ltd.
4880 Lower Valley Road
Atglen, PA 19310
Phone: (610) 593-1777
FAX: (610) 593-2002
E-mail: Info@schifferbooks.com.
Visit our web site at: www.schifferbooks.com
Please write for a free catalog.
This book may be purchased from the publisher.
Try your bookstore first.

In Europe, Schiffer books are distributed by:
Bushwood Books
6 Marksbury Avenue
Kew Gardens
Surrey TW9 4JF, England
Phone: 44 (0) 20 8392-8585
FAX: 44 (0) 20 8392-9876
E-mail: Info@bushwoodbooks.co.uk.
Visit our website at: www.bushwoodbooks.co.uk

Contents

Foreword 4

History of the Ethnic Germans 5

Recruiting Ethnic Germans to the Wehrmacht, Waffen-SS and Ordnungspolizei 14
    The Individual Ethnic Groups 22
        Belgium (Eupen-Malmedy) 22
        Denmark 23
        France (Alsace-Lorraine) 24
        Italy (South Tyrol, Trentino, Kanaltal & Belluno) 26
        Croatia 28
        Luxembourg 30
        Poland 31
        Romania 33
        Serbia 38
        Slovakia 40
        Slovenia 42
        USSR 44
        Hungary 48

The Ethnic Germans in the Wehrmacht 54

The Ethnic Germans in the Waffen-SS 59
    Units with High Ethnic German Numbers 59
        4th SS Police Panzergrenadier Division 59
        6th SS Mountain Division "Nord" 68
        7th SS Volunteer Mountain Division "Prinz Eugen" 74
        8th SS Cavalry Division "Florian Geyer" 80
        11th SS Volunteer Panzergrenadier Division "Nordland" 86
        17th SS Panzergrenadier Division "Götz von Berlichingen" 90
        18th SS Volunteer Panzergrenadier Division "Horst Wessel" 94
        22nd SS Volunteer Cavalry Division 100
        23rd SS Volunteer Panzergrenadier Division "Nederland" 103
        24th Waffen Mountain (Karstjäger) Division of the SS 108
        31st SS Volunteer Grenadier Division 111
        37th SS Volunteer Cavalry Division 112

The Ethnic Germans in the Ordnungspolizei 115

Appendix: Highly Decorated Ethnic Germans 132

Bibliography 135

Foreword

Some 650,000 ethnic Germans from all over Europe served in the German troops during World War II. The concept of *"Ethnic German"* (*"Volksdeutsche"* in German) defined those people were *"of German origin in speech and culture"*[1], but lived in other countries and held foreign nationality. By adding occupied territories to the German Reich, they were obligated to serve, volunteered as natives of allied countries, or were, in a somewhat unjust manner, enrolled in German units by force.

This book is intended to offer an overview and summary of the action of foreign and borderland Germans who served with the Wehrmacht, Waffen-SS and Ordnungpolizei. In the process, such questions will be answered as: When and how were they enlisted? How were the legal prerequisites created? In which units did they serve, and where did they see action?

This publication is not only a work of military history, but also of social history, which also touches on the history of the ethnic Germans before and after World War II. But it cannot reveal the sorrow that the war brought to the people. The flight, displacement and deportation of the Germans and ethnic Germans from 1944 on also cost some two million of them their lives.

In hopes of offering the public an interesting book on this subject, I thank not all of those who contributed to the composition of this book, particularly my father and Herr Möckel for their proofreading.

Rolf Michaelis
Berlin, March 2011

---

[1] Message from the *Reichsminister* and Chief of the *Reichskanzlei* Lammers, dated January 25, 1938, to the Highest Reich Offices to define the term *"Volksdeutscher."*

The History of the Ethnic Germans

The concept of *"volksdeutsch"*[2] was originated in the autumn of 1933 by the founding of the *"Volksdeutscher Rat"*[3] and thus replaced the formerly used designation of *"borderland and foreign Germans."* As an important criterion for whoever was evaluated as such was, first of all, knowledge of the German language. For the so-called Borderland Germans, they were the German minorities that had come into being because of boundary changes after World War I, while the so-called Foreign Germans were designated as those who lived in their own settlement areas in other countries, mostly since the Middle Ages.

The most extensive emigrations from German principalities took place in the 18th century. After the end of Turkish rule in eastern and southeastern Europe thousands of so-called colonists were sought by the Russian and Austro-Hungarian monarchies to resettle the lands that had been won back. The Russian Czarina of German origin, Catherine the Great, made known on July 22, 1763 that she would allow foreigners to settle in the thinly populated part of the Empire along the Volga River in the Saratov district. To make settling in the unprofitable area interesting, she guaranteed special benefits, such as:

- free practice of religion
- no taxes or contributions for 5 to 30 years
- interest-free loans for all purchases
- freedom from military service *"for all time"*
- their own autonomous community and school administrations
- cost-free assignation of 30 to 80 desjatines (= ca. 1.1 ha.) of land by the crown to every family
- payment of travel costs if the immigrants were unable to.

About 27,000 settlers from Hesse, the Palatinate, Northern Bavaria, Northern Baden and the Rhineland followed this call. The reasons were based, above all, on the free practice of religion and, on the other hand, after the many wars, very pragmatically of an economic and political nature.

Czar Alexander I approved, with an act of February 20, 1804, the settling of German colonists in the Black Sea area, the present-day Ukraine. As opposed to the manifesto of 1763, the emigrants had certain requirements to fulfill:

- possession of at least 300 Gulden
- a good character testimonial
- good agricultural knowledge (especially in wine production)
- available training as artisans.

Czar Alexander II, in a decree of June 4, 1871, ended the previous benefits to the German colonists. After military service became obligatory, the pacifistic Mennonites emigrated (mostly to America). A census showed that in 1897 some 1.8 million Germans lived in Russia. The main settlement areas were some 3000 colonies on the Volga, in the Ukraine, Crimea, Transcaucasia and Bessarabia. During World War I an impressive 300,000 Germans served in the Czarist army. The Russian Revolution of 1917 resulted in numerous changes in policy and society. The new minority policy brought about, on February 20, 1924, the founding of an autonomous Socialist Soviet Republic of the Volga Germans. From this area around Saratov and Samara they were deported to Siberia in the summer of 1941.[4]

In southeastern Europe the Hungarian King Geysa II invited German colonists in the 12th century to protect the borders against Mongol and Tatar attacks and for the economic development of the area. As in Russia, the settlers were promised various privileges, such as:

---

2   The opposite was *"reichsdeutsch",* which indicated the Germans living within the boundaries of the German Reich.
3   The *Volksdeutsche Rat* itself was to form a centralization of the German ethnic policy and formed the forerunner of the ethnic German central position.
4   See the chapter "The Individual Ethnic Groups: USSR."

– free choice of judges and pastors
– legal standing according to their own customary rights
– freedom from tolls
– free markets

On the other hand, the German immigrants agreed to pay the king an annual sum and, if necessary, to do military war service. Settled in the Siebenbürgen area, they held autonomous status for a long time. Only the Austro-Hungarian Dual Monarchy set up in 1867 brought the end of their autonomy.

When the Banat, also located in southeastern Europe, became a province of the Holy Roman Empire of the German Nation in 1716 after 150 years of Turkish rule, Emperor Charles VI settled the area with some 15,000 German farmers and artisans. They were supposed to make the desolate region fruitful again. During the following reign of Empress Maria Theresia, a further 22,000 German settlers moved into the Banat. A third wave of colonization under Emperor Joseph II brought another 30,000 Germans into the Banat.

Concepts such as *"Banat Swabia"* and *Siebenburegen Saxony"* did not correspond to their actual origin and were used only as collective terms for the colonists. Most of them came from the Rheinpfalz, Rheinhesse, Trier and Lorraine areas west of the Rhine, as well as from Franconia. Smaller numbers came from Bavaria, Swabia and the Austrian Alpine lands. In the 18th century, the colonists were guaranteed freedom from taxation plus their own government and legal system. After the Banat was assigned to the Hungarian state in 1778, though, a more restrictive policy and Hungarization ensued.

In the 18th century too, the *"Sathmar Swabians"* settled in northwestern Romania. Later this region came under Hungarian rule. Besides the willing settlers, Protestants from the Austrian lands, the so-called Landler, were also forcibly resettled in Siebenbürgen for religious reasons.

The German settlement areas in eastern and southeastern Europe as of 1914.

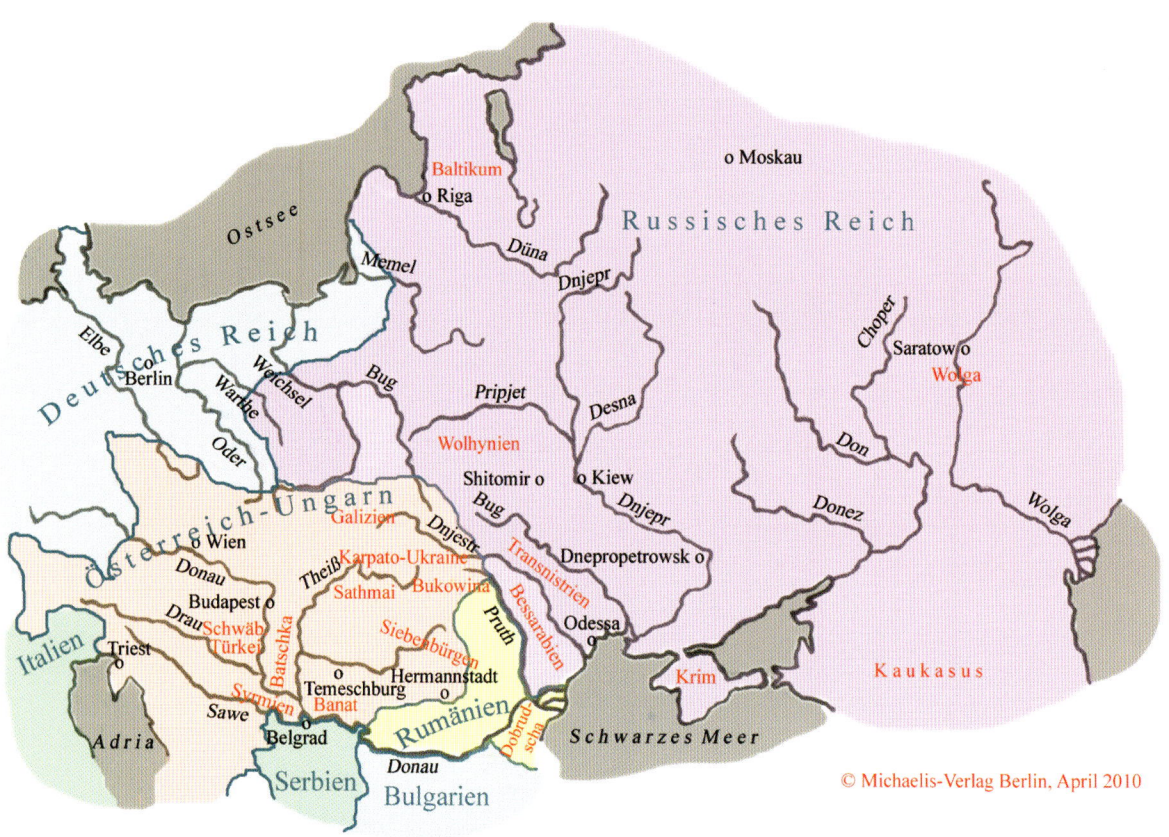

Based on estimates made in 1919, there lived before 1914 outside the German borders:[5]

    2,000,000 Germans in Russia, including
        120,000 in Wolhynia and Podolia (Transnistria)
        400,000 in Bessarabia, Tauria and Cherson
        400,000 on the Volga
        200,000 in the Baltic provinces of Russia.
    500,000 Germans in France
    50,000 Germans in Denmark
    5,000 Germans in Sweden
    2,600 Germans in Norway
    120,000 Germans in Britain
    200,000 Germans in Switzerland[6]
    2,500,000 Germans in Hungary, including[7]
        88,500 in the central mountains of Hungary
        138,000 in Swabian Turkey between the Drava and Danube
        71,000 in Slavonia
        73,500 in Syrmia
        254,000 in Siebenbürgen
        82,000 in Bukovina
        94,000 in Bessarabia
        15,500 in Dobrudja
        404,000 in the Banat
        200,000 in the Batschka
        165,000 in the Carpathian regions
        38,500 in Western Hungary
        34,000 in Slovenia
    50,000 Germans in Romania
    7,000 Germans in Serbia
    25,000 Germans in Bosnia
    3,500 Germans in Bulgaria
    15,000 Germans in Turkey
    1,000 Germans in Greece
    56,000 Germans in Italy
    3,000 Germans in Spain
    1,000 Germans in Portugal.

Here all were counted as Germans who spoke a German dialect. Among the Alsatians in France, for example, this was Moselle Franconian. As also recognizable in Switzerland or Luxembourg, no personal link with Germany need exist. With the end of World War I the Dual Monarchy broke into pieces. The Siebenbürgen Saxons and Banat Swabians voted in 1919 to join the kingdom of Romania. The new Romanian state guaranteed the minorities not very many benefits, but treated them more liberally than, for example, as was the case with ethnic Germans in Hungary. Lower Styria, Southern Carniola and Oberkrain went to the newly created Kingdom of the Serbs, Croats and Slovenes, which also took a chauvinistic policy toward their German minorities. The Sudetenland was given to Czechoslovakia. After their loss in World War I, the German Reich lost:

Alsace-Lorraine	to France
Much of West Prussia (minus Danzig)	to Poland
Much of Posen Province	to Poland
Upper Silesia	to Poland
Eupen-Malmedy	to Belgium
Memelland	to Lithuania

---

5   Class, Heinrich, *Deutsche Geschichte*, Leipzig 1919.
6   According to a census of December 1, 1910, Switzerland had some 3,750,000 inhabitants, of whom 2,600,000 spoke German, 796,000 French, 300,000 Italian and 41,000 Rhätoromanic. The overwhelming majority of the German Swiss, though, oriented themselves socially and politically with France.
7   The figures for the individual settlement areas were taken from the census of 1940-41.

In 1935 the German Foreign Institute in Stuttgart published figures showing how large the portion of German- or German dialect-speaking populations in Europe was:

66,000,000 Germans in the German Reich
400,000 Germans in Danzig
6,500,000 Germans in Austria
150,000 Germans in Belgium with Eupen-Malmedy
5,000 Germans in Bulgaria
60,000 Germans in Denmark with North Schleswig
23,000 Germans in Estonia
6,000 Germans in Finland
1,700,000 Germans in France with Alsace-Lorraine
2,000 Germans in Greece
20,000 Germans in Great Britain
250,000 Germans in Italy with South Tyrol
70,000 Germans in Latvia
10,000 Germans in Liechtenstein
120,000 Germans in Lithuania with the Memel district
290,000 Germans in Luxembourg
100,000 Germans in the Netherlands
5,000 Germans in Norway
1,371,000 Germans in Poland,[8] including

383,000 in Posen-Pommerellen
90,000 in Upper Silesia
40,000 in the Teschen region
60,000 in the Olsa region
360,000 in Central Poland
67,000 in Eastern Poland
71,000 in Galicia

2,000 Germans in Portugal
800,000 Germans in Romania
6,000 Germans in Sweden
2,950,000 Germans in Switzerland[9]
15,000 Germans in Spain
700,000 Germans in Yugoslavia

33,000 in Lower Styria[10]
17,000 in Gottschee
20,000 in Bosnia
170,000 in Croatia and Slavonia
460,000 in Voyvodina (Banat, Batschka and Syrmia)

3,500,000 Germans in Czechoslovakia
600,000 Germans in Hungary
1,000,000 Germans in European Russia

In the process of National Socialistic (ethnic) policies, Austria was taken into the German Reich in March 1938. After discussions in peaceful terms with the victorious powers of World War I, various regions separated by the treaty of Versailles rejoined Germany. In October 1938 the Sudetenland and in March 1939 the Memelland thus became parts of the German nation again.

During the Empire, the foreign ethnic German peoples were looked upon amiably by the state, but this policy changed in the Third Reich. To a great extent, the foreign Germans were supposed to give up their long years of living in other lands and *"come home to the Reich."*

The background for this was described by *Ministerialrat* Globke in 1943:

> The external posts that were worthless or made untenable are … a gain for total Germanism: At some time the national Germanism, which cannot be strong enough for its tasks that arose in Europe, will have new

---

8 This number states the situation as of 1939.
9 See footnote 6.
10 Lower Styria and Gottschee were also called the Drava Banat.

strength added to it; then Germanism, particularly in the newly gained regions in the East will be strengthened by the settling of such Germans, who have proved their colonizing capabilities, sometimes for centuries."

The German settlement regions in the boundaries of 1937.

On October 6, 1939 Hitler announced the return to the Great German Reich of groups of people who had been scattered in Eastern Europe. On the next day he named Himmler to be *"Reichskommissar for the solidification of the German people"*. His main tasks were the return of emigrants and the formation of the new German settlement areas in formerly Polish territory on the Warthe and in West Prussia. Thus the resettlings were a concentration of Germans in Europe. Influenced by the strongly propagandized success of Germany, hundreds of thousands followed, even though with mixed feelings, *"the call of the Führer."* Himmler took over the *"Volksdeutsche Mittelstelle (VoMi)"* originally founded in 1936 and elevated it to a main department in 1941. The leader of the office was *SS-Obergruppenführer* Lorenz.[11]

In October 1939, in the course of the new ethnic policy, the resettling of Baltic Germans began. During December 21, 1939 and January 31, 1940 the return of the Wolhynian, Galician and Narev Germans followed. In September 1940 resettlements from Bessarabia and northern Bukowina, plus Dobrudja and southern Bukowina took place. In the West, the resettling of at first barely 70,000 ethnic Germans from the occupied parts of France to Lorraine began on May 14, 1941. On the very next day, after the end of the Balkan campaign, came a German-Croatian treaty by which southern Styria (North Slovenia) was joined to the German Reich. One can see with what unbelievable speed the resettlements were made. On August 31, 1941 there already came a German-Italian treaty by which the approximately

---

11 Werner Lorenz was born in Pomerania on October 2, 1891, and took part in World War I, ultimately as a lieutenant in the Prussian air forces. Joining the NSDAP (Nazi Party) in 1929 and the SS two years later, he became a member of the Prussian Landtag (Congress) and the Reichstag in 1933. Named an *SS-Gruppenführer* at the end of 1933, he directed the *SS-Oberabschnitt* (superior district) "Nord" (North) in Hamburg from 1934 to 1937. Promoted to *SS-Obergruppenführer*, he became the director of the Ethnic German Liaison Office in 1937, and in June 1941 he was named the chief of the newly formed SS Headquarters of the Ethnic German Liaison Office. Arrested after the war, he was released in 1955. He died in Hamburg on March 13, 1974.

Berechtigt zum tragen einer Faustfeuerwaffe

Gültig für 1941

Dienstausweis Nr. 84

Der Werner Wriedt

geb. am 10.6.02. zu Kiel

wohnhaft in Berlin W Am Karlsbad 20

ist als Mitarbeiter im Umsiedlungskommando der Volksdeutschen Mittelstelle tätig. Alle Staats-, Wehrmachts- und Parteidienststellen werden gebeten, dem Inhaber jeden erforderlichen Schutz und jede Unterstützung zu gewähren.

Berlin, den 25. Jan 1941

Der Beauftragte des Führers für Umsiedlungen

Eigenhändige Unterschrift des Inhabers

Service credentials for a member of the Resettlement Command of the Ethnic German Mittelstelle.

A souvenir book for members of the 8th SS Totenkopf Infantry Regiment who handled the resettlement of the Wolhynian and Galician Germans.

Dienstausweis Nr. R 2001

Der SS-Schütze Eduard Jundt

geb. am 7.8.16.

in Kolmar/Elsaß

ist als Angehöriger

im Kommando des Reichsführers-SS Hauptamt Volksdeutsche Mittelstelle in den besetzten Gebieten der Sowjetunion tätig. Alle Staats-, Wehrmachts- und Parteidienststellen werden gebeten, dem Inhaber jeden erforderlichen Schutz und jede Unterstützung zu gewähren.

Berlin, den 6.10.43.

Der Reichsführer-SS
Der Chef des Hauptamtes Volksdeutsche Mittelstelle

SS-Obergruppenführer und General der Polizei

Eigenhändige Unterschrift des Inhabers

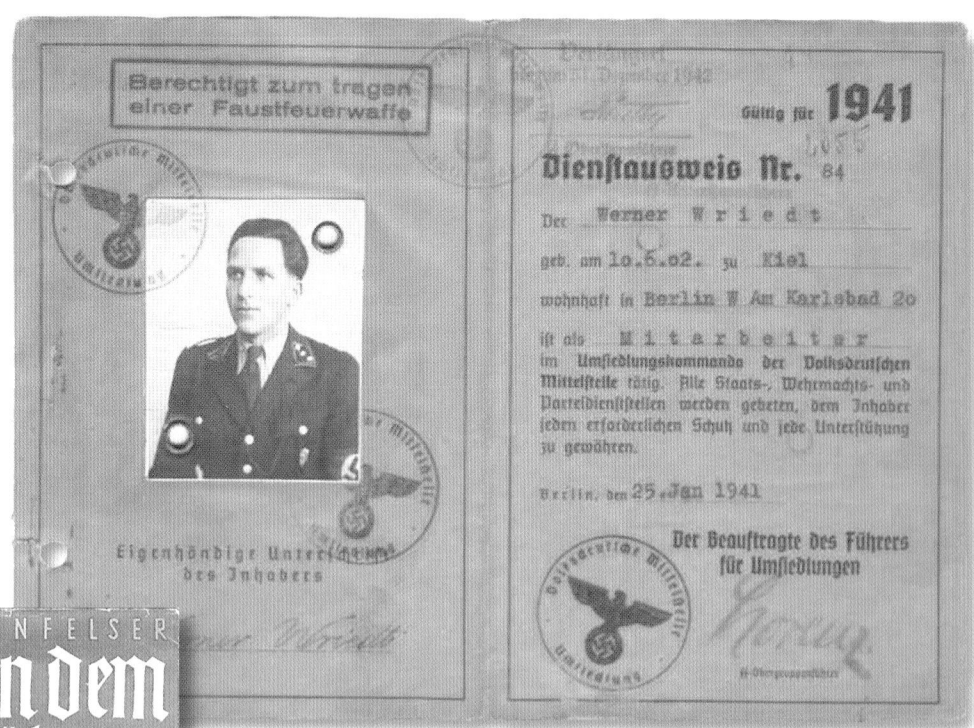

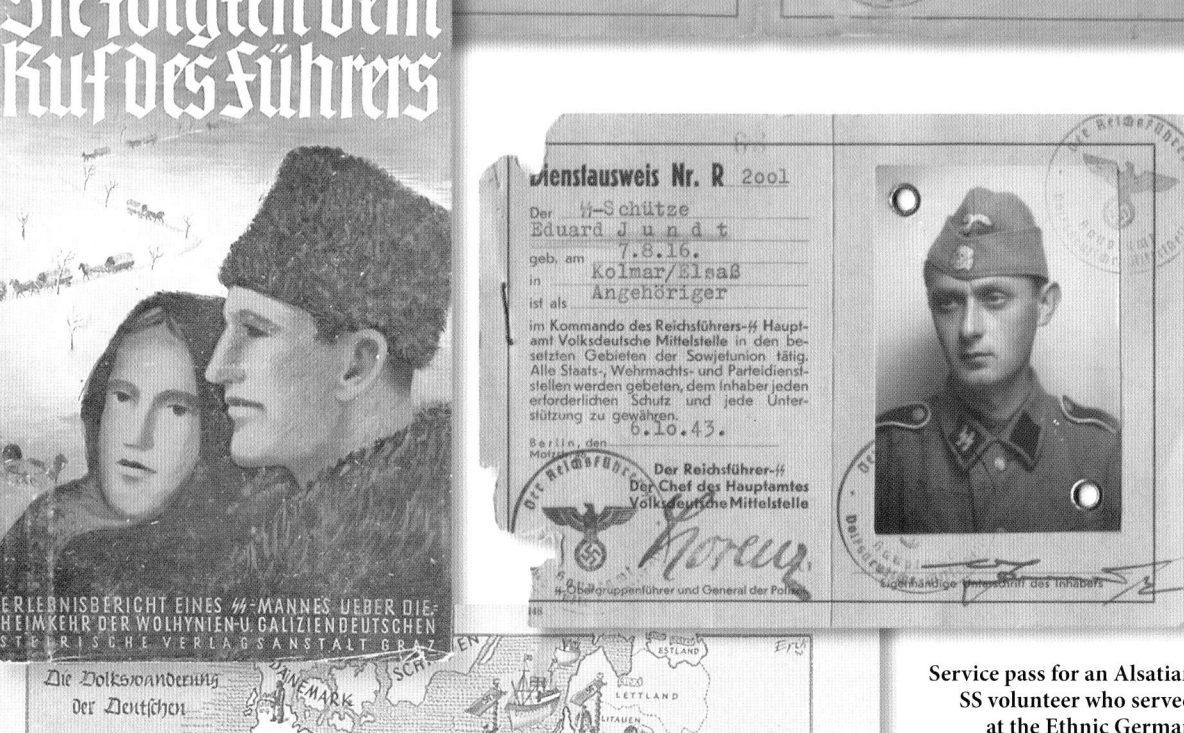

Service pass for an Alsatian SS volunteer who served at the Ethnic German Mittelstelle headquarters.

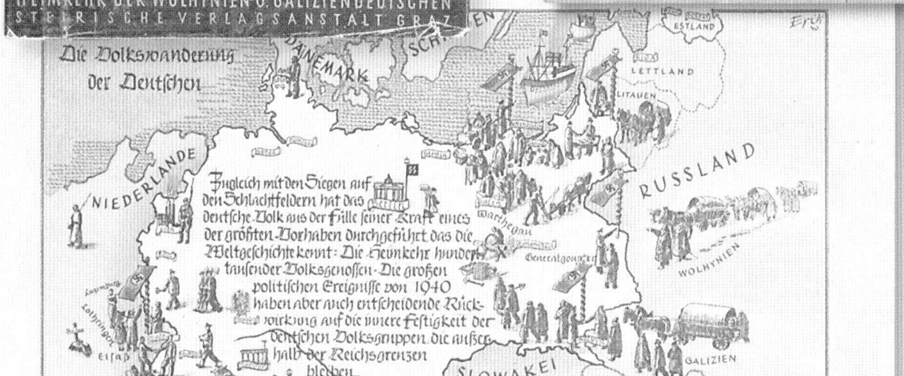

Propaganda material for the *"Umsiedlungen des Führers"* of 1941.

13,500 Gottschee Germans from the Laibach area were to be resettled in southern Styria between November 1941 and February 1942.[12]

The German settlement regions in the borders of 1942.

© Michaelis-Verlag Berlin, April 2010

The resettlers from, among others, the portions of the USSR occupied by the Wehrmacht had already reached the total of barely 500,000 in the Wartheland by the end of 1941.[13] Of them, 120,000 were still housed in sometimes very improvised resettler camps in July 1942. The others had had taken over towns forcibly depopulated by Poland *en masse*. In this respect, the deportation of the Poles into the General Government,[14] plus the murder of the Jewish population, should not be forgotten.[15]

Until July 1, 1942 the Staff Headquarters of the *Reichskommissar* for the unification of German ethnicity made the following numbers of resettlings known in a report:

Estonia and Latvia	72,643
Lithuania	50,744
Wolhynia and Galicia	134,655
Narev Region (eastern General Government)	30,631
Bessarabia	93,548
North Buchenland	43,538

---

12 More exact figures are found in observing the individual groups of peoples.
13 For the ethnic Germans in the absorbed regions, Hitler introduced the *"Staatsangehoerigkeit auf Widerruf"* on April 25, 1943. This meant for the ethnic Germans (especially in the Wartheland and later in northern Italy and Slovenia) that they were now obligated to do military service, but after the war their German citizenship could be renounced again (sic!).
14 By the end of 1942, 365,000 Poles were already pushed out of the absorbed regions.
15 Michael Alberti: *Die Verfolgung und Vernichtung der Juden im Reichsgau Wartheland 1939-1945*, Wiesbaden 2006.

The three stations of the resettlers:

Ethnic Germans leave their former settlement region in Eastern Europe to find a new home in the Warthegau and West Prussia.

On March 16, 1944 the *Gauleiter* of the Wartheland, Arthur Greiser, welcomed the millionth resettler.

In the center of the picture is the Higher SS and Police *Führer* "Warthe", Heinz Reinefarth.

In the late summer of 1944 the flight before the Red Army began.

South Buchenland	52,107
Dobrudja	15,072
Romania (old kingdom)	9,732
Gottschee (city)	14,270
Laibach and scattered settlements in Laibach Province	15,072
Bulgaria	848
Remaining Serbia	1,575
Ingermannland (area between Estonia and Leningrad)	4,344
Greece	144
Total	523,851

When the Red Army won back great portions of the Ukraine including Crimea in the spring of 1944, the evacuation of about 125,000 Black Sea Germans into Transnistria ensued.[16] After the front changed in Romania on August 23, 1944, about 100,000 ethnic Germans also fled from the Banat and Siebenbürgen from mid-September to early October. Those who remained, who believed that the movement of ethnic groups meant that the threatening situation of the German Wehrmacht would soon be set right again, or who did not want to leave their home and property, became victims of being overpowered, expropriated and deported.

Surprised by the political developments in Romania, Hitler forbade any evacuation of the ethnic Germans from the Batschka to the West. The First General Staff Officer of the 31st SS Volunteer Grenadier Division, formed of ethnic Germans, remembers this:

> "The Division Commander Lombard had spent the night of October 5-6, 1944 with the Syr Battle Group. When he came back to Neuverbas in the morning, the Ia reported as a special event that the leader of the ethnic Germans' Mittelstelle Lorenz had gone to the district administration in Sombor with the Führer's order, by which the Vatschka Germans must not be resettled in the West. They must let themselves be rolled over by the Soviets and then create partisan groups if possible. A psychologically dramatic high point almost without equal. Lorenz was asked by Lombard to come to him at once, as the Herren Dr. Kraemer and Spreitzer of the Batschka command had suggested to him during the night. For after all, the division bore the responsibility for the security of the hundred thousand Batschka Germans in the eyes of the population.
>
> Lorenz agreed without delay. The result of the talk between him and the division commander was that both drove to the German embassy in Budapest. The distance was more than 300 km, and for weeks already, no safe discussion could be carried on with Budapest. And only a talk carried on personally with Himmler allowed the hope that this order from the Führer would be lifted.
>
> By means of a 100-watt radio of the division, set at half way, a radio link was set up between Budapest and the Ia. Arrival in Budapest about 10 P.M. The messenger had full understanding. The fast talk was reported. The good fate wanted it; Himmler was reached at once.
>
> **The Messenger:** Reichsführer, with me are Obergruppenführer Lorenz and Oberführer Lombard, who must speak to you on an urgent matter. Before I turn you over to the Obergruppenführer, may I stress that I agree fully with their suggestion? Here he is.
> **Lorenz:** Reichsführer, it is about carrying out the Führer's order, of which you know, regarding not resettling the Batschka Germans. I'll turn you over to Oberführer Lombard.
> **Lombard:** Reichsführer, I beg you most obediently to work it out tonight that the Führer's order be lifted. It concerns the families, parents, women and children, of the men in my division…
> **Himmler:** (He had until then just said "Heil Hitler, Lombard, what is it?") Lombard, You know that an order from the Führer is sacred to me!

---

16   An event that was to be repeated frequently in Southeast Europe, in which not all ethnic Germans did not join those who fled. Some of them even stuck with the Communist Party, hoping (in vain) that in the future, despite the defeat of Germany, they could continue to live in their present settlement areas.

Lombard: I know that, Reichsführer, and that is why I am talking with you. For only the Reichsführer can show the Führer that this order cannot be carried out. The mass of the division will desert, and whether the Hungarian Batschka Germans stay lying there as the order says, might…

The Reichsführer said something, but Lombard spoke on and ended with his final sentence, composed during the whole trip: Reichsführer, it is a matter of the Führer being falsely advised. I stress, so falsely that the advisor could only have been an ignoramus.

A pause for a split second, that seemed like eternity. Then Himmler said he would try it and call back. Lombard should remain reachable where he was now.

Long after midnight a Führer talk from headquarters. Lorenz was requested. Führer's order lifted. Tell Lombard that the Führer makes him responsible for the smooth development of the evacuation of the Batschka until and including setting them across the Danube.

When the division commander got back to Neuverbas at dawn, the Ia reported as a special event: The evacuation has begun!"

A *Führer's* order that sounded the same, the Higher SS and Police Leader for Serbia, Montenegro and Sandzak *SS-Gruppenführer* Behrends, informed the leader of the German ethnic group in Serbia, Dr. Janko. While in resettlements in Croatia since the spring of 1944, about 100,000 ethnic Germans from Syrmia, Slavonia and Croatia had been evacuated out of the partisan areas before the Red Army, this had been neglected in Serbia. On their own initiative, families and communities tried to escape Soviet capture in a well-planned flight. This succeeded for only about 10% of the ethnic Germans in the Banat.

At the end of December 1944, the deportation of some 12,000 ethnic Germans from the Serbian Banat and the Batschka already took place, plus 32,000 from Hungary and some 40,000 from Romania, to forced labor in the USSR. The war's end on May 8, 1945 also often brought, for the resettled ethnic Germans, repatriation to their old homeland and dragging away to Siberia or Asia. In the course of the release of tension between East and West, as of 1986, though, more and more *"Spätaussiedler"* from the USSR could settle in Germany. In 1992 alone there were about 200,000 people. Also from Yugoslavia, Romania and Hungary to Germany, the descendants of the onetime colonists were allowed to emigrate, and so in 1990 out of what once were well over two million ethnic Germans, there were only a meager ten thousand in their old Southeast European settlement regions.

RECRUITING ETHNIC GERMANS TO THE WEHRMACHT, WAFFEN-SS AND ORDNUNGSPOLIZEI

"When a group of people is led halfway passably, then all volunteers report and those who do not report voluntarily have their houses smashed."

So wrote the Chief of the SS Main Office, *SS-Gruppenführer* and *Generalleutnant der Waffen-SS* Berger, on June 16, 1943 in a letter to the Chief of the *SS-Führer* Main Office, *SS-Gruppenführer* and *Generalleutnant der Waffen-SS* Jüttner. It shows clearly what German *"ideals"* amounted to, and that the leadership was interested mainly in a quantitative increase in their possibilities for recruitment.

The enormous losses in the Russian campaign were an important reason for recruiting the ethnic Germans. On February 15, 1942, the Chief of the Army General Staff, *Generaloberst* Halder, stated the total losses on the easternfront from June 22, 1941 to February 10, 1942 as 945,973 men.[17] That was almost one third of the eastern army (3.2 million soldiers). By April 20, 1942 the losses already amounted to 1,148,954 men. That amounted to some 36% of the eastern army. Thus every third soldier had been killed, wounded or reported missing.

---

17 Of them, 21,130 officers and 681,236 other ranks were wounded, 7,872 officers and 191,278 other ranks dead, and 729 officers and 43,730 other ranks missing.

While the Wehrmacht <u>after</u> the collective naturalizing automatically had access to the ethnic Germans, the Waffen-SS was already trying <u>before</u> that to recruit volunteers[18] among the returning men in the immigrant camps. The Ordnungspolizei drew members, primarily older men, from both of the aforementioned groups.

Since the Waffen-SS at first could recruit only in a very limited way among the service-eligible native Germans and naturalized ethnic Germans, they tried as of 1940 to recruit ethnic Germans in allied countries, at least in a small way.[19] Since these men were eligible for service in their native lands, this required discussions with the applicable governments. The majority of the ethnic Germans, though, continued to serve at first in the lands of their birth. For example, there were some 35,000 ethnic Germans in the Romanian armed forces. There were no fewer in Hungary. Surprisingly, this suited Himmler's wishes at first. The Leader of the Ethnic German Mittelstelle, *SS-Obergruppenführer* Lorenz, described this in a letter to Himmler, looking back to August 7, 1942. At this time the *Reichsführer-SS* had basically changed his viewpoint:

> "*Volksgruppenführer* Schmidt had received your order agreed to by the Foreign Office to see to the full-scale induction of ethnic Germans from Romania into the Romanian armed forces. This order, the implementing of which was and is extremely unpopular among the ethnic group has been carried out beyond expectation by the ethnic-group leaders. The ethnic-group leader and his colleagues joined in themselves and expect the highest war decorations."

After negotiations with the Romanian officials, the latter released 1000 ethnic Germans for the first time in June 1940. In 1941 Hungary approved the same thing. During the Balkan campaign, ethnic Germans living in Yugoslavia also volunteered for German units in 1941.

But it took until 1942 before the Waffen-SS could achieve its first success in the inclusive recruitment of ethnic German *"volunteers"*. At the same time, the Wehrmacht had already inducted some 100,000 ethnic Germans from Eupen-Malmedy, the former Poland, and settlers from the USSR and South Tyrol.

From 1942 on, various agreements with the southeast European allies, by which ethnic Germans could join German units. Now Himmler expected every ethnic German to be aware of his *"folkish"* military duty.[20] A full-scale move of ethnic Germans to the Wehrmacht of their native lands was no longer spoken of. Instead, he said on July 13, 1942:

> "The German ethnic groups in the entire Southeast must be clear that for them their military duty is based not on legalities but on the iron law of their ethnicity,[21] and in fact from their 17th to their 50th, and if necessary 55th, year of life."

Himmler's change of mind was of a pragmatic nature. When Romania, among others, very much decreased its involvement on the eastern front at the beginning of 1943 after the debacle at Stalingrad, he wanted at least to secure the service of the ethnic Germans. Thus there were further discussions with the allies. To be allowed to take the ethnic Germans, Hitler advised them to negotiate for the resettlement of the ethnic Germans from the Southeast after the war. Thus he opposed the basic wishes of Romania and Hungary.

With the renunciation of the former high mustering requirements, the Waffen-SS now took in all ethnic Germans from the Southeast. They took in the younger men themselves and made older men available to the Ordnungspolizei. Since those who volunteered were generally not given citizenship, Hitler decreed on May 19, 1943 that foreigners of German ancestry who served in the Wehrmacht, the Waffen-SS, the Ordnungspolizei or the Todt Organization automatically received German citizenship.

---

18 The volunteers thus recruited did not make up significant numbers.
19 On September 27, 1940, a treaty was made on initiative among the German Reich, the Empire of Japan and the Kingdom of Italy. This three-power pact was joined by Hungary on November 20, 1940 and Romania three days later. On November 24 Slovakia joined, as did Bulgaria on March 1, 1941. On July 15, 1941 the independent state of Croatia joined the so-called Steel Pact.
20 Himmler had a particular influence on the leadership of the ethnic groups, also in his position as Reich Commissar for the Unification of German Ethnicity.
21 The political developments in the ethnic groups outside Germany were similar to those in the German Reich. Beyond that, the idea of being German was surely stronger in many ethnic German settlements than in Germany itself!

A former ethnic German recruited by the Waffen-SS described the interesting question of how the various recruitings were handled by the Wehrmacht, Waffen-SS or Police:[22]

> "As for the objections to the mustering and recruiting by the Waffen-SS, nobody made them known to us, and I did not know of any case of objection, or of desertion from this formation. More than enough disagreements on this question existed, and the older men in particular could not understand that there were two armies and why the sons of foreign Germans were preferentially assigned to military units of the Waffen-SS. In addition, one did not at all understand the background and purposes in this matter that applied to the great majority of our countrymen. There were well-read farmers among us who often said: Yes, yes, now we are sold, and if Germany loses the war, we are miserably lost. Unfortunately, this saying came true. Men who avoided service, whether in the SS, Hilfspolizei (Hipo), Einsatzstaffel (ES) or Wehrmacht, just did not exist among us, not even when one saw that the war was 75% lost; they were always accustomed to doing what was ordered from above (the state) because it was the citizen's duty."

Starting with the more than 6.5 million ethnic Germans in Europe on whom the German Reich could have called, they provided some 650,000 men for military service. Of them, the following numbers served:[23]

- 370,000 (57%) in the Wehrmacht, including
    - 310,000 in the Army
    - 40,000 in the Luftwaffe
    - 20,000 in the Navy
- 210,000 (32%) in the Waffen-SS, and
- 70,000 in the Ordnungspolizei

Of the approximately 370,000 Wehrmacht members, there came:

- 6,500 from Belgium (Eupen-Malmedy)
- 118,000 from France (Alsace-Lorraine)
- 15,000 from Italy (South Tyrol, Trentino, Kanaltal and Belluno)
- 2,000 from Croatia
- 8,500 from Luxembourg
- 76,500 from the former Poland
- 3,000 from Romania
- 500 from Slovakia
- 60,000 from the USSR, and
- 2,000 from Hungary

Of the approximately 210,000 ethnic Germans who were inducted into the Waffen-SS, there came:

- 160,000 in the SS Panzer Grenadier and Cavalry divisions, the 6th SS Mountain Division "Nord", the 7th SS Volunteer Mountain Division "Prinz Eugen" and the 31st SS volunteer Grenadier Division.[24]
- 30,000 in the seven SS panzer divisions
- 15,000 in the various work and concentration camps
- 5,000 in smaller contingents (some 1000 men) in SS special units, SS corps Troops and SS main offices.

In terms of origin, the ethnic Germans were especially concentrated in the following units:

1,500 from Denmark	5th SS Panzer Division "Wiking"
	11th SS Volunteer Panzergrenadier Division "Nordland"
25,000 from Croatia	7th SS Volunteer Mountain Division "Prinz Eugen"
	13th Waffen Mountain Division of the SS "Handschar" (Croatian No.1)
	23rd Waffen Mountain Division of the SS "Kama" (Croatian No.2)
	Guard units of work and concentration camps

---

22 Documented by the Center against Expulsion, Wiesbaden.
23 The absolute numbers were calculated from the average recruitment quotas between 1940 and 1945. The relative figures are based on the total numbers of ethnic German volunteers and enlisted men. Reduced to the three parts of the Wehrmacht, they give the following percentages: Army 85%, Navy 4% and Luftwaffe 11%.
24 The actions of these units will be described later.

8,500 from Poland	3rd SS Panzer Division "Totenkopf"
	4th SS Police Panzergrenadier Division
	Guard units of work and concentration camps
58,000 from Romania	4th SS Volunteer Panzergrenadier Brigade "Nederland"
	11th SS Volunteer Panzergrenadier Division "Nordland"
	SS Rifle Battalions 500 and 501
	24th Waffen Mountain (Karstjäger) Division of the SS
	Contingents of various Waffen-SS units
	Guard units at work and concentration camps
17,000 from Serbia	7th SS Volunteer Mountain Division "Prinz Eugen"
	Guard units at work and concentration camps
9,000 from Slovakia	in various Waffen-SS units
70,000 from Hungary	6th SS Mountain Division "Nord"
	8th SS Cavalry Division "Florian Geyer"
	11th SS Volunteer Panzergrenadier Division "Nordland"
	17th SS Panzergrenadier Division "Götz von Berlichingen"
	18th SS Volunteer Panzergrenadier Division "Horst Wessel"
	22nd SS Volunteer Cavalry Division
	31st SS Volunteer Grenadier Division
	37th SS Volunteer Cavalry Division
	Guard units at work and concentration camps
	Various Waffen-SS units
4,000 from Alsace-Lorraine	2nd SS Panzer Division "Das Reich"
	Various Waffen-SS units
500 from Luxembourg	Various Waffen-SS units
500 from Belgium	Various Waffen-SS units
1,000 from Slovenia	Waffen-SS mountain units
5,000 from South Tyrol	24th Waffen Mountain (Karstjäger) Division of the SS
	31st SS Volunteer Grenadier Division
10,000 from the USSR	various Waffen-SS units, particularly:
	10th SS Panzer Division "Frundsberg"
	17th SS Panzergrenadier Division "Götz von Berlichingen"

The different, higher numbers, found mainly in documents of the time and postwar publications, among the ethnic Germans from Hungary indicate that the men were basically taken by the Waffen-SS but then released in part to the Ordnungspolizei or the armament industry. The Germanic Leitstelle in the SS Main Office noted on this subject on September 7, 1943:

> "Between the High Command of the Wehrmacht and the *Reichsführer-SS* there is agreement that the ethnic Germans should serve only in the Waffen-SS. Which units of the Waffen-SS (field units under the command of the OKH or *SS Totenkopf* units under exclusive command of the SS) the ethnic Germans were assigned to is exclusively up to the *Reichsführer-SS*. The ethnic Germans born in or before 1907 should, if possible, not be called into the Waffen-SS at all, but be available to the German Volksgruppenführung for certain tasks. But if there is danger that these older men would be inducted by the homeland, then the applicable ones must also be inducted into the Waffen-SS, but then be placed with the Police."

Of the approximately 70,000 men in the Ordnungspolizei, there came approximately:

```
 6,000 from Alsace
 2,000 from Lorraine
 1,000 from Belgium (Eupen-Malmedy)
 1,000 from Luxembourg
 5,000 from the former Poland
16,000 from the USSR
17,000 from South Tyrol and the "Alpenvorland" and "Adriatisches Küstenland" operation zones
 9,000 from Slovenia
 3,000 from Hungary
 5,000 from Serbia
 5,000 from Croatia
```

Chronologically, the induction of the total of ca. 650,000 ethnic Germans was as follows:

		Wehrmacht
1940	Belgium, Poland,[25] USSR,[26] South Tyrol[27]	26,000
1941	Belgium, Poland, USSR, South Tyrol	28,000
1942	Belgium, Poland, USSR, South Tyrol, Luxembourg, Alsace-Lorraine, Slovenia	55,000
1943	Belgium, Poland, USSR, South Tyrol, Luxembourg, Alsace-Lorraine, Slovenia	91,000
1944	Belgium, Poland, USSR, South Tyrol, Luxembourg, Alsace-Lorraine, Slovenia	92,000
1945	Belgium, Poland, USSR, South Tyrol, Luxembourg, Alsace-Lorraine, Slovenia	28,000
		370,000
		Waffen-SS
1940	Romania, North Schleswig, Poland	4,500
1941	Yugoslavia (Croatia, Serbia), Poland, Hungary, USSR	5,500
1942	Croatia, Poland, Serbia, Hungary, North Schleswig, Luxembourg, Alsace-Lorraine, USSR	45,000
1943	Croatia, Poland, Serbia, Slovakia, Hungary, Romania, Luxembourg, Alsace-Lorraine, USSR	70,000
1944	Croatia, Poland, Serbia, Slovakia, Hungary, Romania, Luxembourg, Alsace-Lorraine, USSR	80,000
1955	Croatia, Slovakia, Hungary	5,000
		210,000
		Ordnungspolizei
1939/40	Luxembourg, Belgium, Poland, USSR	6,000
1941	Luxembourg, Belgium, Poland, USSR, Hungary	6,000
1942	Luxembourg, Belgium, Alsace-Lorraine, Poland, USSR	6,000
1943	Belgium, Poland, USSR, South Tyrol, Luxembourg, Alsace-Lorraine, Slovenia	20,000
1944	Poland, USSR, South Tyrol, Luxembourg, Alsace-Lorraine, Slovenia	29,000
1945	South Tyrol, Slovenia	3,000
		70,000

Recruiting elicited very varied responses among the ethnic Germans. The unusually restrictive policy toward the ethnic groups resulted in their generally having little interest in serving in their homeland. Beyond that, they hoped to be treated better in German units. Many were impressed by the German success and regarded themselves as Germans. The Hungarian German Kurt Schnell recalls:

> "In July and August of 1943 the recruiting took place in North Siebenbürgen – then belonging to Hungary. It was done on the basis of an agreement between the German and Hungarian governments. A recruitment command consisting of SS leaders came to Siebenbürgen and went from town to town. Wherever there were German communities, they enlisted all suitable men between 18 and 35. It was called "volunteering" then. If he had not gone freely to the Waffen-SS, we would have had to do our military service with the Hungarian Army. So it was scarcely difficult for anybody to volunteer.
>
> At the end of September 1943, we were inducted. The departure of those volunteers for the Waffen-SS from Sächsisch-Regen and its surroundings took place in a ceremony at the market place in the presence of the entire populace, the fathers of the church, the Hungarian city commandants, the mayor and the political leaders of the German ethnic group in Hungary. Before the departure there was a service with the Last Supper in the church.
>
> Along with the solemnities, in which many speeches were compelled, we marched to the schoolyard of the German high school, where the women and girls decorated the arrivals with flowers and invited us to a

---

25 From the annexed eastern regions.
26 Resettlers from the Soviet Union, inducted by the Waffen-SS and National police, also in part from the remaining ethnic Germans in the USSR.
27 Until 1943 these were chiefly the so-called "Optanten" (opters).

festively decorated table for dinner. Late in the afternoon we went toward the railroad depot, where we were packed into cattle cars with straw on the floors, and taken to Vienna.

After about three days we arrived in Vienna in the evening and were awaited at the south station. We marched to the arsenal, where we spent the night on planks in a big hall. The next morning we were to turn out at once, and our presence was loudly checked from the prepared lists. Then we were inspected again and X-rayed in order to confirm our usefulness. Then came a division into groups, who were assigned to various units. Some went to Cracow, others to Hamburg, and our group, mostly from Regen and the area, for example Botsch, Zepling, Eidisch, Klausenburg, were ordered to a unit in France. Late in the evening we were loaded into cattle cars again, and after traveling several days we reached Nimes in southern France, where trucks awaited us. From then on we belonged to the SS Field Replacement Battalion 10."

Hans Hedrich enlisted voluntarily as a Romanian German. His reasons are typical of the ethnic German volunteers up to 1943:

"Born in 1924 in Mediasch, Siebenbürgen, I volunteered for the Waffen-SS at the beginning of 1943. I believed I must do my part in the German people's fight for existence, as the war was portrayed to us then. There was, of course, also moral pressure from the organizations of the German ethnic groups in Romania and the social environment."

Among the forcibly recruited ethnic Germans as well as those whose homelands were annexed to the German Reich and thus subject to military service, the motivation was usually much less. There were numerous ethnic Germans who were opposed to Hitler and thus had no interest in war service on the German side. There arose isolated resistance groups who joined partisan groups.

Beyond that, older ethnic Germans in particular did not want to endanger their existence and declined to volunteer. But after all ethnic Germans were rounded up very pragmatically, the operative ability of the units who were filled with them was somewhat decreased. In the end, more than 60% of the Waffen-SS men were forcibly recruited foreign Germans. The former *SS-Unterscharführer* Ludwig Mückl recalls the induction of the ethnic Germans in Hungary:

"At the beginning of 1944 it was suddenly said that we would be taken away from the front and sent to the Reich for new assignment. Such things were said again and again, but this time it was true. In a bad snowstorm we loaded our vehicles at the depot in Winniza, in the Ukraine. The train had no passenger cars, so we were compelled to live and sleep in our vehicles. Fortunately we had fur coats and felt boots. The trip lasted many days, nobody knew to where, but gradually it became clear to us that we were not going to the Reich, but southeastward to Hungary. Via Debrecen and Szeged the trip ran to Esseg in Croatia. The farther southward we went, the more springlike the weather became.

In the Batschka there were very many ethnic German villages, some on the Hungarian, some on the Croatian side. One day the order came to call in and take away all ethnic German men of service age. That was a drama, and often the women acted like hyenas because they didn't want to let their men go."

Though the motivation of the ethnic Germans was varied, so was the attitude toward them in the Reich. Some felt resentment. Here it was all but unimportant whether they had volunteered or been forcibly inducted. Because of the varied social and economic development in the previous decades, the ethnic Germans were often seen as *"somewhat backward"*. The commander of the SS Panzergrenadier Division "Totenkopf", *SS-Gruppenführer* Eicke, said of his unit of ethnic German soldiers:

"Among them are large numbers whom one could describe as mentally of little value. Many cannot read or write German. They do not understand the command language and incline toward disobedience and shirking. Orders given are usually not carried out, with the reason: They don't understand what the superior wants of them. Cowardice is promoted in this way."

"Beloved Parents, 10/13/44

First I greet you, praised be Jesus Christ. I greet all who are at home and still alive. I was wounded at the front and Szymanek was also wounded. We had to draw back and he lay there, so he was captured by the Russians.

So go to Szymena and tell her that he was wounded, we left him behind and he was captured by the Russians. I felt so bad about him, but the Russian artillery fire was so heavy that there are only 40 men in our company. I end this letter, for I must go with a scouting troop, and it is so hard for me to say that if I have no luck I shall never see my homeland again.

I greet you in the name of the Lord,

Your son Paul

Farewell, brothers and sisters, farewell."

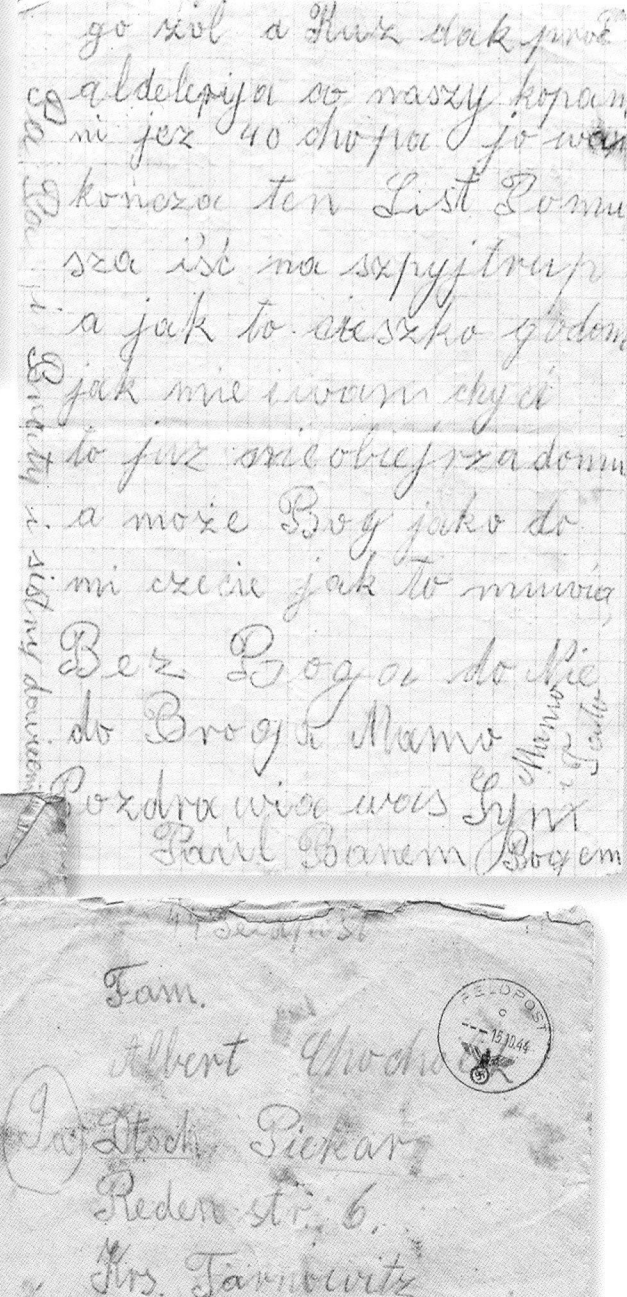

An impressive document of the mood in October 1944. Interesting is the fact that it expresses the thoughts of one who did not know German but was obviously a very devout ethnic German from Poland, presumably a Silesian.

Field mail from *SS-Sturmmann* Paul Chocholik, field post number 12 658 B (1./SS Police Panzergrenadier Regiment 7).

Pawel Palasz Collection

The special problem of language difficulty is also documented by a document from the 225th Infantry Division. By "*Führer's* orders" bearers of the Close Combat Badge in Gold were to be withdrawn from front service to share their experiences with recruits in the replacement army:

> "The Division asks Knight's Cross bearer *Oberleutnant* d.R. Alfons Bialetzki, who is to be assigned to the replacement troop unit by order, <u>not</u> to be transferred there.
> *Oberleutnant* Bialetzki is not suitable for use in the replacement army, because of his abilities and upbringing at home. He is the type of front soldier who is most at home in battle. He is completely unsuited to use in the weapon schools of the Army, since he speaks a very poor, somewhat broken German with a pronounced Silesian accent. Bialetzki was born in Silesia and is probably of Polish ancestry. In my division since March 1944, Bialetzki has since then proved to be an outstandingly brave soldier and an inspiration to his men. He could continue to do exemplary service in combat, but I fear that he will fail to be of any use to the replacement army."

The German command was thoroughly aware of such discrepancies. In order at least to introduce a certain change, Himmler turned explicitly to the handling of ethnic German volunteers in January 1943:

> "The education and treatment of the ethnic Germans and Germanic volunteers in and out of service is a task that more than ever requires the fullest attention of the responsible SS commanders and lower leaders.
> With poor and uncomradely handling, no men will be won for us and the idea of our Führer. This is only possible with understanding for the situation of these volunteers, who, far from the Reich – without German schools and cultural establishments – have led a hard and sacrifice-filled struggle for their Germanity or Germanicity.
> SS commanders and lower leaders must care about every single man and help him in comradely manner at all times. They must take the volunteers on for evening educational hours and enlighten them culturally and politically. These courses also offer a good opportunity to get to know the cares and needs of the young comrades.
> Whoever complains about ethnic German or Germanic volunteers in a garrison, blames them for poor schooling or otherwise treats them as unqualified, commits a crime against Germanity and the Germanic Reich. The lowest punishment in these cases is expulsion from the SS."

In fact, the order brought scarcely any change. On August 30, 1943 173 members of SS Volunteer Mountain Rifle Regiment 2 of the SS Volunteer Division "Prinz Eugen" refused to serve after they had constantly been called "*Gypsies, Serbs and Croatian filth*" by the native German personnel. This led, though, to the former division commander, *SS-Brigadeführer* von Oberkamp, being put on leave at the end of November 1943. In February 1944 Himmler also ordered that the term "*ethnic German*" no longer be used since it was often "*used with a certain debasing tone*". The attitude of many native Germans toward the ethnic Germans is made clear again in the next two reports. A later member of the Waffen-SS at first volunteered without success in 1939:

> "But the mustering for service in the Waffen-SS turned out unfavorable for me. In addition, there came the sudden knowledge that all volunteers who were not yet accepted or were newcomers would be sent back home. At that time the Waffen-SS could not take on any more volunteers, at least not in Hamburg, because there was no possibility of taking them all in, housing and training them. That was a result of the successful campaign in Poland. The units of the Waffen-SS serving there had very simply and very hastily seized all the young ethnic Germans living in Poland, and under "gentle pressure" turned them into men of the Waffen-SS. These forcibly recruited "volunteers", who were all very proud of being taken by the SS, were immediately shipped to their homeland garrisons to be made into long-serving soldiers of the Waffen-SS. If possible, with a service obligation of 12 years.
> Some of the comrades expressed themselves loudly about why these not so "purely Nordic ethnic Germans" who had previously been <u>Polocks</u> were now allowed to serve in the Waffen-SS, the Führer's own very proud

troops. That was not understandable to most of them, could not be grasped. We, the volunteers from the Reich, had reported as genuine Germans to the Führer's elite, the Waffen-SS, and now we had to back off and make room for these "new ethnic comrades", most of whom did not speak German properly, not to mention being able to write. That could scarcely be understood."

The former *SS-Unterscharführer* Albert Schwenn similarly describes his recollections of the ethnic Germans:

"The SS Cavalry Division was already a regular heap of Gypsies. Scarcely a corner in eastern or southeastern Europe was not represented among us. In the 5th Squadron there were two boys who were supposed to have lived as Germans in Russia. Amusingly, one was named Amann and the other Zucker. They barely understood a word of German and slouched around behind all the others. We had no lack of ethnic Germans of all categories, and without wanting to put our comrades down, one must say that they were utilized splendidly in the mounted units. For the most part, this applies to those who were over 25 years old, they had already served in the Serbian Army, had been soldiers in Hungary and Romania, thus had served in armies in which the officer was everything and the man – including non-commissioned officers – was nothing at all. There they were beaten and slugged thoroughly. The old ones had told the young ones about it, and so one day these jerks stood on the barracks grounds before a stern-looking buy secretly grinning *Unterführer* and gaped. Here there was no "beating". One stood straight and looked at one's superiors with respect, and such things pleased the trainers from the Reich – finally their braid and silver trim were sufficiently valued. We native German recruits were different; already processed by HJ and RAD … In our squadron we also had an ethnic German named Franz Kappel. Franzl was undoubtedly a genius at scrounging, cooking and brawling, but after four months of training and two months of special training he had still not learned how to take a rifle apart and put it back together. But under the heaviest artillery fire, Franzl rescued a wounded comrade from a cornfield. We thought he was crazy, but he simply said, *"Well, what should I do if Mother asks, Franzl, why didn't you bring your comrade?"*

There were also other voices, as Heinz Gräber, who served in the 5th SS Panzer Division "Wiking" recalls:

"The *SS Panzergrenadier* Regiment 10 "Westland" consisted almost completely of native Germans, Hollanders and Flemings. The comradeship was great and the situation was outstanding. The later replacements from the Banat were modest, very able to fit in, and we had a good relationship with our ethnic German comrades."

The native German members of the 24th Waffen-Mountain (Karstjäger) Division of the SS also remember their ethnic German comrades from Romania and South Tyrol with praise.

The Individual Ethnic Groups

Belgium

(Eupen-Malmedy and Moresnet)

According to the Treaty of Versailles, the Eupen-Malmedy area, with its 50,000 Germans and 10,000 Walloons, was given to Belgium in 1920. As opposed to the districts which were given to France after World War I, Belgium was open to returning the land to Germany in the ensuing years, but urgent intervention by France prevented it. Unlike other lands, their policy toward the German minority was definitely more liberal.

Twenty years later, after the end of the western campaign, the area was returned to the German Reich on May 18, 1940. The overwhelmingly German population accepted this positively. In May 1940 Hitler announced the reunification of the Eupen-Malmedy and Moresnet regions to the German Reich. Paragraph 2 of the decree read:

> "The inhabitants of German or related blood … become German nationals according to closer determination. The ethnic Germans become Reich citizens by the Reich citizenship law."

On September 23, 1941 there came the order to gather ethnic Germans in eastern Belgium. Military service duty was also reintroduced. Over 8000 Germans from eastern Belgium were thus inducted. Unlike the Luxembourgers and some of those from Alsace-Lorraine, recruiting in Eupen-Malmedy found nobody refusing. From those obligated to serve, about 500 went to the Waffen-SS and some 1000 men to the Ordnungpolizei.

After the war ended, the regions were returned to Belgium and recognized as Belgian by the Bundesrepublik Deutschland in 1956. As opposed to the voluntary Belgian collaborators, the ethnic Germans were not collectively punished by the Belgian government after 1945. On the contrary, the German minority was given extensive autonomous rights.

Denmark

After the Prussian-Danish War of 1866 the Danish duchies of Schleswig and Holstein belonged to Prussia for forty-two years and the German Reich as of 1871. After World War I plebiscites ensued, as a result of which Holstein stayed in the German Reich and Schleswig was split into a northern and a southern part. The approximately 40,000 Germans living in North Schleswig, later organized into an ethnic group under Jens Möller, thus became Danish citizens. In all, some 60,000 Germans lived in their northern neighbor country. The partially desired reunification if North Schleswig with the German Reich was declined by Hitler, since he did not want to provoke hostility from Denmark.

From the German ethnic group in Denmark, about 100 men volunteered for SS service even before World War II. They were persons who had maintained their German citizenship even after 1918. When in April 1940 Denmark – *"for its own protection"* – was occupied by German troops,[28] the Waffen-SS began to recruit among the approximately 5,000 17- to 35-year-old ethnic Germans. Around 1400 of them applied, of whom some 600 were suitable for the SS and were inducted into the Waffen-SS during the course of 1940.

A second recruiting campaign in the spring of 1942 for those born in 1924 and 1925 also brought some 600 volunteers. One year later those born in 1926 were called, and the age was otherwise raised to forty-five years. By December 31, 1943 a total of 1,292 men served in the Waffen-SS. By the war's end there were some 1,500 ethnic Germans, most of whom were placed with Danish nationals in the "Danmark" Free Corps and later in the SS Volunteer Panzergrenadier Regiment 24 "Danmark" (11th SS Volunteer Panzergrenadier Division "Nordland").

These 1,500 men represented about 3.75% of the ethnic group. A basic calling of ethnic Germans from Denmark to serve in the Wehrmacht was not done by the Germans for the sake of ethnic folk rights, and so it remained with the exception of the volunteers who joined the Waffen-SS.

After the war the German ethnic group in Denmark was dissolved, and on November 22, 1945 the *"Union of German North Schleswigers"* was set up as an organization for the German minority. This organization, numbering only about 4,500 members, had its roots already in November 1943. At that time ethnic Germans opposed to the German regime had been organized in the underground. Along with an oath of loyalty to Denmark, they rejected a reunion of North Schleswig with Germany on principle. Attempts to weaken the legal prosecution of numerous ethnic Germans, both SS volunteers and civilians, could scarcely be carried out. Only in 1948 was the situation normalized. Today some 20,000 so-called North Schleswigers of German ancestry live in Denmark.

---

28 In case of war, Hitler feared an occupation of Denmark by the Western Allies, mainly by British troops, and had the country occupied by German troops to "protect" it from British occupation (sic!).

France

(Alsace and Lorraine)

Alsace and Lorraine, formerly belonging to the Kingdom of France, fell to the newly formed German Reich in 1871 after the Franco-Prussian War. France agitated among the populace in favor of leaving the territory. The "Optanten" were offered, among other things, free land in Algeria and three years' freedom from taxation. Perhaps because of that, more than 100,000 persons, who did not feel like Germans anyway, left the region. When the land was returned to France after World War I, a resettling of the formerly emigrated francophone inhabitants began. At the same time, about 200,000 Germans who had immigrated after 1871 were forced to depart. Thus in 1939 about 1.9 million people lived in Alsace-Lorraine.

In the course of the western campaign, the region was occupied by German troops as of June 19, 1940 and finally joined to the Gau of Baden. After Hitler directed on October 18, 1940 that *"the Alsatian and Lotharingian districts … be won back to the German people in the shortest time;"* instructions followed. But Alsace and Lorraine were not reunited but only annexed and given civil governments. Thus Lorraine and Lorraine *de jure* did not belong to the German Reich. But on August 23, 1942 the instructions as to nationality in Alsace, Lorraine and Luxembourg followed:

> "Those German Alsatians, Lotharingians and Luxembourgers receive the nationality according to law who a) are or will be inducted into the Wehrmacht or Waffen-SS, or b) are recognized as proven Germans."

With that the approximately 2,100 Alsatians who volunteered or were enlisted in the Wehrmacht or Waffen-SS received German citizenship. The general induction for defensive and service duty was problematic for a legal standpoint and only covered by their being granted German citizenship. Thus by 1944 those born from 1908 to 1928 were mustered, and in all about 100,000 Alsatians and 30,000 Lotharingians were inducted. In January 1944 the induction of former reserve officers into the Waffen-SS followed through emergency service orders, whereby forty-two refused and were confined at the Neuengamme concentration camp. Of them, twenty-two lost their lives.

Of the approximately 130,000 mobilized men, about 4,000 born between 1908 and 1910 were called into the Waffen-SS[29] and some 8,000 into the National police through emergency service orders. The way to the Waffen-SS is described by the former *Ortsgruppenleiter* Friedrich Amos:

> "I was born on February 10, 1904 in Wolfskirchen, Alsace and lived through World War I as a small boy. When as a result of the defeat, Alsace-Lothringen had to be given back to France, there was great joy at first, because the murder of peoples was ended and the thought of red wine and white bread still made many mouths water. Many also remembered the speech of Marshal Joffre at Tann in 1914, where he assured them that France would respect the customs and habits of Alsace. In 1924 I went – still a minor then – with my father to recruiting in Saarburg. Then I went to the deuxiem Compagine of the Mitrailleuses in the 67th Infantry Regiment in Soissons, Aisne. At the beginning of the thirties I joined the Young Men of the Progress Party of Alsace-Lorraine. In thisd organization, which was German-oriented, I became the leader of the 22nd Town Group. When France was mobilized in 1939, the then mayor Henri Lader came to me and said the Gendarmes had been to see him and I should give up the flag of the Young Men; otherwise I would be interned for the duration of the war. I told him that I could hardly do that, since I did not know what was happening. The flag bearer was also called in, and his old mother did not want to know where she had come to. I experienced the western campaign in great movement. I was to report in Chateauroux on June 12, 1940. That did not work, as the German Wehrmacht was faster than our train moved. When I went back home, there was already a German town commander there, to whom I reported. I was sent to the Alsatian Help Service, whose task above all was seeking and bringing back whoever was still in German imprisonment or held in the interior of France as being from Alsace-Lorraine. On the basis of my previous activities as leader of the 22nd Town

---

29 Alsatians were involved in the revealed German revenge action in the Oradour-sur-Glane.

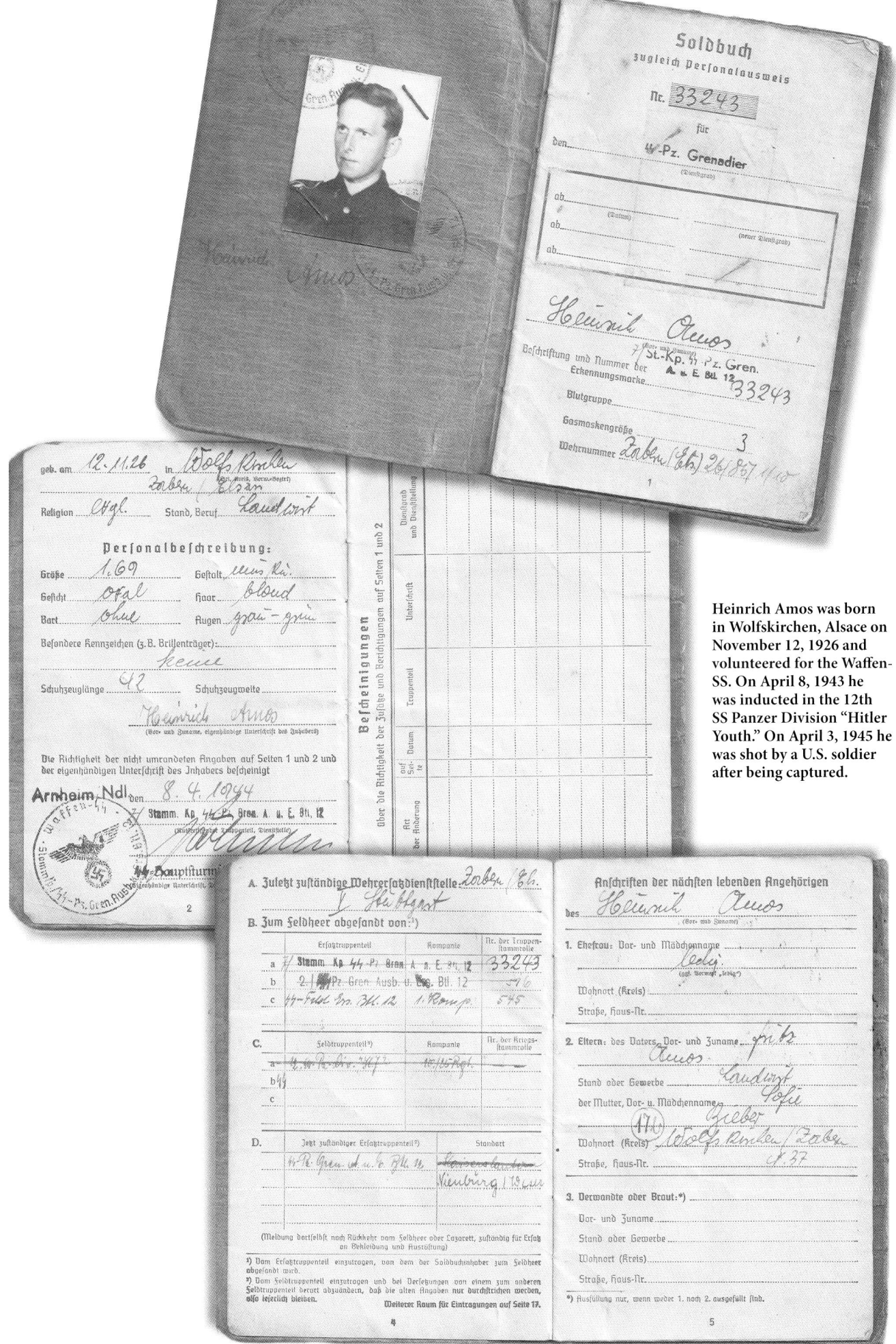

Heinrich Amos was born in Wolfskirchen, Alsace on November 12, 1926 and volunteered for the Waffen-SS. On April 8, 1943 he was inducted in the 12th SS Panzer Division "Hitler Youth." On April 3, 1945 he was shot by a U.S. soldier after being captured.

Group of the Alsace-Lorraine Young men, I was named Town Group Leader by the country leader on October 1, 1940. In May 1941 I and others went to the Gau School in Frauenalb for a week, and in March 1942, after I had become a member of the NSDAP, was named mayor.

In a gathering at the county building in Zabern one day, one of the town group leaders said that some of his people were afraid they would be inducted again. The County Leader said that if the Alsatians were inducted, the war would be lost. Then it was not very long before military duty was introduced; then the men were inducted, and soon the first news of deaths arrived. Now I was supposed to go to the parents or wives and tell them the bad news, and convince them of the necessity of taking part in this fateful battle. I went twice, Then another matter came up, which shook my trust in the party's work. Then I made up my mind to withdraw from my offices. At a meeting I asked the County Leader what would be done to someone who wanted to withdraw from the party. He replied, that person would sign his death sentence. Now I knew for sure. My oldest son had already reported to the Waffen-SS, so I also volunteered in 1943. At a mayors' meeting in Gulgweiler, Landrat Müller took me aside. He said I should distance myself from my voluntary reporting. He had spoken with the County Leader, and he also thought that I could accomplish more here than at the front as a common soldier. But my mind was made up. Early in February 1944 I was ordered to report to the SS Infantry Gun Training and Replacement Battalion 1 in Breslau-Lissa. Shortly before my transfer to SS Panzergrenadier Regiment 7 of the 4th SS Police Panzergrenadier Division in December 1944, I was ordered to my company chief. There I had to sign an explanation that I had been made aware that a father of eight children did not need to be on the front. Then I wrote that I, as having made the application, nevertheless wanted to go to the field army. In Slovenska Lubja I then became a helper of the armorer and made my way with the division via Pomerania and Danzig back to Eberswalde. On the night of May 2-3 it was said we were surrounded by Americans and should prepare to surrender. Our weapons were thrown away, the SS collar emblems removed, which probably meant nothing, since we had our service books, as well as our blood types tattooed under our arms. Turned over to the British, things went relatively well for us. One day it was said that Alsatians should report to the writing room. The Alsatians and Lotharingians were turned over to the French. There we were not guarded by soldiers, but by civilians of the 'force francaise d'interieur.' First they compelled us to pull out the grass between the paving stones with our fingers. Then our suspenders and belts were taken from us, and we had to run around a house with our hands behind our necks. Naturally our trousers fell down to our shoes, and then the shoelaces were also taken away from us, so our shoes flew off. But the debasing procedures were not over yet. My son Heinrich, born on November 12, 1926, was shot on April 3, 1945 by the Americans with two other soldiers *after* being taken prisoner in Höchstberg near Heilbronn. His service book was kept at the city hall in Höchstberg, where we could pick it up later."

In 1945 Alsace-Lorraine came back to France, which immediately instituted a strict assimilation policy. Among other things, there was a general ban on teaching the German language in the schools of Alsace and Lorraine. This was lifted only in 1972. In the legal prosecution of collaborators, France omitted, after protests, the men who were inducted by force, and limited itself mainly to the volunteers.

Italy

(South Tyrol, Trentino, Kanaltal and Belluno)

After World War I, South Tyrol along with Trentino and the Kanaltal were given to Italy according to the Treaty of St. Germain. While the population of South Tyrol was almost completely German, in Kanaltal in the Province of Udine and in Trentino there were separate ethnic German language islands. In the Province of Belluno there were smaller, so-called scattered settlements.

The Italian policy toward the German inhabitants was extraordinarily rigid and resulted in much tension in the area. After the so-called Steel Pact between Hitler and Mussolini, it was agreed on June 23, 1939 to resettle over 200,000 ethnic Germans. This was supposed to end the existing problems. The Germans living in northern Italy were to decide by December 31, 1939 whether they chose German citizenship and then wanted to leave Italy. After certain pressure from the party, a total of 185,085 ethnic Germans from South Tyrol, Trentino, the Kanaltal and Belluno decided to do so. They were gathered in the "Work Community for Opters for Germany."

By October 1940, about 56,000 people left their homeland and were settled for the most part in Austria. The number of those willing to be resettled from South Tyrol and Kanaltal rose by mid-1942 to 222,018, that of the emigrants to 76,824 people. Of these, 55,768 settled in the districts of the Ostmark, especially in Tyrol-Vorarlberg (27,308) and the rest in the Altreich. At the end of 1942 there were also some 6000 ethnic Germans from the southeast area and 600 Luserners from South Tyrol in the Protectorate of "Bohemia and Moravia."

Through the Italian swing to the Allies, South Tyrol was combined with the provinces of Belluno and Trentino in the Operation Zone "Alpenvorland", and the approximately 135,000 remaining ethnic Germans were left in the region as an ethnic group under Peter Hofer. The administrative regime was taken over by Gauleiter Rainer of Tirol-Vorarlberg. At the same time, the so-called Windischen, who lived in the Kanaltal, were also regarded as ethnic Germans after long discussions with Italy.

While some 7,500 South Tyroleans who had been resettled since 1940 were required to do military service by their gained German citizenship and were inducted by the Wehrmacht and Waffen-SS, the introduction of military duty in the "Alpine Foreland" Operations Zone followed on November 6, 1943. At first those born in 1924 and 1935 were inducted, then those of 1894 to 1927 on April 10, 1944. Some 17,000 men were turned over to the Ordnungspolizei. In addition to numerous training battalions, there ensued, especially for those born in 1900 to 1912 (31 to 45 years old), the founding of the Police Regiments "Bozen", "Alpenvorland", "Brixen" and "Schlanders". About 1,000 ethnic Germans went to the planned 24th Waffen Mountain (Karstjäger) Division of the SS or other training and replacement units of the Waffen-SS.

At the same time as the establishment of the "Alpine Foreland" Operation Zone, the "Adriatic Coastland" Operation Zone was established on October 1, 1943 of the Italian provinces of Friaul, Görz, Istria, Laibach, Trieste and Quarnero. Although military duty in the "Adriatic Coastland" was already introduced in November 1943, it is interesting that only in March 1944 were those born in 1923 to 1925 were mustered. In July 1944 those born in 1914 to 1926 were inducted.

The motivation for the older ethnic Germans inducted as of November 1943 was usually meager. In the assignments to the Waffen-SS, force was used and any volunteering was omitted. This is shown, among other things, in the case of Josef Mayr-Nusser. He was born in Bozen on October 27, 1910 and appointed first diocese leader of the Masculine Catholic Youth in the German part of the bishopric of Trient in 1934. Working as a mercantile employee in a Bozen firm, he was called into the Waffen-SS at Konitz at the beginning of September 1944. There Mayr-Nusser refused on religious grounds to take the oath to Hitler on October 4, 1944. As a draft resister, he was delivered to the prison camp of the SS and Police at Danzig-Matzkau and died in Erlangen on February 24, 1945 while being transferred to the Dachau concentration camp. At the beginning of October 2005, the process of Mayr-Nusser's beatification began in the diocese of Bozen-Brixen. After its successful conclusion, the status of a martyr will be requested for him in Rome.

In all, including those ordered from the Ordnungspolizei to the Waffen-SS, some 5,000 ethnic Germans from Italy served in the Waffen-SS. This number also includes those men resettled since 1940, mostly to North Tyrol. At the same time, some 15,000 men were sent to the Wehrmacht and 17,000 to the Ordnungspolizei.

After the war ended, great tension arose between the ethnic Germans living in northern Italy and the Italian government. The chicanery toward the German-speaking population grew to such an extent that the German speakers demonstrated actively against it. Among other things, there were explosive attacks. Only some forty years after the end of World War II did a certain relaxation set in, which remains in the process of opening borders within the European Union.

Croatia

As a result of the Balkan campaign of 1941, the country of Yugoslavia disintegrated. On April 15, 1941 the independent state of Croatia was already proclaimed. Within its borders lived some 200,000 ethnic Germans.[30] they were mostly gathered in the ethnic group under Branimir Altgayer.

On September 16, 1941 a German-Croatian agreement was made, by which the great majority of ethnic Germans were to do their military duty in the Croatian Army, while 10% volunteered for German military service. Altgayer tried along with other ethnic-group leaders to keep these volunteers in their own area. Since it was clear to him that if they were recruited into the Waffen-SS, the young men of his ethnic group would be taken away he agreed, among other things, even to subordinate his service echelon of 3,000 men to the *Deutsche Mannschaft*[31] under the Croatian Ustasha. The service echelon was set up in August 1942 of volunteers 17 to 22 years old and divided into a staff guard in Esseg and the "Prinz Eugen" available battalion of 1,500 men. There were also three readiness battalions, "Ludwig von Baden", "General Laudon", and "Emanuel von Bayern" with 1,500 men in all. The service time of the volunteers was recognized as a serving of the active Croatian military duty.

The Chief of the SS Main Office had no understanding of Altgayer's position. He was supposed to obtain personnel replacements for new units of the Waffen-SS. Thus in September 1942 the German-Croatian agreement allowed the Waffen-SS to recruit 17- to 30-year-old ethnic Germans in Croatia. The contingent recruitment of 10% of the eligible men a year before thus came to an end. Of the fourteen age groups with some 20,000 eligible men in all, 6,529 volunteers were already inducted into the 7th SS Volunteer Mountain Division "Prinz Eugen" by the end of November 1942.

In the course of the steadily worsening war situation, the SS Main Office, from 1943 on, put more and more pressure on the German ethnic group in Croatia. Without the Croatian government being in a position to oppose them, the service echelon and others were totally inducted into the Waffen-SS. Besides the eligible men born in 1925, recruiting was also extended to those born from 1903 to 1913. On December 28, 1943 there were, in all, 32,158 ethnic Germans from Croatia in military service. Of them, there were:

 2,636 in the Croatian Army
17,538 in the Waffen-SS
 4,500 in work service in Germany
 1,385 in the German Wehrmacht
 3,488 in paramilitary units
   410 in Croatian work service
 2,200 in the Todt Organization

In 1944 those born in 1927-28 were mustered, as well as those 41 to 50 years old. The latter were mainly assigned to the Ordnungspolizei. In 1945 those born in 1929 were taken. In all, some 25,000 members of the German ethnic group in Croatia were taken into the Waffen-SS, some 2,000 into the Wehrmacht, and around 5,000 into the Ordnungspolizei. Most of them served in the 7th SS Volunteer Mountain Division "Prinz Eugen". Older men and younger men not fit for army service were also assigned to guard concentration camps. Smaller contingents also went to the 13th Waffen Mountain Division of the SS "Handschar" (Croatian No.1). The ethnic German volunteer Zvonimier Bernwald recalls:

> "I was born in 1924 in Brod on the Save. My grandparents were named Bärenwald, but this became Bernwald in Croatian. We were Roman Catholics and had the status of ethnic Germans. In 1938 several changes were made in eastern Croatia. Previously dominated by Serbs, now only Croatian flags could be flown, Croatian written and spoken. When Croatia became an independent state, the Serbs and Jews disappeared from public life. In May 1941 the Leibstandarte Adolf Hitler came into our city and handed out Greek Papastratos cigarettes. We were excited. In September 1942 it was announced in our school that whoever joined voluntarily would be inducted into the Leibstandarte. Since we all were afraid the war would end before we were there, we

---

30 About 20,000 ethnic Germans who lived in Bosnia also belonged to it. From there they were resettled *en masse* in the Reichsgau of Wartheland.
31 The *Deutsche Mannschaft* corresponded to the SA, the Service Echelon to the SS,

volunteered. In October 1942 I was actually called to Berlin to join the Leibstandarte. At the end of the year came the transfer to the SS Panzergrenadier Division "Das Reich" in northern France. Here I was trained on the 3.7cm antitank gun. We ethnic Germans were not badly treated, but the drill and the tricks were generally so great that some of us were sent back to Croatia. After I went to the SS Motorcycle Rifle Replacement Unit in Ellwangen in January 1943, I was ordered to the SS Translator Replacement and Training Conmpany in Oranienburg in March 1943. From here I was transferred to Unit VI of the Division Staff of the newly formed Croatian SS Volunteer Mountain Division. I worked on the Division's newspaper 'Handzar' which was published in Zagreb."

The path for men who were originally in the Croatian Army to the Waffen-SS is described by a former ethnic German in the typical patois. It is clear to see that a general volunteering cannot be spoken of. If war service was seen by the men as a duty, the interest of getting them into the Waffen-SS was obviously very meager:[32]

"I was born in 1920 and drafted into the Vojni Okrug (Defense District Command) Sr. Mitrovica on June 15, 1942. From Mitrovica I was sent with 40 other men from the whole district, all ethnic Germans, to Sarajevo and the 9th Croatian Artillery Unit. Men from the districts of Osijek, Valpovo, etc. also came there, so that there were about 80 of us.

After spending a week with the Croats we were turned over to the German Wehrmacht, the 4th Mountain Battery (the number of the artillery unit is unknown to me). In the 4th Mountain Battery there were already 40 ethnic Germans whop had been sent from the rifle battalion in Ruma. Then came 14 men from Virovitica from the Croatian Cavalry and 20 men from Esseg, the Croatian Field Artillery, also ethnic Germans, so that we were 160 ethnic Germans; two of them were sergeants; the other officers and lower commanders were native Germans, although the majority came from the Sudetenland.

The training was tough and fast; the uniform and pay were Croatian, food and weapons German. The training was never finished, for after four weeks cam the first partisan action, thank God, with no dead. With six weeks we had the first dead. And so it went with the Wehrmacht until March 1943.

Then suddenly a mustering commission from the Waffen-SS came for the SS Mountain Division "Prinz Eugen". At that time we were in Konjic, Herzegovina after the end of the so-called fourth offensive. All the ethnic Germans there were found to be acceptable for the Waffen-SS. Only a single one was allowed to stay with the unit as a translator. At the beginning of April (before Easter) we all got a furlough until called, and we were told that we would find out where we were to report. And two days before Easter came a telegram: I had to report to the Rifle Battalion in Ruma on Easter Tuesday. There we met almost all the men on furlough. Then on the second day we took off the Croatian uniforms and received complete SS uniforms with all the equipment except the weapons. The same day we were taken on a special train under guard to Betschkerek; during the trip nobody was allowed to leave the train at any station. We arrived in Betschkerek at night, slept in a school. After two or three days was a parade; officers came from various service arms, and every one of them looked for men that he could use; the rest went to the infantry in Lissa. I myself with 20 other men went to the Tank Destroyer Unit in Weisskirchen at the former air force barracks, for our commander could not find more than 150 men who suited his taste.

The training itself lasted from May through June 1943 in Weisskirchen. In July we went to the action area: Bosnia, Herzegovina, Montenegro, Dalmatia etc. Then in November 1943 a question suddenly came of who was volunteering for the SS and who wasn't. But only those from the Croatian area were asked, and the result was very disappointing for the officers, for 80% of the men asked were not willing, despite the threats of the concentration camp at Dachau and many other tricks. Nobody from our unit went to the concentration camp, which was understandable, because the company would not have been ready for action then."

---

32 Documentation by the Zentrum gegen Vertreibung, Wiesbaden.

After the war ended, most of the ethnic Germans were gathered in work and internment camps. Here there was mishandling, shooting and brutality. After the Federal Republic of Germany was founded, 367,348 ethnic Germans could emigrate from Yugoslavia until 1968. Almost three-quarters of them emigrated into the Federal Republic. The war and postwar losses of the German population in Yugoslavia amounted to over 90,000 persons, about half of whom died in the camps. Today only about 8,000 people who call themselves German live in the territory of what once was Yugoslavia.

Luxembourg

Luxembourg declared its neutrality in 1867. Economically it belonged to the German Customs Union until the end of World War I. It was not just because of the German defeat that about 60% of the population wanted a link with France and over 20% with Belgium. The fact that the majority of Luxembourgers turned more and more toward France was already seen in a German history book in 1919:[33]

> "Luxembourg, which is actually not a Low German language area but may be handled here because of connections on account of its location and history, provides a sad counterpoint to Flanders. The small country has, other than not quite 4,000 immigrated Frenchmen, a population of a quarter million, which is of purely German ancestry. Despite that, the German character is completely obliterated, and the Luxembourgers look upon the native Germans with hostility while being amicably disposed toward the French – and this although they belonged to the German Bund from the Congress of Vienna until 1866, although until the Treaty of Versailles they belonged to the German Customs Union and owe their prosperity to it, and although in 1867 Bismarck rescued their independence from the rapaciousness of France. … The country has been neutral since 1867. In the book of totally German culture, Luxembourg is a dead person; the gap between the native Germans and Luxembourgers was even deepened by the events of the war."

In May 1940 the neutral Luxembourg was occupied by German troops in the course of the western campaign. At the end of June 1940 the Gauleiter of Koblenz-Trier, Gustav Simon, took over the civil government of the small country. Despite the obvious antipathy, the German ethnically-oriented policy sought the annexation of Luxembourg to the German Reich. And in fact, on August 23, 1942 came the integration of Luxembourg into the former Gau of Koblenz-Trier, known since January 24, 1941 as the Gau of Moselland.

The majority of the approximately 300,000 inhabitants, as could be expected, were completely opposed to this step. Only about 10% of the inhabitants sympathized with Germany. Opportunism, though, resulted in even previously reserved citizens suddenly becoming members of the Ethnic German Movement (VdB) under Damian Kratzenberg. In 1941 the VdB already had 62,450 members.[34] In 1943 a publication appeared that, again according to the officially desired perspective, reported on the annexation of the small neighbor land to the German Reich:[35]

> "As already stated, pure German blood flows in the veins of Luxembourg's population, it belongs with our Mosel lands to one and the same ethnic group and also speaks the same dialect as they do. But it would nevertheless be extreme to claim that the Luxembourgers had greeted their new national political situation with jubilation and vigorous enthusiasm. On the contrary, they behaved very restrained and hesitant at first, which after all had its basis in the fact that more than half of the inhabitants of the country are amiably minded toward France…
>
> After Luxembourg had been occupied by German troops and become a part of the Great German Reich, the German government was introduced in this country as also in Alsace-Lorraine. The maintenance of quiet and order was taken over by bands of the German police, which even watched over the borders with France and Belgium as well as with the Reich area – customs duty was not yet lifted. This surveillance of traffic toward

---

33 Class, Heinrich, *Deutsche Geschichte*, Leipzig, 1919.
34 In 1942 about 84,000 Luxembourgers were organized in the VdB, which remained in existence as an organization despite the annexation of the country into the German Reich.
35 Richter, Hans, *Einsatz der Polizei*, Berlin, 1943.

the Reich area applied only to checking merchandise, while the borders with France and Belgium had to be closed against an influx of French and Jews. For this purpose it was thus advisable to transfer stronger police forces to Luxembourg. The arrival of a police battalion in the city of Luxembourg itself took place shortly after the armistice with France. Countless persons lined the unit's line of march. In part they behaved very restrained and had presumably come only out of curiosity to attend the military spectacle of the green police troop marching in. Not very many raised their arms in the German salute…"

With the annexation of Luxembourg to the Reich area, German citizenship was first granted, as organized by the Ethnic German Movement. As of August 30, 1942, citizens were also required to serve in the German Wehrmacht. While the annexation of the small country to the German Reich had already resulted in strikes in all parts of the country, the mustering of men born from 1920 to 1924 resulted in a further escalation of the situation. On August 31, 1942 there was already a general strike throughout the land. On October 18, 1942 the first 2,200 young men of Luxembourg were finally inducted. On March 25, 1943 those born in 1925, and on December 8, 1943 those of 1926 were mustered. The youths of 1927 followed on July 14, 1944.

As opposed to Alsace-Lorraine, though, the older men were not called into the Wehrmacht. It was feared that this could bring on another general strike. In all, over 10,000 men of the approximately 150,000 born between 1920 and 1927 identified by the VdB were inducted. About 500 of them joined the Waffen-SS more or less willingly. About 3,500 eligible men withdrew from service by leaving the country and/or going underground, or deserted shortly after induction. Some 1,000 Luxembourgers were called into the Ordnungspolizei.

A sovereign land again after the war ended, Luxembourg again oriented itself toward France plus Belgium and the Netherlands. Legally, action was taken first against army volunteers and agitators for the National Socialist policy. The majority of those who were included in the Ethnic German Movement remained untouched by further legal prosecution.

Poland

After World War I, Poland, according to the Treaty of Versailles, received large parts of Pomerania, West Prussia and Silesia. The policy of the country toward the minorities, including the German, was remarkably restrictive in many ways. In 1935 the German Foreign Institute made known that around 1,150,000 Germans lived in Poland. The counting of the Reich Commissar for the unification of the German ethnic group in September-October 1939 showed more than twice as many. According to it, about 2,310,000 ethnic Germans lived in Poland. After only some 930,000 persons had applied to be on the list of people desiring German citizenship, it was clear that the Ethnic German Mittelstelle was obviously working with overly high statistics.[36] It is noteworthy that even among the 930,000 ethnic Germans, a great number entered their names on the list only after considerable pressure. The People's List (VL) set up the prerequisite for gaining German citizenship and was divided into four categories:

    I: Ethnic Germans who had promoted their German character in the past,
    II: Ethnic Germans who had provably maintained their German character but had not promoted it actively.
    III: Ethnic Germans who had entered into affiliations with non-Germans, or children of these mixed marriages, and
    IV: Ethnic Germans who had actively opposed the German character (Communists or Social Democrats).

Of the 930,000 applicants, 340,000 were on Lists I and II, 535,000 on List III and 55,000 on List IV. Without successful integration, the ethnic Germans kept their Polish citizenship. Thus they were *de facto* not obligated to serve in the German Wehrmacht. But they could volunteer freely as soon as they had received a People's List certificate, even if German citizenship had not been granted. Since majority in Poland began only at the age of twenty-one, registering by younger volunteers had to be attested by their parents. The Waffen-SS also attempted to influence the parents. The Leader of the SS Replacement Office Vistula wrote accordingly on December 3, 1941 to the father of a volunteer:

---

36   One reason for this can be that the office wanted to emphasize the extent of their task. It is recognized that statistics from documents of the time should be examined critically.

Roman Neujahr was born on October 20, 1921 in the Litzmannstadt (Lodsch) district and, even before his German citizenship was granted, joined the II./Artillery Regiment 240 (340th Infantry Division).

Temporary permission to wear the Ethnic German Medal for applicants to the People's List.

> "Your son Johann has reported voluntarily for admission to the Waffen-SS and informed the Weichsel office (XX) that you do not want to give your permission. With this voluntary reporting, your son has recognized, along with thousands of others, the necessity of fighting with weapons for a great, strong Germany against our greatest enemy. You are thereby urged to consider your decision again and to authorize your agreement on the enclosed application form, as well as on the declaration of service (which is still in the hands of your son), with your signature. Should you, though, still withhold your consent as before, the reasons are to be given on request. It is hereby noted that your son, being born in 1921, soon has to expect being drafted by the Wehrmacht."

The parents did not always let themselves by persuaded by such letters. The father of the volunteer Johann Chynacki of Gotenhafen wrote tersely and to the point:

> "To the letter of December 3, 1943 I state the reason that we are not yet ethnic Germans, though I have applied since 1939, but unsuccessfully to date."

After being made citizens, most of the ethnic Germans served in the Wehrmacht. Assuming from this that some 10% of the people on Lists I to III were drafted, there were still some 90,000 men. It can be estimated that some 8,500 reported voluntarily to the Waffen-SS and were for the most part placed in the 4th SS Police Panzergrenadier Division or used as guards at the concentration camps in Defense Zones XX and XXI or in the General Government. Presumably some 5,000 older men were taken into the Ordnungspolizei and used in large numbers for guardian tasks, including the Jewish work camps.

When the war ended, the expulsion of the Germans and ethnic Germans from Poland began. One statistic gives the following numbers: Some 672,000 people were expelled, while 436,000 ethnic Germans remained in their homeland, now under Polish rule again. They were, presumably, mainly members of the earlier People's Lists III and IV, who had entered their names in the lists only after certain pressure from the native German officials.

Romania

In Romania in 1935 there lived some 800,000 foreign Germans, who had settled mainly in Siebenbürgen and the Banat.[37] The latter was in the three-country angle of Romania, Hungary and Serbia, between the Danube, Theiss, Marosch and the streams from the southern Carpathians.[38] Through the second Vienna Separation Declaration of 1940 northern Siebenbürgen, with a mainly Hungarian population, was joined to Hungary. Thus some 550,000 ethnic Germans still lived in Romania.[39]

For the post part, they were gathered in the ethnic group under Wolfram Bruckner (as of September 27, 1940, Andreas Schmitt), and received the status of legal persons with public rights. Their relationship with the Romanian government was more liberal than the chauvinistic minority policy of Hungary. Thus Andreas Schmitt, who as representative of the Ethnic German Mittelstelle was also responsible for recruiting for service in Germany, was already able to remove 1,000 (SS) volunteers from Romania by June 1940.

---

37   By the Trianon Treaty (June 4, 1920), this closed settlement area of the collapsed Habsburg monarchy had been divided into three parts. The larger eastern part, with Temeswar and the Arader Komitat (66.5%, 18,966 sq.km.) went to Romania, the southern part (32.5%, 9,276 sq.km.) to the kingdom of the Serbs, Croats and Slovenes (renamed the Kingdom of Yugoslavia in 1929), and the northern part of Marosch-Theiswinkel (1%, 284 sq.km.) remained in Hungary.

38   West of the Banat lay the Batschka, also formerly part of Hungary. This region, by the Treaty of Trianon, was also divided. The smaller northern part remained in Hungary, the much larger southern part went to Serbia. The last large settlement area was the Swabian Turkey, which lay between the Plattensee, the Danube and the Drava.

39   According to an intermediate report on the work of the farmers in the German ethnic group in Romania in 1941, almost 400,000 of the approximately 550,000 Germans in the country were farmers. The total number of places in Romania occupied by Germans was over 800. Only 400 of them could be said to be mainly German or to have a considerable number of German inhabitants according to their establishment or combination. In the other 400 there were scattered Germans living in numbers up to ten families. Of the 400 towns designated as German-populated, seventy-eight had a non-agrarian German population (industrial and mine workers, German officials, etc.). In all towns in which at least ten German farm families lived the *Landesbaürnschaft* founded a local unit and named a local farm leader.

Enthusiasm over Hitler's political and military success had brought them, approved by Romania (officially as volunteer workers for Germany), together quickly. During the 1941 Balkan campaign, volunteers also reported to the German units. After a mustering, 600 men were sent to the SS "Schönbrunn" barracks in Vienna. There they were united to form a battalion of the SS Division "Reich" (mot.).

Since service in the Romanian Army had little attraction for the eligible ethnic Germans, what with the bad treatment, training and equipment, there was generally a strong desire to serve in German units. The Foreign Affairs Office reported to the Ethnic German Mittelstelle on March 9, 1943:

> "In the most recent times, some 10,000 ethnic German members of the Romanian Army in the southern sector of the eastern front have reported to German units. They have made known there that in their previous troop units they were treated very badly, in particular, have often been beaten, and thus have urgently requested to be allowed to enter the German Wehrmacht."

The approximately 10,000 men used the collapse of the Romanian 3rd Army at Stalingrad to leave their units. Since they were *de jure* deserters, Hitler arranged an amnesty for the soldiers with Antonescu.

After it was shown that Romania, after the defeat at Stalingrad, only wanted to continue in the war with a limited contingent, Himmler tried to take at least the whole body of Romanian ethnic Germans into the Waffen-SS. In return for this, armament deliveries were scheduled, and the resettling of all ethnic Germans after the war was advised.

On May 13, 1943 the treaty between the countries concerning the induction of the ethnic Germans in the Waffen-SS was made. The treaty stated, among other things:

"I. Mustering
1. Entry into the German Army, into the units of the Waffen-SS, is voluntary for all Romanian citizens of German ancestry who, on April 1, 1943, had completed at leas the minimum age of 17 years. Those who enter the German Army, in the units of the Waffen-SS, on the basis of the present agreement retain their Romanian citizenship with all resulting duties and rights; the same rights are also retained by those volunteers who, at the mustering, were found unsuitable or were sent back to their homeland for other reasons.
2. The establishment of the following categories of Romanian nationals of German ancestry is ruled out:
    a) All active officers and non-commissioned officers, reserve officers and reserve non-commissioned officers, may be placed only on the basis of specific permission of the Army General Staff.
    b) The officers, non-commissioned officers and men, and the troops that are active or reserves and who are subordinated to the command offices and the units and formations which are located at Taman, Kuban, Crimea and the district as far as the Dniester. In addition, those who are in the marching formations of the Army within the country, who are intended for the larger units for Taman and Kuban, are also eliminated.
    c) The corporals and sergeants who serve actively with the homeland troops for the years of 1942 and 1943. Exceptions are the students in the officer schools and the reserve non-commissioned officers.
    d) All specialists of any rank active in 1942, 1943 and 1944, specifically: telephone mechanics, radio-telegraphers, measuring engineers, altimeterists, meteorologists, flamethrower men, aiming gunners, cannoneers of the artillery and the infantry guns, grenade launchers, tank gunners, armorers, tank drivers and all members of the Navy and the Air Force.
    e) All specialists of any rank and any age who are needed by the army and national industry, specifically: opticians, druggists, vehicle drivers, mechanics, electricians, radio technicians, vulcanizers and iron founders.
3. The Romanian citizens of German ethnicity who have the desire to be taken into the German Army, in the units of the Waffen-SS, have until May 30, 1943 to report to the mustering commissions of the German ethnic group in Romania, for which they are to submit the written declaration for this purpose, which will be examined by delegates of the defense district command. In the declaration for voluntary reporting it is to be stated precisely that the applicable man reports "of his free will" for placement in the German Army

The gate of the Sachsenhausen concentration camp.

The ethnic German in Romania, Klemens Altmann, reported to the Waffen-SS in 1941. Serving for a short time in the SS Cavalry Brigade, he was then used at the Sachsenhausen concentration camp.

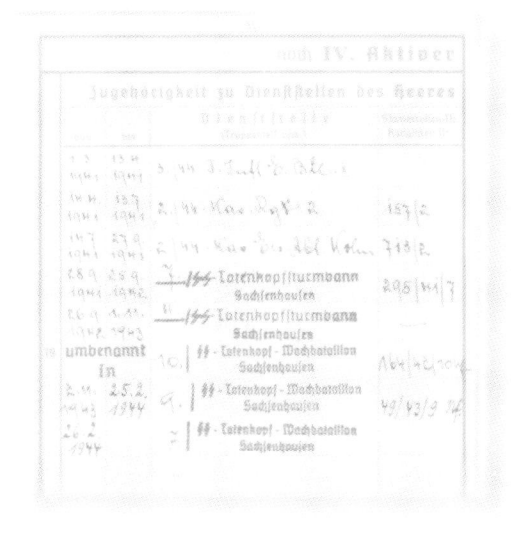

in the units of the Waffen-SS. The Romanian government guarantees all of those who do not want to enter the German Army that they will not be threatened with punishment from any side."

The carrying out of the musterings was the job of the SS Replacement Command "Southeast" in Vienna. Responsible in Romania was *SS-Sturmbannführer* Dietz, who traveled through all areas in which ethnic Germans lived with a small staff plus doctors of the German ethnic group between May and August 1943. Mustered according to the announcements of the Wehrmacht, an outside position at the SS Replacement Command in Kronstadt followed the induction.

By June 2, 1943, 47,580 volunteers had already been seized, which cannot have come about because of their wish to serve in the Waffen-SS. Instead, the majority of the men chose general service in the German Wehrmacht. Characterized by propaganda, the *Völkische Beobachter* yet reported on May 22, 1943:

"Ethnic Germans from Romania in the Waffen-SS. With great enthusiasm, the men of the ethnic group in the German settlement areas of Romania, in Siebenbürgen, the Banat and the hill country, are now being mustered for the Waffen-SS. The first transport of SS recruits was already sent off from a depot near Kronstadt by ethnic group leader Andreas Schmidt, who indicated in his speech that the great majority of the Germans in Romania have fulfilled their duty to date in the Romanian Army on the eastern front, and most of them wear Romanian medals for bravery on their field-gray coats."

After the ages were first limited from 18 to 30, there were:

17,748 eligible for the SS
12,743 capable of Army service
 2,031 capable of garrison service
 1,429 capable of work service.

After the calling of five more age groups (31 to 35 years), about another 14,000 men could be gained. In addition, the barely 10,000 ethnic Germans who had formerly served in the Romanian Army and had joined German units at the beginning of 1943 were taken over.

The men were first taken to Vienna and remustered there. Whoever was classified as unqualified was given duty in the armament industry. Of the remaining men, some 17,000 were assigned to the new III. (Germanic) SS Panzer Corps. The SS-qualified volunteers went mostly to the basic units of the Waffen-SS, such as the 1st SS Panzer Division "Leibstandarte Adolf Hitler." Contingents with the mustering classification of Army capability were also assigned to the 7th SS Volunteer Mountain Division "Prinz Eugen" or the SS Karstwehr Battalion.

Unlike the ethnic group in Hungary, there was no general mobilization in Romania in the spring of 1944. But in the summer of 1944 the mustering of those born in 1926 and 1927 took place. In all, some 61,000 men of the Germans living in Romania were in German units. Of them, some 58,000 were in the Waffen-SS and come 3,000 in the Wehrmacht.

A former ethnic German member of the Waffen-SS recalls, writing in his typical patois, his induction and first training:[40]

"Through the German-Romanian military agreement for our German ethnic group in Romania, a mustering of so-called volunteers from 18 to 35 years old was carried out. In Gross Komlosch it took place on May 20, 1943 at the Young Men's Club. The communities of Ostern and Lunga were added. Because it was Easter, some farmers' sons did not want to be mustered, but they were brought from their towns by roll commands. In the local offices it was made public on the bulletin board: Only those who volunteer of their free will, thus without pressure or "must", need to be mustered. Again the German Ethnic Group leadership gave out orders on a "must" basis. Thereupon I though, as so many did: That looks as if the German ethnic group were a state in the state.[41]

---

40 Documented by the Center against Expulsion, Wiesbaden.
41 By the "state in the state" was meant that the ethnic group leadership gave the orders, not the Romanian state, whose citizens the ethnic Germans in fact were.

The Romanian officials scarcely got involved in the matter. For the command decree by Marshal I. Antonescu, in agreement with the great General Staff, was read before the troops in the daily orders of all regiments: On order of Marshal I. Antonescu and in agreement with the great General Staff we received the order to deconcentrate all soldiers of German ethnic status from our regiment as of today. The regimental commander gave a short speech: Comrades! Soldiers! With heavy heart I must release you from our regiment today as ordered. To this day you were good, honorable and brave soldiers and comrades, and I wish you to remain the same in the future – Hurrah!" The same day all the ethnic Germans were deconcentrated, as were so many who did not want to or for whom things went better and who held good posts or positions. At home they awaited the mustering commission. So it went from spring to summer.

The mustered men were taken by the local service-office leader with the block leader to house gatherings, to collect the required money support. Then I went house to house twice with Block Leader Stuhlmüller to collect the support money. The money was determined by a list of support amounts according to the value of possessions. So many owners complained more than non-owners and did not foresee that soon everything would be involved, as it later happened. As a collector, one gained many experiences and opinions.

On July 16, 1943 at 6:00 A.M. the first transport of inducted young men was to be ready at the Young Men's Club to depart with about 29 mustered men to Gross Sankt Nikolaus on horse-drawn wagons. Our wives also went along, if there was room, to Gross Sankt Nikolaus to see us off. It was a hot, sunny Friday. About halfway through the trip we stopped in the shadows of the berry trees along the road for a short rest, and a pause to eat and drink; one had already suspected an urge to travel. At about 11:00 A.M. we arrived at the main depot in Szentmiklosch. In the afternoon there was a parade through the city. At 8:00 P.M. we were loaded into freight cars and seen off for the last time, so many forever. Then we went via Perjamosch, Arad, Cirtici; early in the morning the border check of identifications plus papers and cars, then everybody got in, via Loekoeshaza, Szolnok (washing and delousing facility), then Vienna East Station, everybody out. There was a small crowd of people asking: "Where are you from? From Romania? You war-lengtheners, do you have any pork?" Each one got one kilogram, collected in baskets, then we marched, not in step, to the arsenal, there we were organized and counted, those up to 165 cm tall to the right, those over 165 cm to the left. Given food and quarters for the night.

Early next morning to the station. Departure for Agram, out of the cars, walk out of step outside the city to the cattle market. Quarters with a wooden roof over us. Wood shavings. Blanket; that was our sleeping place. Food from the goulash pot. Unpeeled potatoes, salted potatoes, vegetables, stew, margarine for breakfast and supper, coffee without sugar, jam; a complete change. (At home margarine was an almost unknown food.) After several days we received fatigues, shoes, socks, caps, underwear. Then the recruit training began with native German instructors. In mid-August our Company chief, SS-Hauptsturmführer Müller, introduced himself. Among other things, he spoke to us: "Dear comrades, I come from Germany and have the task of introducing myself as your company leader. You will shortly be taken to Germany, and in fact to Wahn near Cologne. An advance command of 8 to 10 men can already get ready to travel. In about a week we all go there." So the whole company traveled to Cologne-Wahn: Troop training place, airport, barracks. There the recruit training really started without mercy. Strict, factual, either/or. As for food, it was very short, constant coal gas, hungry from the hard training. In November we received cloth uniforms and took the oath to the colors."

In 1944 ethnic German families already fled to the west in front of the Red Army. After the war ended there came expulsion or deportation, so that in a first census at the end of January 1948 only about 345,000 people of German ancestry were registered. In the now-Communist regime the ethnic groups were collectively deprived of their rights for years and exposed to the will of state offices. This included deportation to the Soviet Union in January 1945 and deportation to the Baragan Steppe in June 1951.

As a result of a land reform law of March 1945, the Romanian Germans were dispossessed of their land. Only through a ministerial decision in December 1955, which regulated the homecoming of the Baragan deportees, were the fields and houses returned. Despite the relaxing of repression at times in the sixties and seventies, the majority of the Romanian Germans tried to leave the country. From 1967 to 1989 the German government "bought" the departure of 226,654 Romanian Germans to the Federal Republic of Germany.

Serbia

In Serbia, which was under German military command since the Balkan campaign of April 1941 and the resulting dissolution of the kingdom of Yugoslavia, there lived about 123,000 foreign Germans. They were mostly organized in the German People's Group under Dr. Sepp Janko and were categorized similarly to, for example, the ethnic Germans in Poland:

Group A: Character ethnic-politically without objection, socially secure
Group B: Character without objection, ethnic-politically unreliable, as in or from mixed marriages. No guarantee of German education of their children.
Group C: Too much Serbian blood, absolutely unreliable, asocial

On July 3, 1943 Dr. Janko reported in a telegram to Himmler how the number of ethnic Germans in Serbia was composed:

> "Our efforts in the years before the war to include all of our fellows in an organization approved by the state and train them in an outlook on life encountered difficulties in Belgrade and the Serbian area (the part south of Belgrade). Only the more valuable once came then. The socially very sunken ones, those who had made mixed marriages or came from mixed marriages, stayed away. So did some of the ethnically aware ones, who are kept very much under pressure. After the entry of the German troops, those elements also reported freely, because we set up food centers both in Belgrade and in the other Serbian cities. Whoever was German got food more easily. When I noticed that, I ordered at once that all these people might be taken up not as regular members. Only as "Preservation Members"! In the course of the last two years they were sifted constantly. Until a certain stock remained. Two months ago I ordered a last head count, so as to find out for each of the remaining ones whether he could be regarded as a German or not."

The military use of ethnic Germans in Serbia began in the summer of 1941. After little confidence in the Serbian police then in service, the German military commander used ethnic German volunteers to secure the transit intersections against partisan attacks. These had already taken part in the disarmament of the Serbian Army in April 1941 and were originally called the *Bürgerwehr*, somewhat later the "*Deutsche Mannschaft*." The Wehrmacht trained them at first in a weekly "marching and shooting".

When the plans of the Waffen-SS were changed to establish a 26,000-man SS mountain division of the unused potential of the ethnic Germans in the southeastern area, they turned to the members of the *Deutsche Mannschaft*. The legal justification was *de jure* made clear with the Serbian Prime Minister installed by the Germans, General Nedic, who gave a free hand to the ethnic-group leadership. In the course of setting up the SS Volunteer Mountain Division "Prinz Eugen", the ethnic-group leader Dr. Janko made known:

> "The German Wehrmacht has taken our villages and residences under their protection in the spring of the past year. Germany is fighting with its soldiers a hard battle to free all of Europe from Bolshevism. In our country too, the Bolshevik enemies tried in the past months and weeks to lift their heads, make the roads unsafe and burn our villages. German troops, in unity with us and all order-loving elements in the country, have opposed this danger. For us it is now a point of honor that we, following the traditions of our fathers, take over the protection of house and land ourselves. Therefore I call on you for all men from 17 to 50, as soon as the applicable year of birth is called, to report to your mayor, and in Belgrade to the district leadership of the ethnic group, to serve with weapons to protect our homes. Nobody who is healthy can withdraw from this service. German ethnic comrades, show your fathers you are worthy through manly service and deeds!"

With barely 1,000 eligible men per year of birth, this meant that thirty-four birth years with a total of some 34,000 men were mustered. Since 50-year-old men were scarcely suitable for service in an SS mountain division, some 12,000 members of the ethnic group, 17 to 35 years old, came to establish the 7th SS Volunteer Mountain Division "Prinz

Eugen."[42] By the end of 1942 there came the mustering of a further 2,500 men in ages up to forty-five years, so that at first some 14,500 ethnic Germans from Serbia served in the Waffen-SS. The older men, plus those who were mustered as capable of garrison or work duty were generally placed in so-called Help Police battalions.

On June 16, 1943 the Chief of the SS Main Office, *SS-Gruppenführer* Berger, wrote to the Personnel Staff of the *Reichsführer-SS* about the problems of military duty for ethnic Germans in the southeastern region – specifically in Serbia:

> "With the question of the military duty of ethnic Germans we went to bring one thing to clarity which is not yet ready and does not need clarification at the moment at all. The Reichsführer-SS has, for the ethnic group in the Serbian area – meaning Dr. Janko – announced the general military duty. The Serbian region is a German-governed area, since it is occupied by Germany. By state law, nothing is to be done against this announcement, except that no man cares about what we do with our ethnic Germans. The establishment of the "Prinz Eugen" Division took place not only by the principles of the general military duty, but also by the principles of the Tyrolean Landsturm Order of 1782."

According to the conditions of December 28, 1943, a total of 22,118 ethnic Germans from Serbia served in the Waffen-SS, the Police and the Help Police as well as in the Wehrmacht. By the war's end, three more birth years (1925 to 1927) were mustered, and men of 46 to 50 were called, so that again some 2,500 men were integrated into the Waffen-SS. Walter Neuner recalls:

> "In 1944 I was (born in 1925) in the 7th grade of the Realgymnasium in Gross-Betschkerek, the capital of the Banat. At first we did not have to go away from the school – like all the other boys – to military service in the "Prinz Eugen" Division. We were to graduate from school and only then be drafted as Fahnenjunker (officers' aides). Thus we were seen as officers' aides by the former head of the "Swabian-German Culture Club", Johann Keks, who was in Gross-Betschkerek as the *SS-Obersturmbannführer* Leader of the SS Replacement Command Serbia. When the situation in the Banat worsened and Romania withdrew from the alliance, we were inducted on August 10, 1944 into a readiness troop of the German People's Group in the Banat, the Standarte "Michael Reiser". This unit consisted mainly of mere boys, and we were, I believe, divided into four companies and quartered in bigger towns in the Banat. Here the training with Yugoslavian rifles and Czech and Italian machine guns began. I went to the 1st Company in Gross-Kikinda, which was led by a teacher named Wilhelm. The 2nd Company was led by my Uncle Joseph Koch, who was also a teacher. He fell at Stefansfeld in October 1944 during the fighting against the Russians advancing from Romania. Our uniforms were of mixed colors: blue pants (apparently from Czech supplies) and German field blouses of duck canvas without any emblems, and German coats. When the Russians reached the border of the Banat, we were subordinated to the Police Battle Group "Behrends". This battle group, under the Higher SS and Police Leader of Serbia, Montenegro and Sandzak, was composed of Police and Help Police forces, members of the Deutsche Mannschaft (Volkssturm), and a company "Otto" composed of furloughed men. On September 13, 1944 the advance on Temeschvar, Romania began with this pushed-together heap. We recruits were moved ahead to Schuple but did not take part in the combat. A week later we reached the other unit at the edge of Temeschburg, but were pushed right back again. On September 30, 1944 we were moved on horse-drawn wagons (without steel helmets, tent canvas, etc.) to St. Georgen on the Bega (some 20 km northeast of Gross-Betschkerek). Actually, we were supposed to escort the refugees from Romania through Gross-Betschkerek to the Theiss at Aradac. But since Betschkerek was already occupied by the Red Army on October 1, 1944, we were supposed to withdraw through Deutsch-Elmer to the Theiss. On the next day, at the first light of dawn, I was taken prisoner by the Russians along with six men of the rear-guard. We were turned over to the partisans, who wanted to shoot us at once, like so many others. Fortunately there was also a Russian officer, whom the partisans chased at once. Anyway, we were turned

---

42 In order to reach the necessary specified strength, ethnic Germans from Croatia and Romania were also taken into the division.

over to other partisans and, after being hit 100 times on the feet with a stick on October 10, 1944, taken to a big internment camp in my home town, from which I was able to flee in August 1946 through Romania to Austria."

In all, some 17,000 ethnic Germans served in the Waffen-SS between 1942 and 1945. There were also some 5,000 men taken into the Ordnungspolizei. The number of ethnic Germans in Serbia who served in the Wehrmacht was marginal.

After the war, the ethnic Germans in particular who had been in the List A group in the Nazi times suffered from mishandling, robbery, murder and deportation. This happened in milder form to the ethnic Germans on List B who were married to a Serbian spouse. The conditions led to the majority of the affected people trying to travel to the Federal Republic of Germany over the course of time. Today fewer than 5,000 people who regard themselves as Germans live in Serbia.

Slovakia

In Slovakia, which first formed Czechoslovakia along with Czechia in 1918, there lived around 130,000 ethnic Germans in 1939. In the country set up as an independent Slovakian Republic on May 14, 1939, though, only some 56,000 persons of the German ethnic group lived, under Franz Karmasin, a relationship that reflects an obviously lacking interest.

The service-eligible ethnic Germans at first served in the Slovakian Army, which took part in the 1941 Russian campaign with some 42,000 soldiers. There it was combined into special troop units. After Slovakia was already reduced to a strength of some 16,000 soldiers in its engagement with the USSR by the end of 1941, Himmler tried at least to hang onto the ethnic Germans. On August 2, 1942 there came an agreement with the Slovakian Prime Minister Tuka, by which the 17- to 35-year-old ethnic Germans could volunteer for the Waffen-SS. Excepted, though, were those who were already serving in the Slovakian Army.

The first to join the Waffen-SS were some 750 members of the *Einsatztruppe* (ET) of the Volunteer *Schutzstaffel*.[43] By December 28, 1943 there were, in all, 5,390 men inducted into the Waffen-SS. In all, 8,367 ethnic Germans from Slovakia served in the war. Besides the Waffen-SS volunteers, there were:

    1,740 in the Slovakian Army
    3,500 in work service in Germany
      237 in the German Wehrmacht
    1,000 in paramilitary units.

This represented about 6.4% of the ethnic Germans in Slovakia. When the two Slovakian divisions still in the USSR were reorganized into building brigades at the start of 1944 because of their unreliability, an agreement was made on June 7, 1944 by which the military duty of the ethnic Germans *had to be done* in the Waffen-SS. This also applied to the two purely ethnic German units in the Slovakian Army. The approximately 1,740 men were thus transferred to the Waffen-SS.[44] This was the last attempt to take soldiers from Slovakia for war service.

Since many of the mustering orders never took place, the ethnic-group leaders prepared lists in which so-called "Drückeberger" were named. Actually, this was also a precarious situation. On the one hand, they wanted to go along with the ethnic Germans' wishes for military potential; on the other, they did not want to weaken the ethnic group. In some cases the Slovakian police then had to take the men called by the Waffen-SS to the branch office of the SS Replacement command in Pressburg. A particular incident took place in Drexlerhau. A group of unwilling ethnic Germans was taken away in a truck by the Slovakian Gendarmery, and as they rode through their home area they held their shackled hands high and shouted, *"That is our free will!"*

---

43 The Volunteer *Schutzstaffel* corresponded to the usual SS in Germany. Under the command of Walter Donath, there were some 5,500 men, divided into six *Sturmbanne*, in it in 1939.

44 These ethnic Germans had already seen action on the eastern front in the Slovakian fast divisions in the union of the "German Battalion" (originally an artillery regiment on Käsmark and an infantry regiment in Kremnitz), mainly with Slovakian officers and non-commissioned officers.

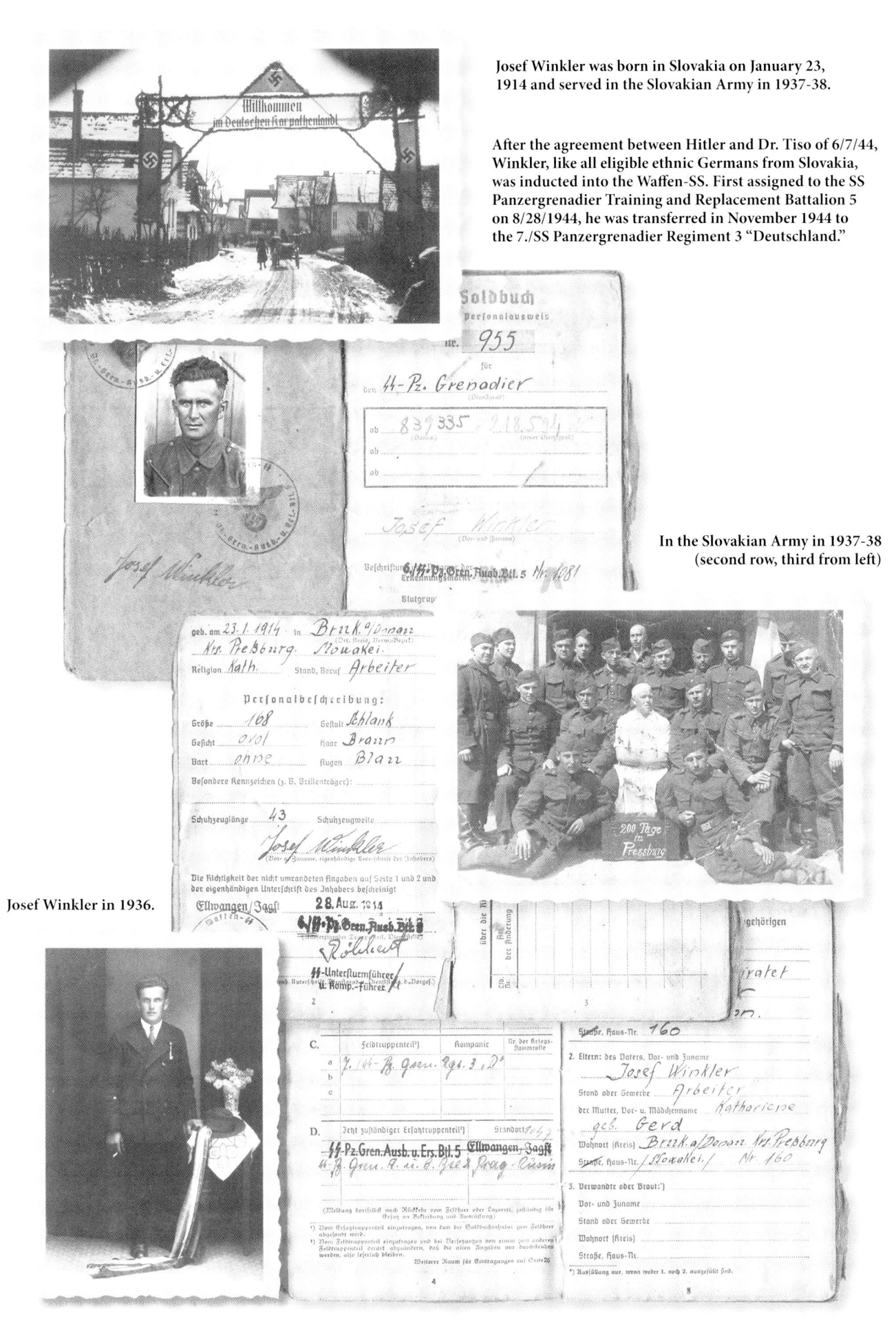

Josef Winkler was born in Slovakia on January 23, 1914 and served in the Slovakian Army in 1937-38.

After the agreement between Hitler and Dr. Tiso of 6/7/44, Winkler, like all eligible ethnic Germans from Slovakia, was inducted into the Waffen-SS. First assigned to the SS Panzergrenadier Training and Replacement Battalion 5 on 8/28/1944, he was transferred in November 1944 to the 7./SS Panzergrenadier Regiment 3 "Deutschland."

In the Slovakian Army in 1937-38 (second row, third from left)

Josef Winkler in 1936.

Surely this was a sort of compensation for the Slovakian officials. The German First Class Ambassador in Slovakia, Hanns Ludin, stated in a letter about the introduction of military duty:

> "The possible readiness of the Slovaks will be increased mainly by their happy thoughts of removing the Germans completely from their positions and chasing them off for the duration."

When the Security Headquarters called for volunteers from the German ethnic group in Slovakia, Ludin remarked:

> "By the experiences that we have had with voluntary recruitment in the last few months, I scarcely believe that the Security Headquarters will attain the desired number (of 800 volunteers for guarding tasks)."

Finally, ethnic Germans were given the mustering evaluation of *"capable of garrison and work use"* and ended at last in the guard crews of the concentration camps.

In the process of the Slovakian national uprising on September 2, 1944 the "German Home Guard" was set up, to which all service-capable but not serving masculine ethnic Germans from 16 to 50 years old belonged. This "Volkssturm" was called to do ditch-digging work for the "Pressburg" fortress in 1945.

At the beginning of 1945 there were 17,175 men in war service, but almost half of them were in reduced-time home guarding. Yet the total of militarily utilized man amounted to 19.1% of the ethnic Germans in Slovakia. Of them, there served:

    8,222 in the Waffen-SS
    8,116 in the Home Guards
      292 in the German Wehrmacht
      545 in paramilitary units.

The numbers called into the Ordnungspolizei could not be found.

Even before the war ended, a great many of the Carpathian Germans fled into the Sudetenland. After May 8, 1945 about one-third at first returned to Slovakia. As of August 2, 1945 they were denied Czechoslovakian citizenship, along with the Sudeten Germans in Czechia. Internment in gathering camps was followed in 1946-47 by the expulsion of some 33,000 Germans as a result of the Potsdam Accord. In 1947 there remained some 20,000 persons in Slovakia, most of whom had a Slovakian spouse. According to a census, fewer than 6,000 Germans live in Slovakia today.

Slovenia

Belonging to the Habsburg realm since the Middle Ages, Slovenia split off from Austria in 1918 and joined the Serbs and Croatians in the kingdom of the Serbs, Croats and Slovenes. In the Treaty of St. Germain in 1919, further Austrian regions, such as Lower Styria with its capital of Marburg (Maribor), Carniola, and parts of Southern Carinthia, were assigned to the new kingdom because of their overwhelmingly Slovenian populations.

The population of Slovenia included some 1.7 million people, of whom there were some 35,000 ethnic Germans in Lower (or Southern) Styria, some 35,000 in the Gottschee region (Upper Carniola), about 15,000, and in Southern Carinthia some 30,000.[45]

After the Balkan campaign, Slovenia was divided among the German Reich, Italy and Hungary in 1941. Southern Styria, Upper Carniola and Southern Carinthia were first given a civil government and were annexed to the German Reich as of October 1, 1941. Southern Styria was administered by *Gauleiter* Uibereuther and Upper Carniola and Southern Carinthia by *Gauleiter* Rainer:

---

45 In addition, the Windish ethnic group numbered some 45,000 people. Ethnically, they were Slovenes who in the past had not belonged to the Kingdom of the Serbs, Croats and Slovenes, but were oriented to Austria. In the course of the *"total war"* these Windish people, partially Germanized, or regarded as capable of being Germanized, were also forcibly recruited by the Wehrmacht.

After the Yugoslavian campaign, Southern Styria was included in Defensive Zone XVIII, and thus military duty was introduced for the population there.

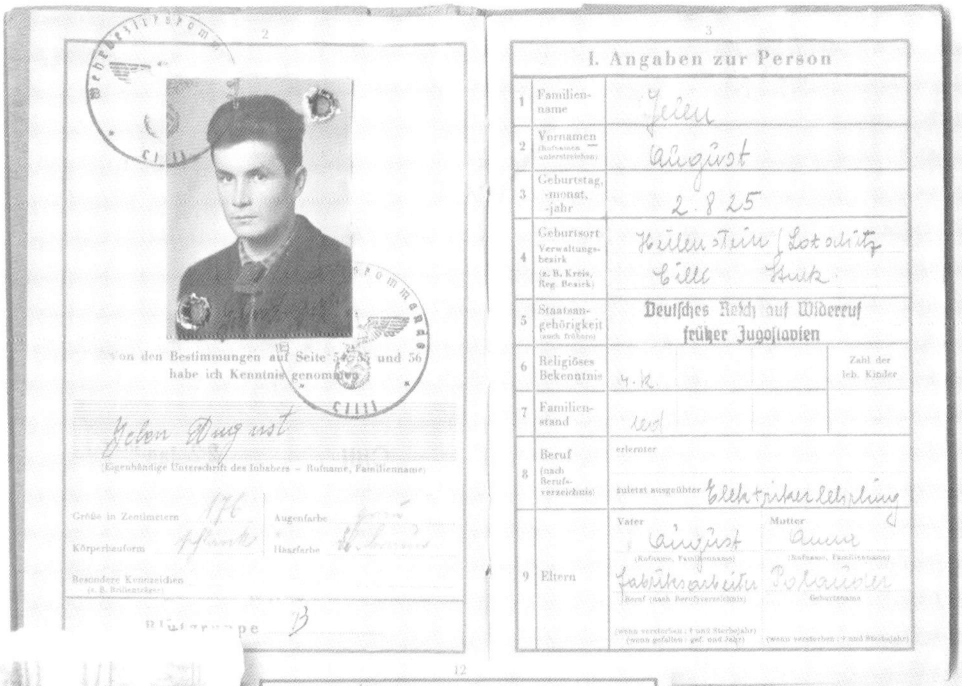

August Jelen received "revocable" German citizenship and, at the age of seventeen, entered the Waffen-SS. As of 6/1/43 he belonged to the 6th SS Mountain Division. No tragedy was spared when Jelen, in the withdrawal from Finland, fell in a fight with allied Finnish troops.

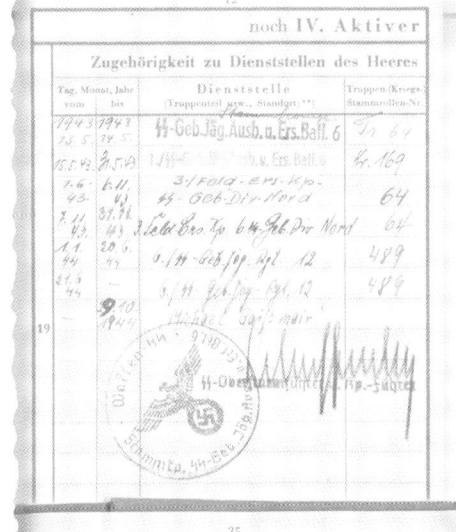

> "The Führer has given the Gauleiters of Styria and Carinthia the task of making the regained regions of Lower Styria and Carniola German after the victory of German weapons against Yugoslavia. Here it is a matter of winning back to the Great German Reich and the German people German blood, which in part because of the historical events and thanks to fully falsely understood state leadership in the times before the World War were lost to the German people."

Then came the formation of the Styrian Homeland League on May 10, 1941 and the Carinthian People's League on May 24, 1941. Both gathered the inhabitants and divided them into lists of people for the granting of German citizenship. For fear of being expelled, most of the Slovenians also joined. On October 14, 1941, with the orders for the gathering of them, ethnic Germans in Southern Styria, Southern Carinthia and Upper Carniola were given German citizenship.[46] In November of that year the resettling of the German ethnic group out of Gottschee in the Italian part of Styria began. On the other hand, the approximately 80,000 Slovenians who had not signed the People's List were settled shortly thereafter.

On March 24, 1942 the introduction of military duty in Southern Styria began with the mustering of man born between 1906 and 1922. On July 7, 1942 military duty was also introduced in Upper Carniola and Southern Carinthia. In the autumn of 1942 those born in 1923 and 1924 were mustered, plus those of 1926 on July 1, 1943 and those of 1927 on December 1, 1943. Finally even those born in 1928 were called. In all, some 70,000 Slovenians were forcibly recruited for the Wehrmacht, Waffen-SS and Police, plus the *Wehrmannschaften*.[47] A large number escaped here by fleeing to Croatia or joining the partisans.[48] Of the approximately 70,000, only about 8,000 were ethnic Germans. About 1,000 of them reported to the Waffen-SS. Some 9,000 older men were drafted for the Ordnungspolizei.

At the war's end, many fled from the partisans to Austria. Numerous ethnic German families, though, were interned in Sterntal (Strnisce) near Ptuj and Tuechern (Teharje), where a large number died in the overcrowded camps. Finally the interned ethnic Germans were expropriated and shoved off to Austria until 1946. In 1971 a census showed only about 700 inhabitants to be German.

USSR

According to a census in 1897, about 1.8 million Germans lived in the Russian Empire. Some 300,000 of the Germans lived on the Volga, around 342,000 in the south, some 237,000 in the west and about 18,000 in Moscow. At the beginning of the 1920s there was a great weave if emigration (mainly to the USA). By a census of 1926, there were 1,238,539 Germans in the USSR. In September of 1939 there were circa 1.4 million, divided as follows:

Russian Federated Soviet Republic	700,231
Ukrainian Soviet Socialist Republic	392,458
Autonomous Soviet Socialist Republic of the Volga Germans	366,685
Autonomous Soviet Socialist Republic of the Crimea	51,299
Region of Ordshonikidse	45,689
Region of Krasnodar	34,287
Azerbaijan Soviet Socialist Republic	23,133
Georgian Soviet Socialist Republic	20,527
White Russian Soviet Socialist Republic	8,488
Kirghiz Soviet Socialist Republic	8,426
Region of Chabarovsk	5,696
Autonomous Soviet Socialist Republic of the Kabardines and Balkars	5,327
Dagestanish Autonomous Soviet Socialist Republic	5,048
Kalmuckish Autonomous Soviet Socialist Republic	4,150

---

46 In November 1942 83% of the population had German nationality. Of them, 27,059 were final and 415,694 revocable. 82,365 were stateless and forcibly protected.

47 Some 28,000 men belonged to the Carinthian and around 6,000 to the Lower Styrian *Wehrmannschaft*. These two security forces were under the command of the SA and corresponded in structure and function to it. The members were taken forcibly, and not a few of them lost any and all service.

48 Not least, the chauvinistic Germanization policy led to strong rejection of being German; for example, all Slovenian names had to be Germanified.

Bashkirish Autonomous Soviet Socialist Republic	3,299
North Ossetish Atonomous Soviet Socialist Republic	2,924
Region of Primorye	1,911
Autonomous Soviet Socialist Republic of Chechens and Ingushens	858
Armenian Soviet Socialist Republic	433
Autonomous Soviet Socialist Republic of the Tchuvachen	10,223

After the Polish campaign, in September 1939, the three Baltic states of Estonia, Latvia and Lithuania became soviet republics. The parts of eastern and southern Poland occupied by the Red Army were added to the Ukrainian Soviet Socialist Republic. Thus the German-speaking population in the USSR increased by about 280,000 people.

In October 1939, though, the resettlement of some 51,000 members of the Baltic German ethnic group under Erhard Kröger[49] from Latvia began, as did that of 16,000 Baltic Germans from Estonia. They were settled mainly in the new Reichsgau of Wartheland created after the Polish campaign. The emigration aroused mix feelings in the Baltic Germans. Most of them had established themselves and achieved high prosperity. The interest in leaving their homeland suddenly and having to go to a strange land was mostly meager. The Baltic Germans were especially surprised by Hitler's resettling action, as until then they had been politically supported as *"German outposts."* Heinrich Bosse writes spiritedly about it in his book, *The Führer Calls*:[50]

> *"On October 9, 1939 the German newspapers of the country announced the cry for resettlement. Nobody was calm about it. The more glowingly and passionately the news was given to the nation, the more naturally the demand to hold the worn-out outpost for the German people was linked with it. All of that meant nothing any more from one day to the next."*

On November 16, 1939 Hitler also agreed with Stalin that the ethnic Germans living in the recently annexed regions of eastern and southern Poland could also emigrate. Some 58,000 ethnic Germans left Wolhynia, circa 60,000 Galicia and around 40,000 the Narew district around Bialystok. On April 30, 1940 the law about the introduction of German military duty in the annexed eastern regions (Wartheland, West Prussia and Upper Silesia) was abolished, retroactive to March 1, 1940. With that the resettlers who received German citizenship (sometimes revocably) were called into the Wehrmacht.

Further resettlements followed as of September 1940, after Romania had surrendered Bessarabia and northern Bukovina to the Soviet Union. Around 90,000 ethnic Germans from Bessarabia and 45,000 from northern Bukovina left their homelands then. After the signing of a German-Romanian treaty, 14,500 ethnic Germans from Dobrudja, on the Romanian-Bulgarian boundary near the Black Sea,[51] and 45,000 from southern Bukovina were resettled. Finally there came the German ethnic group in Lithuania (Lithuanian SSR), with some 35,000 members. In all, 420,000 ethnic Germans were moved into the Warthegau, Silesia and West Prussia within a year.

After the Russian campaign began in the summer of 1941, Stalin had some 640,000 ethnic Germans deported to Kazakhstan and Siberia.[52] He feared that they could become a danger. Some 250,000 escaped the same fate by the quick advance of the German troops. According to the general plan "East",[53] some 65,000 of them were ethnic Germans from eastern Wolhynia (part of the USSR since the Peace of Riga in 1921), who formed three settlement areas between Schitomir and Vinniza.[54] About 135,000 more Black Sea Germans found themselves in Transnistria,[55] which

---

49 Erhard Kröger was at first the leader of the Baltic German movement in Latvia and was named an SS-Standartenführer by Himmler. He finally became the leader of all the ethnic Germans in the Baltic states.
50 Bosse, Heinrich, *Der Führer ruft*, Berlin 1941.
51 The Bulgarian part of Dobrudja was annexed by Romania in the 1913 Baltic War and returned to Bulgaria in 1940 by the Treaty of Craiova.
52 Other documents speak of 949,829 ethnic Germans who were resettled in special settlements. Of them, 446,480 came from the dissolved Volga republic, 82,900 from the Ukrainian regions not yet conquered by the Wehrmacht, and 46,356 from Transcaucasia.
53 Among Himmler's extensive resettlement conceptions, which included the large-scale settlement of the eastern area with Germans and ethnic Germans, consult applicable publications, such as *Czeslav Madajaczik* et al, (editors), *Vom Generalplan "Ost" zum Generalsiedlungsplan*, Berlin 1994.
54 In the new areas, large numbers of the ethnic German men were organized by the SS into so-called self-protection. In the spring of 1942 there were already some 20,000 men who, among others, were to protect the villages from partisan attacks.
55 From 1941 to 1944 the area between the Dniestr and Bug was called Transnistria, under Romanian administration.

Ethnic German resettlers from Bessarabia.

Command Book for a member of the Ethnic German Mittelstelle. The Special Command "R" (Russia) was responsible for resettling the ethnic Germans in Transnistria, which was under Romanian rule since 1941.

had been annexed by Romania in the summer of 1941. They received similar ethnic-group rights to the ethnic groups in Romania on December 13, 1941, after German-Romanian negotiations. They were taken by the Special Command "R" of the Ethnic German Mittelstelle and given a classification like the well-known People's Lists. In March 1943 the planned mustering and induction of the eligible men who were to undergo the *"Folkish Military Duty"* began. Of the approximately 9,000-man-strong Ethnic German Home Guard in Transnistria alone, some 3,000 young men were inducted into the Waffen-SS.

One year later, the evacuation of the Black Sea Germans via Romania, Serbia and Hungary to the Wartheland began. Their first station there was the resettler camp in Litzmannstadt (Lodz). On March 17, 1944 the National Socialist press euphemistically reported on the evacuation:

> "Lodz, millionth resettler in the Wartheland! Over a million German settlers in the Wartheland. In connection with the securing of the German living space in the East, initiated four years ago, by bringing the outer German ethnic groups home and settling them in the expanded Reich borders, the Wartheland Reichsgau has put an important section of its ethnic policy work behind it. Gauleiter and Reichsstatthalter Greiser could report to the Führer and the Reichsführer-SS as Reich Commissar for solidifying of the German people that in the process of the presently careful resettling of the Black Sea Germans the number of Germans in the Wartheland has reached the million mark. After taking in the Black Sea Germans, who are still in transit, the German population in the Wartheland will rise to 1.1 million."

Thus in all, more than a million ethnic Germans from the region of the USSR were resettled or evacuated into the Great German Reich. Among others, they included the Baltic Germans as well as the Wolhynian and Galician Germans, the Black Sea Germans or the Bessarabian Germans. If one assumes that these people were added to the agriculture, then there were still some 78,000 men inducted into the Wehrmacht. The Waffen-SS was already recruiting for volunteers in the resettler camps <u>before</u> the settlement. In September 1944 came the forced induction, especially of those who had not yet received German citizenship, to the Waffen-SS. This involved some 7,500 men. About 1,000 of them came in October 1944 to the newly established SS Panzergrenadier Training Regiment in Neweklau. In all, about 10,000 former residents of the USSR (including the Baltic Germans, etc.) served in the Waffen-SS. The former Baltic German *Standartenführer* George Beckmann recalls:

> "After our resettlement from Riga (Latvia) to Posen in the Wartheland, I was inducted into the RAD (Work District XIII) in Magdeburg in 1942. In February 1943 I reported voluntarily to the Waffen-SS under the prerequisite of joining the cavalry. The reasons for it were, for one thing, the elite concepts propagated through "comradeship and reliability", plus a talk with my father, who had been a cavalryman under the Russian Czars and told me, "Go to the Cavalry; it is bearable there." In the late summer of 1943 I was then called to Schiratz near Litzmannstadt to the 3rd Regiment of the SS Cavalry Division. Until the new year, we stayed at the troop training camp but received more infantry training and sat on a horse only now and then. In January 1944 I had to go to the hospital and thus missed the regiment's departure to Kowel. Along with some 30 or 40 other comrades, I then formed the regiment's rear command, which mainly brought along equipment, food and armaments. The regiment was not mounted and was divided as "corset bones" into several hundreds that had been made up of railroaders, engineers, etc. Since almost all the commanders and officers had died, an SS Unterscharführer led my hundred. My squadron leader Willi Geyer commanded a battle group (strength" one battalion). In Kowel I was promoted to SS-Sturmmann and received the Assault Badge and bronze Close Combat Badge. And the Iron Cross II for one action southwest of Kowel as a Gruppenführer. Our hundred was moved to the west bank of the Turija and had taken up positions and a kolkhoze. On the same night we were attacked by strong Soviet troops and had to retreat. The west bank was very steep, while the east one was flat. I secured the withdrawal of the individual groups and platoons, since they would otherwise have been left to be shot at as if on a platter. With my group I was the last to leave the west bank. On the night before Easter Sunday, shortly before units of the 5th SS Panzer Division opened the pocket, I was wounded by a shot through the lower arm."

In the National police as well, some 10,000 ethnic Germans from the USSR were inducted. One part of them came after June 22, 1941 in the non-evacuated areas of the Ukraine. During the war the ethnic Germans living under Soviet authority again were deported to Siberia, Kazakhstan and other regions. Before the Red Army captured the Wartheland, the evacuation of the ethnic Germans settled there into the West began. Some of them were forcibly repatriated from here back to the USSR after the war. The numbers were very varying. For example, of the 350,000 Russian Germans, some 250,000, and of the 80,000 Bessarabian Germans some 10,000, went forcibly back to the USSR. In 1950 there were still some 670,000 Russian Germans listed as being forced into the Soviet Union. Some 100,000 lived in German reception camps.

Hungary

In Hungary there lived some 845,000 Germans after the Viennese agreement of 1940 and the connected annexation of the northern part of Siebenbürgen (formerly Romanian). They were mostly organized in the ethnic group under Dr. Franz Basch, which was given the status of a public, legal organization in Hungary. New rights were involved. The members recognized by the ethnic group, for example, could take back their German names. In the course of the formerly chauvinistic minority policy, the first names and some last named had been Magyarized and the German schools and culture oppressed.

Because of the existing discrimination, the ethnic Germans eligible for service had little interest in serving in the Hungarian Army. So after the 1941 Balkan campaign some 1,000 young volunteers from Hungary joined the Waffen-SS in a more or less illegal action.

The Hungarian government, under Prime Minister Bardossy, was not opposed in principle to the growing interest of the Waffen-SS in ethnic German volunteers. It saw therein the possibility of weakening the German ethnic group, and so on February 1, 1942 an agreement made between the countries declared that that the SS volunteers would be stripped of their Hungarian citizenship. All ethnic Germans born from 1912 to 1925 (17 to 30 years old) were inducted, as long as they were not already serving in the Hungarian Army.

With some 6,000 eligible men per year. 25,709 of the theoretical total of 84,000 reported. Of these, 17,860 were mustered as qualified. If one subtracts form the total the approximately 30,000 ethnic Germans serving in the Hungarian Army at that time, about every other man reported voluntarily in 1942.

From March 22, 1942 to May 3, 1942 16,527 men left their homes and went to the SS troop training base of "Heidelager". The majority of the men were used to form the SS Cavalry Division and the SS Mountain Division "Nord". SS-capable volunteers also went to the original Waffen-SS divisions. The recruiting action had had great success, for with some 17,000 new recruits the Waffen-SS had received the strength of a division in five weeks.

It was hoped that this result could be repeated a year later. But after those born in 1926 had brought about 6,000 potentially able men, the second effort, on June 1, 1943, raised the maximum age to 35. Thus there were six more birth years available, with some 35,000 men to be mustered. Since some of these were already in the Hungarian Army, the new Hungarian Prime Minister Kallay approved their release for voluntary reporting. The first transport trains left Hungary as of September 7, 1943. In this action, which lasted until February 8, 1944, about 20,000 men were taken for the Waffen-SS. Volunteer Kurt Schell recalls:

> "In July and August 1943 the mustering took place in northern Siebenbürgen (belonging to Hungary since 1940). A command made up of SS leaders came to Siebenbürgen and drove from town to town. Wherever there were German communities, all eligible men between 18 and 35 were mustered. It was called "voluntary" then. If we had not gone to the Waffen-SS, we would have had to do our service in the Hungarian Army. So it was not hard for us to report voluntarily. At the end of September 1943 we were inducted. For the sake of simplicity, we were picked up at once by SS lower leaders and taken to Vienna in cattle cars. The departure of the Waffen-SS volunteers from Sächsisch-Regen and its environs took place formally at the market place in the presence of the entire population, the fathers of the church, the Hungarian city commander, the mayor and the political leaders of the German ethnic group in Hungary. The departure was preceded by a supper at the church. Along with the ceremony, in which many speeches were made, we marched to the schoolyard of the German high school, where the women and girls decorated the men with flowers and invited us to eat at a fancily set table. Later in the afternoon we went to the railroad station, where we were loaded. The trip

Departure of the Hungarian ethnic Germans who reported in the second recruiting action, October 20, 1943.

to Vienna took three days. At the south station we were awaited and marched from there to the arsenal with our baggage on our backs. We slept the first night on wood shavings. On the next morning we turned out, and our presence was recorded again according to lists, and we were checked for capability. The only barely capable men stayed in Vienna and then, in part, went into the armament industry (Author's note). The rest were transferred to Cracow, Hamburg and France. I went with others from my home area to Nimes (southern France). At the barracks there, the commander of SS Field Replacement Battalion 10 (SS-Hauptsturmführer Dietrich) awaited us, welcomed us in a short speech, and informed us that we were assigned to the already existing five companies composed of ethnic German volunteers from Hungary and the Banat. After a few days many of us began to feel a certain disappointment. The tone that prevailed in the companies was not what we had expected. We were called "war-lengtheners" (sic!), "cannon fodder" and "starvelings" by a lower leader. This resulted in expressions of displeasure among the ethnic Germans. It only became better or was abolished when some of the men had the courage to speak to the commander and report this situation to him."

On December 28, 1943, 62,845 Hungarian Germans were in military service. They made up about 7% of the ethnic group. Of them, there were:

35,000 in the Hungarian Army
22,125 in the Waffen-SS[56]
3,500 in work service in Germany
1,729 in the German Wehrmacht
459 in paramilitary units
32 in work service

In February 1944 some 35,000 ethnic Germans were serving in the Waffen-SS. With the losses to date, there were barely 40,000 members of the ethnic group in the ranks of the Waffen-SS. Only a few weeks later, on April 14, 1944 a third agreement with the new Prime Minister Sztojay introduced universal military duty with the Wehrmacht and Waffen-SS for ethnic Germans from Hungary born from 1894 to 1927. It was stated in this agreement:

"1. In the course of increased war service together against the mutual enemy, stronger Waffen-SS units are being set up at once.
2. To assure the hastened establishment in personal terms, the following process will be used:
3. Hungarian citizens, stateless persons, ethnic Germans from other countries born in any year are turned over, according to mutual agreements, for the duration of the war, in the way of military duty, to the German Wehrmacht and Waffen-SS. The military duty begins with the completion of the 17th year of age.
4. In the application of this agreement, whoever shows himself to be such through his life style and ethnic characteristics, or voluntarily accepts German status, is viewed as an ethnic German.
5. For the establishment of the SS units, men from the civilian sector (reservists and non-serving) and from the Honved are considered.
6. With consideration for the production capability of the industry, mining, and readiness of the Honved, the necessary specialist workers with special training are held back by the Honved Ministry for their own use. This retention may, as in the first two Waffen-SS actions, not exceed 10.5% of the qualifying mustered men.
7. Necessary barracks and troop training camps will be made available by the Honved Ministry. Likewise – when possible – arms, equipment, materials, etc.
8. The locating, mustering and inducting are carried out by the SS Headquarters, Replacement Inspection Southeast Region, SS Completion or Replacement Command in Hungary, in cooperation with the Royal Hungarian Honved Ministry.

---

56 The small number of some 22,000 ethnic Germans from Hungary in the Waffen-SS on December 28, 1943 worked out as follows: some 17,000 men were inducted in 1942. In their service of about 1.5 years until the end of 1943, some 4,000 died or were released from service because of wounds. From September to December 1943, about 10,000 men were inducted newly into the Waffen-SS. The remaining approximately 12,000 men followed in January and February 1944.

The German-Hungarian Mustering Commission.

Departure at the market place in Sächsisch-Regen.

Rail transport to Vienna, where the post-mustering took place.

9. The decision
    a) about sending back takes place immediately after the mustering by the Waffen-SS
    b) about holding back, the Honved Ministry decides within 14 days after the mustering. Those sent back must also be left in their civilian occupations by the Hungarian state.
10. The Hungarian Honved Ministry receives from the SS Replacement Command Hungary transport lists of the inducted in the same manner and preparation as before.
11. The care and supplying take place according to the existing agreements.
12. The men inducted into the German Wehrmacht or Waffen-SS retain all the rights of a Hungarian citizen and remain Hungarian citizens. Through their entry into the German Wehrmacht or Waffen-SS they also qualify as members of the German Reich. The same also applies to those previously inducted into the German Wehrmacht or Waffen-SS. Thus for the applicable ones, the previous renunciation of Hungarian citizenship or the already undertaking los of citizenship is reversed. The members of the inducted enjoy the same rights and privileges as the members inducted into the Honved."

Thus all men from their 17th to their 50th year of life became eligible for service. The then higher SS and Police Leader in Hungary, *SS-Gruppenführer* and *Generalleutnant* of the Police Winkelmann recalled after the war:

"In the spring of 1944 – I do not know exactly if it was in April – I heard that negotiations to set up an interstate agreement concerning the service of ethnic German in the Waffen-SS were being held at the German embassy. The negotiations were led by the Commander of the Waffen-SS in Hungary, SS-Gruppenführer Keppler, and the Leader of the SS Completion Command in Hungary, Heermann. I learned the following: Himmler had advised the SS Headquarters (Berger) to make sure in an agreement between Hungary and Germany that the ethnic Germans in Hungary were inducted into the Waffen-SS. I note that there were previously – before March 19, 1944 – two actions to induct ethnic Germans into the Waffen-SS. These, though, concerned voluntary reporting. The SS-FHA passed the order above on to the SS Replacement Command in Hungary and turned to Keppler with the request to support the order. Thus Keppler spoke with Honved Minister Csatay and received the agreement in principle of the Hungarian government. After several textual changes, service in the Waffen-SS became obligatory for all those who, by their ancestry and life style, belonged to the ethnic Germans. A standpoint that the affected men should again attest to their German ethnicity was not foreseen. Between the Hungarian War Ministry and the SS Completion Command in Hungary the following process was set: The local organs of the German Ethnic Union listed applicable ethnic Germans in local registers. These registers went to the SS Completion Command, which provided them to the Completion Department of the War Ministry.

The latter presented the register to the local notaries for action. They deleted the persons whom they no longer regarded as ethnic Germans. But it also happened that they suggested names. The registers went back to the War Ministry, which brought them to the attention of the SS Replacement Command. Since Heermann complained almost daily that the notaries definitely deleted German men from the lists and the War ministry did nothing about this situation, I told Heermann he should temporarily be satisfied with those for whom authorization had come. Later we would be able to negotiate for the others. This is what happened. Meanwhile, Himmler advised me to hasten the realization of the agreement with all powers. He had the feeling that the Hungarian offices rejected everything and I allowed it. I tried to set him right: The Hungarians do their duty and so it is natural that there are differences of opinion. This must be cleared up mutually after the agreement. Beyond that, the process is committed to a laborious method which cannot be shortened. I said it would still take some 4 to 6 weeks until the medical examination could take place. Only after that would the inductions by the Hungarian War Ministry take place. The inducted men, up to the age of 45 years, would be assigned by the SS Replacement Command, which was subordinate to the SS-FHA,[57] to the Waffen-SS and also the Ordnungspolizei."

---

57 As opposed to the so-called *"Germanic"* countries, the recruiting was handled by the SS Headquarters, Department VI, the former *"Germanic Volunteer Administration."*

Since the men eligible for war service from the ages of 17 to 35 were already in military service, the German ethnic group in Hungary still numbered about 350,000 men at that time. The men from 36 to 45 who had not served should be taken by the Waffen-SS, and the 46- to 50-year-olds for the Ordnungspolizei. Beyond that, ethnic Germans serving in the Hungarian Army could and should also report, which the Hungarian Army did not always make possible. Of the first group, out of about 50,000 mustered men, some 30,000 were inducted into the Waffen-SS, while some 3,000 of the 30,000 older men went to the Ordnungspolizei. A larger contingent came from the Hungarian Army, so that as of September 1944 at least 60,000 ethnic Germans from Hungary were taken for the Waffen-SS and Police.

Over 10,000 of them were used to set up the 22nd SS Volunteer Cavalry Division. In October 1944, 15,000 formed the 31st SS Volunteer Grenadier Division, and about 5,000 were called to form the 37th SS Volunteer Cavalry Division. Some 5,000 men also went to the 6th SS Mountain Division "Nord" in the first half of 1944, and large contingents went to the 11th SS Volunteer Panzergrenadier Division "Nordland" and as replacements to the SS panzer divisions after their losses in Normandy.

The inductions brought very different reactions, in which the basic political inclination of the ethnic Germans had to be considered. There were the "Browns", who were Nazi-inclined, the 'Blacks', who were Christian conservatives, and the Magyarones, who were strongly oriented to Hungary. An ethnic German described the situation of the time impressively:[58]

> "I myself was at the front in the Pripyet Swamps of White Russia in 1944 as a Hungarian Honved soldier in the Hussar Division, when I got mail from home in which my brother wrote specifically of how the mustering for the Waffen-SS was going. The minor judge brought six summonses to the house for the German mustering at the end of August: for our father (then 46 years old), World War participant and father of 12 children) and for his five sons. On being told that the two eldest sons were on the front as Hungarian soldiers, the messenger took their summonses away, plus my father's. My three younger brothers, Franz (1924), Philipp (1925) and Stefan (1926), were not willing to join voluntarily, so that they also, after repeated urging, did not go to the mustering. Since they, along with other "refusers", went into hiding, our father was summoned at night and interned with other parents of unwilling ones in a guest house, so to speak, as hostages. The Hungarian police helped in the action firmly. Then the boys and men reported to the mustering commission, where they were received appropriately and naturally had to listen to what was said. This would not have been surprising, except that a Hungarian officer stood out especially in the snottiness, which seemed somewhat surprising.
>
> The course of this story also bothered me somewhat, and I wrote right back that, if the matter goes on like this, then Franz and Philipp should go to the Waffen-SS if they were called. That is about how it happened, although Franz and Philipp were not inducted right away, but had to be rounded up by the Bosniaks[59] and taken away to Karawukovo. From then on they were good soldiers, and did their duty loyally and properly. Franz, in fact, lost his life when he died of his wounds on February 22, 1945 after a dive-bomber attack on the transport train near Maria Saal in Carinthia, while Philipp spent the whole war as a messenger in Silesia.
>
> I told the youngest, Stefan, that he was too young to be a soldier, and he should see about getting to Kalocsa to continue his education in the beginning new school year. That is what he did, but when the Russians came at the end of October and the school was closed, he set out for home again. On November 25, 1944 our father and Stefan, along with 210 men from Filipova, were murdered by a Serbian partisan command. Mother and my six sisters were sent to the concentration camp in Gakova."

In all, some 70,000 ethnic Germans from Hungary served in the Waffen-SS, about 3,000 in the Ordnungspolizei, and 2,000 in the German Wehrmacht. In the course of World War II, about 8,000 Hungarian Germans fled to Germany; some 45,000 were deported to the Soviet Union by the Red Army. After the war ended came the expulsion of some 200,000 ethnic Germans. After the rebellion of 1956, a further wave of emigration ensued. In 2002 there were about 62,000 people still claimed to be Germans. This amounted to circa 10% of the ethnic German population of 1939.

---

58 Pencz, Rudolf, *Vor Haus und Hof und Kind und Weib*, Frankenstadt 2010.
59 These were members of the 23rd Waffen Mountain Division of the SS "Kama" (Croatian No.2), which was being set up in that area. It can be assumed that the German personnel were called in because the Bosnian men were also only recruits.

The Ethnic Germans in the Wehrmacht

Around 370,000 ethnic Germans served in the Wehrmacht, some 310,000 of them in the Army, 40,000 in the Luftwaffe and 20,000 in the Navy. Based on the annexation of border areas into the German Reich, they became obliged to serve when given German citizenship. From the defense zone in which they lived, at least in the case of the Army, their induction generally sent them to a troop unit that was in touch with the defense zone. Here the Wehrmacht differed from the Waffen-SS. In the latter, a homogeneous regional unit was not rare, but an organization of a large unit by a defense zone essentially did not happen.

An exception in inductions for the Wehrmacht was the total of about a million ethnic Germans from Russia who were settled in the Wartheland. Because of their lack of their own units in Defense Zone XXI, they were called to Zones I, II, III and VIII, or as of the summer of 1942 also to the newly formed Reserve Divisions.[60] The reason for this was that in the Warthegau, unlike the "old" regions of Germany, the structures for inclusive new establishments were lacking, and besides, they did not want to set up any complete divisions of ethnic Germans because of their sometimes doubtful motivation.

On the basis of the quantity of Wehrmacht units in which the ethnic Germans served, a description of the individual formations would explode the limits of this book. Since some 85% of the ethnic Germans were inducted into the Army, the divisions that were formed in the defense zones in which the majority of the ethnic Germans were called for military service shall be listed below. Those called into the Luftwaffe mostly went to the (homeland) Flak units and the Luftwaffe field units. Only a very small group reached the flying units. In the Navy the ethnic Germans were used both on ships and in the coast artillery.

Alsace	Zone V	Infantry Divisions 5, 25, 35, 77, 78, 125, 198, 205, 215, 245, 260, 266, 282, 305, 323, 335, 344, 355, 365, 554 and 715; Panzer Divisions 10 an 23.
Luxembourg and Lorraine	Zone XII	Infantry Divisions 33, 34, 36, 65, 72, 79, 85, 91, 112, 132, 197, 246, 263, 342, 348, 389, 462, 556 and 712; Panzer Divisions 15, 22 and 27.
Eupen and Malmedy	Zone VI	Infantry Divisions 6, 16, 26, 39, 47, 64, 69, 70, 84, 86, 106, 126, 176, 196, 211, 227, 240, 253, 254, 264, 306, 326, 329, 361, 371, 385, 393, 526, 555 and 716; Panzer Divisions 6, 16, 25 and 116.
Silesia	Zone VIII	Infantry Divisions 8 (later 8th Rifle), 18 (later 18th Panzer-Grenadier), 28 (later 28th Rifle), 41, 62, 81, 102, 148, 158, 168, 213, 221, 226, 252, 286, 320, 332, 358, 370, 708, 544-567; 573rd Volksgrenadier Division; Panzer Divisions 5, 11 and 232.
Wartheland	Zone XXI	Divisions z.b.V. 429 and 430; Infantry Division 399.
	Zone I	Infantry Divisions 1, 11, 21, 61, 121, 161, 199, 206, 217, 228, 244, 274, 291, 311, 340, 349, 383, 395, 521, 542 and 714 (later 114th Rifle); Panzer Division 24.
	Zone II	Infantry Divisions 2, 12, 32, 59, 60, 75, 122, 156, 162, 207, 242, 258, 272. 281. 292, 302, 328, 338, 353 and 702; Panzer Division 12.
	Zone III	Infantry Divisions 3, 23, 50, 68, 76, 93, 123, 263, 203, 208, 218, 223, 257, 270, 273, 278, 293, 303, 333, 359, 386, 430, and 719; Panzer Divisions 3, 8, 26 and 233.
	Zone VIII	(see above)
South Tyrol, Carinthia, Stryia, Slovenia	Zone XVII	Infantry Divisions 44, 45, 92, 137, 182, 243, 262, 277, 297, 327, 328, 331 (Div. z.b.V.), 351, 357, 369 (Croatian), 373 (Croatian), 392 (Croatian) and 717 (later 117th Rifle); Rifle Divisions 42 and 187.
	Zone XVIII	Infantry Divisions 538 (z.b.V) and 718 (later 118th Rifle); Mountain Divisions 2, 3, 5, 6 and 188.

---

60 These were 141, 143, 147, 148, 151, 153, 154, 156 to 160, 165, 166, 171, 173, 174, 182, 182 (new), 188, 189, 189 (new), and the 191st Reserve Division.

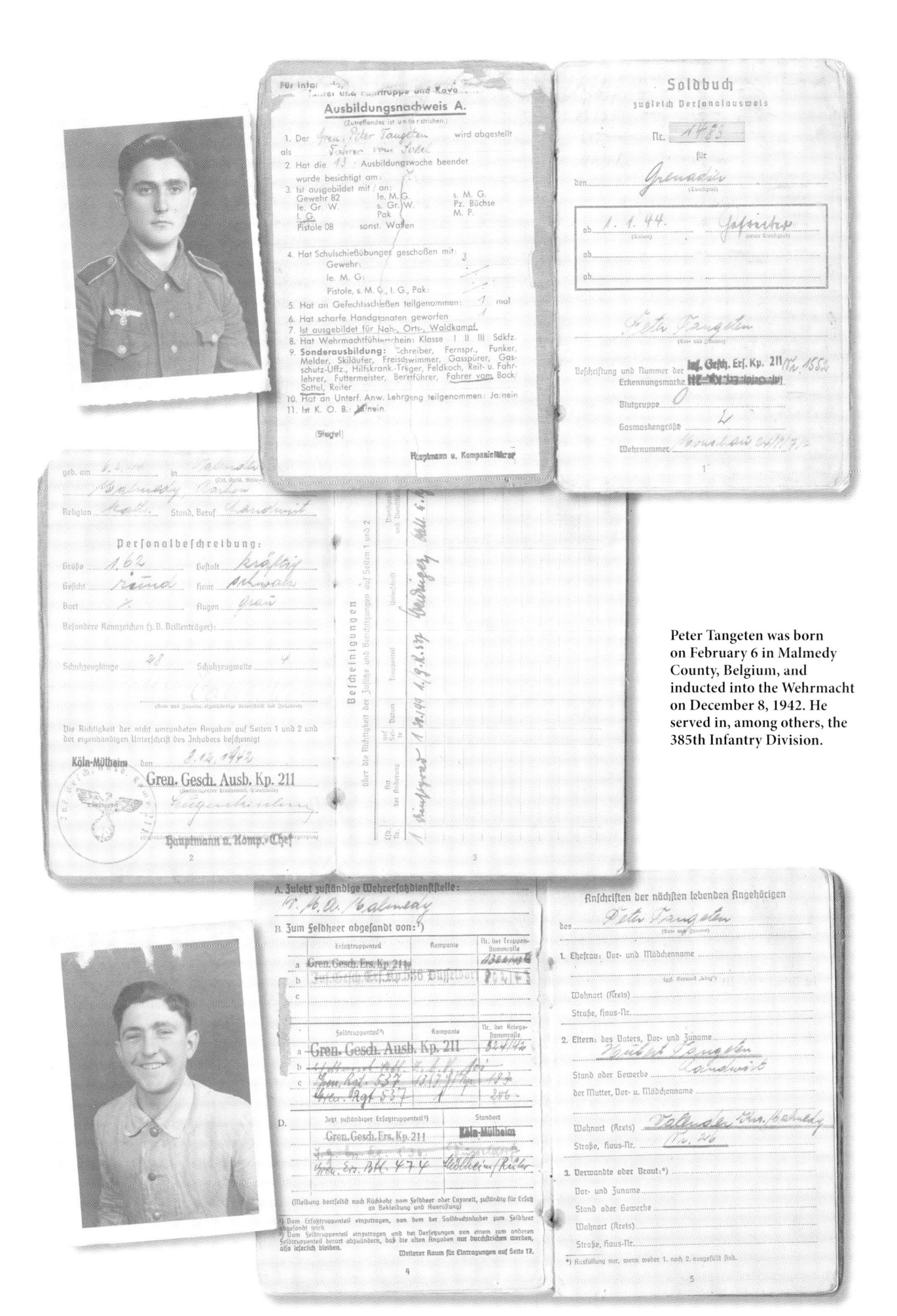

Peter Tangeten was born on February 6 in Malmedy County, Belgium, and inducted into the Wehrmacht on December 8, 1942. He served in, among others, the 385th Infantry Division.

Unlike the Waffen-SS, as already noted, there were no divisions completely of ethnic Germans. Instead, contingents were assigned when needed to the various new or refreshed units. During World War II there were usually between 1,500 and 4,000 ethnic Germans in the various units. The former company leader Berthold Vogt recalls the personnel when Engineer Battalion 114 (114th Rifle Division) was being formed:[61]

> "The core of the new battalion was formed by the former Engineer Company 714. In its ranks there must have been a certain number of Banat Germans, since at least in the new 1st Company two "translators" were assigned. The men came mostly from Defense Zone I, including a considerable number of "ethnic Germans from List 3". The composition by age I would now estimate as being as such" 1/3 of the men were born in 1924, 1/3 from 1920 to 1922, and 1/3 older, to about 1915."

The average ethnic German portion of the whole manpower of a division usually amounted to between 5 and 20%. According to the experience of the German command" *"The higher the number of ethnic Germans in a unit, the lower its fighting value,"* this proportion was not usually exceeded. But that not only the units organized in the Defense Zones received ethnic German replacements is shown by the statement of the commander of the 276th Volksgrenadier Division. *Generalleutnant* Badinski explained after being captured by U.S. troops in Normandy that at least 15% of his division were ethnic Germans. The 352nd Infantry Division, set up in northern France also consisted of at least 15% ethnic Germans. There were also some 10% Soviet volunteer helpers (so-called *Hiwis*). In the 302nd Infantry Division stationed in Dieppe there were about 20% ethnic Germans from Poland, *"who barely understood German."* The language problem was also noted by Army Panzerjäger Unit 463 (subordinate to the 274th Infantry Division) in a monthly report of February 1, 1945:

> "1.) Training Situation:
>   The replacements sent in December 1944 needs three more weeks of training on the antitank gun (some are ethnic Germans with defective language knowledge); its infantry training is satisfactory.
>
> 2.) Morale of the Troops:
>   The difficult defensive fighting in the East is followed with keen interest. 82 members of the unit come from the eastern border areas and are concerned as to whether their families can be resettled at the right time. Among the ethnic Germans, there was recently no change to be seen in their attitude under the impression of events in the East. The morale of the Alsatians was strongly influenced by the lack of and connection with their families. Very many soldiers constantly express the wish to see service in their threatened home area."

After the greatest percentage of the ethnic Germans came from Poland, a guidebook was issued in the Army to get around the language problems. In this three-part publication the training of the recruit, from explanations of the weapons to drill and combat service, were explained in German and Polish.

---

61 Voth, Berthold, *Das Pionier-Bataillon 114 der 114. Jäger-Division (vormals 714.Infanterie-Division)*, Lahnstein 1996.

Stanislaus Hlisnikowski was born on April 14, 1917 in Orlau near Katowice, Poland and entered Rifle Replacement Battalion 28 in Defense Zone VIII on May 19, 1943. In November 1943 he was transferred to the 245th Infantry Division.

Although he was "only" included in People's List III, the judgment of the company leader was "conception of service *without exception.*"

Polish passport of 1936.

After Jozef Hermann was placed on the German People's List on January 28, 1942, he was inducted into Navy Artillery Unit 115 in Pillau on April 21, 1942. From August 2, 1942 to the end of the war he served with M.A.A. 512 in Tromsoe, Norway.

The Ethnic Germans in the Waffen-SS

Unlike the Wehrmacht, the Waffen-SS had a modest number of divisions in which ethnic Germans served during the course of the war. Here those units in which at least 5,000 ethnic Germans served will be described in detail. When divisions of the Waffen-SS are described, it will not be one-sided, but rather refer to the percentages. The approximately 370,000 ethnic Germans in the Wehrmacht were divided among at least 250 different divisions, while the majority of the 210,000 ethnic Germans in the Waffen-SS were divided among only thirteen divisions, plus the SS economic and administrative main office.

In the SS economic and administrative main office, not fully combat-capable ethnic Germans from eastern and southeastern Europe were mainly used as guards in the concentration camps. On January 15, 1945, some 10,000 of the 41,182 SS members thus used were ethnic Germans. The total from 1942 to the war's end was about 15,000 ethnic Germans, of whom there came approximately:

>   2,500 from Croatia
>   4,000 from Poland
>   2,000 from Romania
>   1,000 from Serbia
>   1,000 from Slovakia
>   2,000 from the USSR and
>   2,500 from Hungary.

They served at all the concentration camps[62] (Auschwitz, Bergen-Belsen, Buchenwald, Dachau, Floßenbürg, Herzogenbusch, Kauen, Lublin, Mauthausen, Mittelbau, Natzweiler, Neuengamme, Niederhagen, Plaszow, Ravensbrück, Riga, Sachsenhausen, Stutthoff and Vaivara) and as a rule belonged to the guard units. The number of ethnic Germans in the commands was rather low. Like the ethnic Germans in the ranks of the Ordnungspolizei, some of whom were used to guard the Jewish ghettos and work camps, the ethnic Germans did not usually volunteer freely for the Waffen-SS. They were generally ordered there because of lacking combat ability. Many a one observed atrocities there.

Units with Large Ethnic German Numbers

4th SS Police Panzergrenadier Division

On September 18, 1939 Hitler ordered the Chief of the Ordnungspolizei to form a horsedrawn infantry division of members of the police. The idea of using policemen militarily was not new. In 1938-39 parts of the German Police had been organized into units and groups and taken part in action on Austria and the Sudetenland.

On October 1, 1939, under the command of *Generalleutnant* of the Police Pfeffer-Wildenbruch, the establishing began at the Wandern troop training camp near Frankfurt on the Oder. The division, whose "soldiers" remained members of the Ordnungspolizei, and which was only set up in the framework of the Army, was later assigned to Artillery Regiment 300 (Army) and Intelligence Unit 300 (Army).

The assigned policemen received the ranks and uniforms of the Army. While the ranks were retained, an original type of uniform was created a short time later. The police eagle was again attached to the caps, and the collar emblems and belt buckles were also those of the police. The German emblem, though, was usually worn, as in the Waffen-SS, on the left upper arm. Members of the SS also wore the embroidered Sig-runes[63] under the left breast pocket. Externally, the Army membership was now recognizable only from the markings of the vehicles, which unlike the Police (Pol) and Waffen-SS (SS), bore WH for Wehrmacht-Heer.

---

62 For the history of the individual concentration camps, see Michaelis, Rolf, *Die Waffen-SS: Mythos und Wirklichkeit*, Berlin, 2006.
63 This was also introduced in the 7th SS Mountain Division "Prinz Eugen."

After three months the Police Division was transferred from Wandern to the Westwall in January 1940 and relieved the 205th Infantry Division within the XXV. Army Corps. Shortly after the western campaign began it was ordered to the XVII. Army Corps.

On June 9, 1940 the units crossed the Ardennes Canal southwest of Sedan and moved toward Vouziers. On June 14, 1940 the troops reached Les Islettes without facing much combat. East of Bar de Duc the unit crossed the Rhein-Marne Canal and pursued the retreating French troops past Neufchatel and Besancon in the direction of the Swiss border. There the report of the armistice agreement reached them on June 22, 1940. On July 10, 1940 the units were transferred to the St. Dizier area, From there they were ordered to the troop training camp at Suippes (50 km north of St. Dizier) on August 2, 1940.

Here the restructuring and renaming of the unit as the SS Police Division took place. The Army units were removed and replaced by newly established police units. Numerous ethnic Germans from Poland were already there. Along with the new Police Artillery Regiment and the Police Intelligence Unit, a Police Reconnaissance Unit was also formed from the former Police Bicycle Squadron, and a Police Flak Unit was formed.

The added "SS" indicated Himmler's wish as *Reichsführer-SS* and Chief of the German Police to show the close connection between the SS and Police. On November 12, 1940 *Generalleutnant* of the Police Mülverstedt took command of the SS Police Division. After talks with *SS-Obergruppenführer* Daluege, *SS-Gruppenführer* Jüttner and the *Reichsführer-SS*, the SS Police Division was subordinated to the Waffen-SS on April 17, 1941 with a strength of some 17,000 men.

Two months later the order came to transfer from France to East Prussia. At the beginning of the Russian campaign on June 22, 1941 the Division, as in the French campaign, was not in action on the foremost front, but crossed the Lithuanian border only on June 30, 1941. The advance routes were generally completely jammed, and so the march went slowly in the hot summer days. After some 600 of the 5,000 horses of the horsedrawn infantry division were lost within a few days, horses were requisitioned in Latvia.

On July 14, 1941 the Duena was crossed near Dryssa. Two days later the Artillery Regiment was the first unit to be sent into combat. In the night of July 23-24, 1941 the Division marched through Ostrow. Then came a march through a completely swampy forest. Subordinated to the VVI. Army Corps, the SS Police Division finally moved out to take Luga on August 1, 1941, under its new commander, *SS-Brigadeführer* and *Generalmajor* of the Police Walter Krüger. The enemy had built up the Luga position extensively with bunkers, mine belts, tank traps and wire barriers. Fortunately, part of the area was a former troop training camp. In the outstanding defense, the SS Police Division suffered high losses. Since Luga could not be taken frontally, the Division moved southwestward past Sopolje on August 22, 1941 to attack on the flank. To avoid being surrounded, the Red Army evacuated the city on September 1, 1941. The SS Police Division had lost about 1,000 dead and over 2,000 wounded by that time.

Again assigned to the L. Army Corps, the fight for Krasnogwardeisk began on September 9, 1941, a main obstacle before Leningrad. Five days later the SS Police Division captured the city. On October 18, 1941 the Division received 3,000 men of native and ethnic German origin as replacements for its losses to date. In the following weeks there were constant supply problems. Not only did the artillery remain without shells, but the soldiers had no winter clothing or food. By February 1942 the Division, now commanded by *SS-Brigadeführer* and *Generalmajor* of the Police Wünnenberg, was in the Puschkin-Pulkovo area in the siege ring around Leningrad.

When the Red Army broke through on the Volchov, some 40 km north of Novgorod, on January 13, 1942 on the line between the 16th and 18th Armies, the SS Police Division was ordered to move to the Volchov. Except for the Police Artillery Regiment, the Division turned the positions before Leningrad over to the 121st Infantry Division on February 19, 1942 and marched to the Tschudovo area. Subordinated to the I. Army Corps, the unit, which was taken over by the Waffen-SS on February 10, 1942,[64] was supposed to reestablish the connection with the XXXVIII. Army Corps. On March 15, 1942 the SS Police Division arrived, and four days later it was able to close the so-called Volchov Pocket. The heavy and constant attempts by the Red Army to open the pocket from inside and outside with the unfavorable weather conditions, withtemperatures down to 50 degrees below zero,

---

64 Regarding this, Himmler noted in his diary/appointment book that the reason for taking the unit into the Waffen-SS was the constant difficulties with the Ordnungspolizei head office and Daluege's interference in the command of the division. When the division became part of the Waffen-SS its members were given corresponding Waffen-SS ranks. A *Gefreiter*, for example, became an *SS-Sturmmann*.

caused the combat strength of the three rifle regiments to sink to a combined total of some 500 men by the end of April 1942. When the enemy pocket had been smashed in the heavily wooded area at the end of June 1942, the Division was again subordinated to the L. Army Corps and transferred northward to the Sablino area.

From there the unit moved back to the front before Leningrad and took up positions near Krasny-Bor. On July 23, 1942 the Red Army also made a major attack there. After the end of the costly defensive combat, one battalion each of the three regiments was ordered to the "Heidelager" troop training camp for restructuring on August 8, 1942. For the troops staying on the main battle line, another Soviet major attack ensued in the Kolpino area. To make up for its losses, the Division was assigned 2,000 men of ethnic German origin as reserves on August 20, 1942.

When AOK 11 from the Ukraine was moved before Leningrad in order to attack the Soviet metropolis on September 1942, the Red Army again went on the offensive. By the beginning of October 1942 there were extremely heavy defensive battles, in which the German troops were able to smash enemy forces.

In mid-October 1942 the SS Police Rifle Regiments were renamed as SS Police Infantry Regiments and the SS Police Reconnaissance Unit became the SS Police Cycle Unit. In November 1942 the unit reported a total strength of 10,479 men, with three infantry regiments of two battalions each.

The three infantry battalions then being set up anew at the "Heidelager" SS troop training camp had a total of over 2,920 members. With around 13,400 soldiers, the SS Police Division thus had about 80% of its intended strength of some 16,500 men.

On January 12, 1943 the soviet winter offensive began on the northern front. When enemy troops were able to break through by the XXVI. Army Corps to the southeast, the SS Police Division was given the order four days later to free the connection with Schlüsselburg. The German troops enclosed there were to be freed, and at the same time the ring around Leningrad was to be closed again. But the German troops could not oppose the powerful attack of the enemy with artillery and tanks. Schlüsselburg had to be given up. In the heavy fighting in the Ssinyavino area the SS Police Division was almost wiped out. The fighting strength of the battalions was only 30 to 50 men. When the battle escalated to an inferno on January 28, 1943, there was panic flight before the enemy at times. On the next day, the survivors were taken out of action and sent back to the LIV. Army Corps. Gathered in Sablino, the three Infantry Regiments that had been called SS Police Grenadier Regiments since February 1, 1943 were formed into three weak battalions. In all, the SS Police Division had lost about 3000 men in the past few days.

From the SS "Heidelager" troop training camp, one newly formed battalion of 1,200 men reached the Division on February 9, 1943, while the other two battalions were transferred to the southern front at the end of 1942. On February 10, 1943 the Red Army pushed its offensive again, but the German troops were able to hold almost all of the territory. At the end of February 1943 the battles simmered down and remained like that along the Tossna until mid-March 1943.

The grenadiers, heavily burdened anyway by the difficult weather conditions, got no rest in the area south of Kolpino. On March 18, 1943 the enemy attacked again with heavy artillery and many men. When the front was held for two weeks, the Red Army halted its attacks. For about a third of the SS Police Division this finally meant being taken out of the front during April 1943. While cadres in particular were sent to the Panzergrenadier Division at the SS "Heidelager" troop training camp for scheduled new formation and restructuring, parts remained under the command of *SS-Standartenführer* Bock as a battle group in the Leningrad siege ring. Here there were no more major battles at first. As of October 21, 1943 the three battalions still in action were collectively named the SS Police Grenadier Regiment 3.

In November 1943 parts of the 225th and 24th Infantry Divisions took over the positions of the battle group, which was subordinated to the L. Army Corps, on the western front of the Oranienburg Pocket between Kernovo and Gorbovizy. When the III. (Germanic) SS Panzer Corps, coming out of Croatia at the end of 1943, arrived in the area, the battle group, with a strength of 5,067 men, went under the new command. When the majority of the battle group arrived at the Oranienburg Pocket, the battle group was taken out of the front on January 10, 1944 and again moved almost 200 km to the east on the Volchov. Subordinated to the XXVIII. Army Corps, it replaced parts of the 96th Infantry Division and took up positions at the mouth of the Tigoda.

In the course of the new Soviet winter offensive, there were heavy fights there on January 16, 1944. Since one focal point of the attack was farther south, near Novgorod, the group, now called the SS Battle Group "Bock", was taken off

After the end of the Soviet summer offensive in 1942, Paul Koryciorz received the Infantry Assault Badge.

For his action in holding off the Soviet winter offensive of 1943 on the Tossna, Paul Koryciorz received the Iron Cross II from *SS-Gruppenführer* Wünnenberg on April 20, 1943.

The Wound Badge for one wound during the Soviet winter offensive on February 16, 1943.

Documents of the ethnic German from Poland, Paul Koryciorz.

the main battle line five days later and ordered to the XXXVIII. Army Corps. In the following battles the Red Army was able to smash the battle group. Having lost their heavy weapons, the men drew back through Sapalje to Oredesh. Along with Latvian SS volunteers, the town was defended until it was surrounded. With heavy losses, the battle group was able to break through the enemy lines and reach the German main battle line via Luga and Turkovice.

Without the possibility of forming an ordered defense, the troops withdrew in the direction of Pleskau and, on March 2, 1944, occupied provisional positions in the Panther position. Just two days later the Red Army attacked the desolate units along the Velikaya. Without support from heavy weapons, the action of the SS Battle Group "Bock" ended in holding off Soviet attempts to break through between Pleskau and Ostrov on the Pleskau Lake. Seen as no longer capable of combat, the remainder was ordered via Opotchka to the SS troop training camp of "Kurmark" at the end of March 1944.

In April 1943 the reformation of the still horsedrawn Infantry Division into an armored grenadier division had begun. Because of the frost situation, though, some 2,500 men were transferred to the SS "Heidelager" troop training camp or to special training (such as engineers). The full strength of 17,005 men was to be realized mainly from the newly inducted ethnic Germans from Romania. While the SS Battle Group "Bock"[65] was still fighting with the Army Group "North", the setting up of the new troop units began.

In April 1943 units from the SS "Heidelager" training camp (General Government) were called on for action against polish partisans. When Mussolini was overthrown in July 1943, the OKW also ordered the transfer of parts of the SS Police Panzergrenadier Dvision to the 2nd Panzer Army in the Balkans. It was to fill the developing vacuum there.

At the end of July 1943 the SS Police Panzergrenadier Regiment 1 took up barracks in the Valyevo area southwest of Belgrade and the SS Police Panzergrenadier Regiment 2 in the Misar/Sabac area (70 km west of Belgrade). After the Italian III. Army Corps was ordered back home from eastern Greece in the course of the new political developments, the two Panzergrenadier regiments received the order to move into that area. Subordinated to the XXII. Mountain Corps along with the 1st Mountain and 104th Rifle Division, the units were supposed to take up, in particular, securing tasks against the Greek ELAS and EDES partisans in Thessaly while receiving further training.

But large-scale active partisan fighting was scarcely possible. In the Larissa area only rail and road intersections were secured at support points. Often the German occupation troops were attacked by Greek partisans, and often the smaller support points could be relieved only after the arrival of the assault guns of the SS Police Armored Unit in the spring of 1944.

Problems with the hygienic conditions caused trouble during the entire occupation time. Some 80% of the soldiers caught malaria or suffered diarrhea from the impure water. Besides the lack of training for the young recruits, this strongly limited their combat ability. Effective October 22, 1943 the Division, in the course of renumbering the Waffen-SS, now was designated the 4th SS Police Panzer-Grenadier Division. While the Division's units also added the number 4, the Panzergrenadier Regiments were numbered 7 and 8.[66] The term "Polizei" was dropped by all units except for the name of the Division. On December 31, 1943 the Division, minus the Battle Group still at the front, reported a strength of 10,709 men.

Barely a year after the motorized SS Division began to be set up, the new commander, *SS-Brigadeführer* and *Generalmajor* of the Waffen-SS and Police Schmedes, reported that on the basis of the lacking weapons and equipment plus fuel shortages, the unit's training could not yet be finished. Aside from that, a tactical cooperation of the entire Division through the occupation tasks was not possible. The units were almost all utilized separately of each other in the area.

---

65   The SS Police Panzergrenadier Regiment 3 was not formed anew at the troop training camp; rather, the infantry units of the SS Battle Group "Bock" formed the third Grenadier Regiment.
66   The division was later operated with two Panzergrenadier Regiments. The SS Police Panzergrenadier Regiment 3, still in action in Russia, was later divided between the first two regiments.

On May 23, 1944 Army Group "E" ordered parts of the 4th SS Police Panzergrenadier Division to relieve SS Police Mountain Rifle Regiment 18 on the Gulf or Corinth. Along with the I./SS Artillery Regiment 4, SS Panzergrenadier Regiment 7 traveled the 120 km southward to there. In the securing and pacification tasks, the power escalated. When in the town of Distomon, a few kilometers from the coast, some Green civilians fell victim to a German retaliatory action, this led to a military legal investigation of the responsible company and battalion leaders.

After the majority of the former SS Battle Group "Bock" came from the SS "Hurmark" troop training camp and joined the troop units in Greece, a strength of 15,891 men could be reported on June 30, 1944. The units, some 50% of whose members had gained experience in Russia, and about 50% who had a year's experience as occupation troops, could be blended into a strong combat division with appropriate training.

In July 1944 parts of the two SS Panzergrenadier Regiments were sent to fight independently in the area of the southern Pindus Mountains. At the end of August 1944 the situation worsened drastically from the fall of Romania. To support the threatened front and prevent the German troops to the south from being cut off, the 4th SS Police Panzergrenadier Division was to move some 600 km northward into the region of the Army Group "South Ukraine" at Werschetz near Belgrade.

During the transport from Larissa via Saloniki to Serbia, Bulgaria also declared war on Germany. Parts of the Division were then used in the Skople (Kosovo) area to disarm the former Bulgarian occupation troops there. While one battle group saw action with the 21st Waffen Mountain Division of the SS "Skanderbeg" (Albanian No.1), the majority of the 4th SS Police Panzergrenadier Division secured important transit lines from Serbia to Kosovo.

Divided into battle groups, the Division reached the Belgrade area beginning on September 11, 1944. The withdrawal route through Gnjilane, Pristina and Mitrovica was lined with burned-out vehicles and wagons with dead horses. Arriving in Belgrade, the vehicles had to be overhauled after the difficult march. In particular, the tires were no longer up to the pressure and had to be replaced. The assault guns had been left behind in Saloniki and reached the units only later. They left Belgrade in a pouring rain and crossed the Danube on a ferry at Pancevo. From there they were transported by rail to the Romanian Banat around Temesvar.

Subordinated to the LVII. Panzer Corps, the 4th SS Police Panzergrenadier Division was supposed to win back Temesvar, which was already occupied by the Red Army. Because of the situation, *SS-Brigadeführer* Schmedes did not carry out the attack, but left his unit near Szeged to take up a bridgehead position over the Theiss. When this became weak because of the already successful crossing of the Red Army, they transferred to the Szolnok area about 100 km away. Here the Soviet thrust at Budapest was to be held up. On October 24, 1944 the Red Army succeeded in crossing the Theiss. After vigorous fighting, the 4th Police Panzergrenadier Division had to withdraw into the Jasz-Ladany area. Here the 18th SS Volunteer Panzergrenadier Division "Horst Wessel" was subordinated to it, only to collapse completely in the fighting on November 11, 1944. By November 25, 1944 the troop units moved off via Hered to Ecsed. Here the units were at least able to refresh themselves personally thanks to men from the SS Field Replacement Battalion 4.

For a long time the German troops could only react, and in the ensuing battles the Division was under the command of *SS-Standartenführer* Harzer since December 4, 1944, and was almost surrounded south of Kis-Terenye. Subordinated to the "Feldherrnhalle" Panzer Corps, the unit them moved to the Slovakian-Hungarian border area and was ordered in mid-January 1945 to block a soviet breakthrough in the Divin area (some 20 km from the border).

In the next few days the subordinated units of the 18th Volunteer Panzer-Grenadier Division were also released from the group. After the 4th SS Police Panzergrenadier Division had lost much of their heavy weapons, they took over the equipment of the subordinated units were also strengthened by the I./SS Volunteer Panzergrenadier Regiment 40.

In the Schemnitz area at the end of January 1945, there came the order to transfer to Pomerania. Here soviet troops were already pushing toward Berlin along the Netze and Warthe. The SS Panzergrenadier Regiment 8 was first to arrive in Stargard on February 1, 1945 and was deployed at once southeast of Greifenhagen. Here between the Oder and Madue Lake the whole division gathered in the first week of February.

Josef Meinzinger was born in Genna, Hungary on July 21, 1924 and reported, upon the second government agreement, to the Waffen-SS in the summer of 1943.

After his first training in the SS Artillery Training and Replacement Regiment in Prague, he was transferred in the autumn of 1943 to the 4th SS Police Panzergrenadier Division.

For the planned Pomeranian offensive the 4th SS Police Panzergrenadier Division moved into the area south of Stargard and served under the XXXIX. Panzer Corps. In the battles that followed on and after February 16, 1945, the group could advance on Dölitz along with the SS Panzer Unit 4, which had meanwhile become combat-ready again. On February 19, 1945 the offensive was halted because of the Soviet superior power. The 10th SS Panzer Division took over the positions of the 4th SS Police Panzergrenadier Division the next day, which was *"because of its very good equipment ... to take over the protection of the city of Danzig."*

On February 25, 1945 the division was loaded on a train and transported to the VII. Panzer Corps in the Dirschau area. Even before the destination. The 4th Police Panzergrenadier Division was unloaded in the Rammelsburg area. Here the VII. Panzer Corps was supposed to restore the meanwhile broken connections to the 3rd Panzer Army. On February 28, 1945 the Division made a counterattack and could at least achieve some relief. The Soviet pressure forced the German units, though, to draw back steadily. To prevent a rolling-up of the main battle line along the coast toward Danzig, the 4th Police Panzergrenadier Division moved to the Stolp area and then back via Laünburg to Neustadt. Here the roads were fully overcrowded with refugees and Wehrmacht vehicles.

On March 9, 1945 the Commander of the 2nd Army judged the units subordinated to him. The 4th Police Panzergrenadier Division he described as an *"experienced combat division with young replacements who still lack combat experience ... in action at the focal point of the defensive fighting, high losses. Daily strength: 4,767; combat strength: 2,744."*

At this point the Division still had one Panzer IV, 8 Assault Gun III, 6 Assault Gun IV and 11 7.5 cm (mot.Z.) antitank guns. After the troop units had only a combined combat strength of a small regiment, they were only used as a battle group. Consisting of 5 battalions, one engineer battalion, one field replacement battalion and three subordinated companies of French SS members, the group moved into the area of the Putziger Wiek to Rahmel.

When the Red Army was able on March 12, 1945 to take Neustadt, German soldiers and civilians streamed out in a desperate flight toward Oxhoefter Kaempe and Gogenhafen. There the VII. Panzer Corps was temporarily able to stabilize the front. The masses of back-line units, civilians and vehicles were gathered on the Kaempe so that the enemy's massive artillery fire caused particularly high losses.

The Red Army was able to split the Danzig-Gotenhafen defense zone on March 20, 1945. Four days later Hitler ordered the unqualified holding of the fortresses of Hela, Gotenhafen. Danzig and Königsberg. The events caught up with the order quickly, for on March 28, 1945 the Red Army as able to occupy Gotenhafen. The situation north of the Oxhoefter Kaempe grew worse and worse. In order to rescue the approximately 20,000 men of the VII. Panzer Corps and parts of the civilian population from defeat and imprisonment, the Commanding General, *General* of the Panzer Troops von Kessel, ordered a move to Hela on April 4, 1945. During the evacuation over the Putziger Wiek, all the airplanes still at the Oxhoefter Kaempe airfield were destroyed. In a splendid performance, the Navy was able to evacuate all the soldiers and numerous civilians to the peninsula by the next day.

The 4th Police Panzergrenadier Division took over the coastal defenses in the area around Heisternest in the Hela General Command, and reported on April 9 a combat strength of 3,110 men and a daily strength of 4,871 men. At this strength a temporarily subordinated Navy gun battalion and a Luftwaffe battalion were included. Heavy weapons were no longer at hand. Because of the still *"notable"* personnel strength of the Division, the OKH ordered it transported to the Army Group "Vistula".

To strengthen the Oder front before the expected Soviet major attack, the shipping of the 4th SS Police Panzergrenadier Division to Swinemünde began on April 13, 1945. Unloaded there in the next day, the units gathered near Heringsdorf at first and, on April 18, 1945, were subordinated to the III. SS Panzer Corps in the Gramzow area. When the Army Group "Vistula" was ordered by its Commanding General, SS-*Obergruppenführer* and *General* of the Waffen-SS Steiner to secure the boundary between the 3rd Panzer Army and 9th Army between Liebenwalde and Oderberg, what was left of the 4th SS Police Panzergrenadier Division was restructured and strengthened by Army units. It was then called the SS Battle Group "Harzer".

While the SS Panzergrenadier Regiment 7 was the first troop unit to march into the Eberswalde area, the Red Army was able to break through toward Bernau. The speedy advance of the enemy tanks on Oranienburg led to the order not to let the rest of the SS Battle Group march into the Eberswalde bridgehead, but to Eberswalde at once. Thus the Battle Group was divided in action. The SS Panzergrenadier Regiment 7, because of the Soviet breakthrough of the Randow position, was ordered to the XXXXVI. Panzer Corps in Mecklenburg-Vorpommern. After heavy fighting near Prenzlau and Neubrandenburg, the rest moved through Waren-Karow to Hagenow and went into US captivity there. The SS battle Group "Harzer", after heavy fighting between Oranienburg and Berlin, first drew back to the Kremmen-Behrensbrüch-Foersterei Kuhbrücke line. From there the last of the onetime 4th SS Police Panzergrenadier Division tried to reach the Allied demarcation line at Schwerin-Ludwigslust via Kyritz and Perleberg, and went into U.S. captivity there.

Set up hastily and improvised with German policemen as a horsedrawn infantry division, the unit at first was more useful as an occupation troop. After exchanging men and regular ethnic German replacements, a more functional unit was formed in Russia, which came through heavy fighting successfully on the Volchov and before Leningrad. The later 4th SS Police Panzergrenadier Division became a melting pot for ethnic Germans from Poland as of 1940. As of 1942-43 there was also the addition of many Romanian and Hungarian Germans, so that in 1945 the great majority of the men were ethnic Germans.

6th SS Mountain Division "Nord"

In view of the coming war against the Soviet Union, Himmler ordered of February 24, 1941 that the SS Totenkopf Standarten 6 and 7 plus an SS Intelligence Unit be united into the SS Battle Group "Nord". For this, the SS Totenkopf units were taken into the Waffen-SS and renamed SS Infantry Regiments 6 (mot.) and 7 (mot.).

Around six weeks later, the units, under the command of *SS-Brigadenführer* Richard Herrmann, were transferred some 1,500 km northward to AOK "Norwegen". The then 1. General Staff Officer, *SS-Hauptsturmführer* Ruoff, recalls the tactical value of the battle group:

> "There existed neither intelligence connections with and command offices nor from the staff to SS Infantry Regiment 7. During the ship transport I already noticed formal deficiencies in the appearance of the soldiers. My 1st Ordnance Officer, to whom I mentioned it, replied, "Yes, you don't know that the men have had absolutely no combat training ... The officer corps consists almost without exception of leaders of the general SS, the lower officer corps of the same origin. All of them were taken over with their rank in the general SS. A plan worked out in the assembly room showed that the command corps did not know even the simplest basics of tactics. It was absolutely clear that the unit was not usable in the field. The commander determinedly denied these findings. His presentations when the plan was made showed that in combat he would run the unit by means of giving orders to the command corps daily at 10:00 A.M. He met my strong objection with complete lack of understanding."

While the SS Battle Group "Nord" crossed the Norwegian-Finnish border in mid-June 1941 and marched toward Rovaniemi, *SS-Hauptsturmführer* Ruoff reported the conditions to the AOK "Norway". Then *SS-Brigadeführer* Demelhuber took command of the battle group on June 17, 1941.

On the same date, the setting up of the motorized SS Division "Nord" as a three-unit group was ordered, thus with three infantry regiments. The SS-FHA thought, completely naively, that through mere combining of the failing troop units a combat-ready division could be formed. The necessary practice of the working together of the units in larger and smaller groups on a troop training field was not considered. *SS-Brigadeführer* Demelhuber reported on June 30, 1941 on the condition of the division:

> "The very first impression showed that the basis of the troop – the single and single-combat training – is on a very poor footing, and thus the group's training is completely lacking. … The mass of the commanders and company chiefs are reserve officers with very little or absolutely no troop or war experience in modern warfare. The battalion commanders are not at all sufficient in their ability to measure up as to the conduct of modern infantry combat and fighting with the involved weapons.
>
> The artillery was fired only once in Jüterborg and never together with the infantry. The tank destroyers have not fired live bullets, ditto the light grenade launchers and, for the most part, the Flak batteries. Drills in mixed units have never taken place. …
>
> The human material is good, in part very good. The non-commissioned officers must be trained. The training of specialists is very meager. The Division will be fully ready for action when it is given the chance, as is and was the case with all other new units, to be trained for two or three months at a good troop training camp."

Instead of being removed, the Division was subordinated to the Higher Command z.b.V. XXXVI in the area between Maerkajaervi and the border of the USSR, and on July 1, 1941 to a focal point of the offensive. The inexperienced men set out in the morning to attack the fortress of Salla and remained lying before the well-built and well-staffed enemy positions. Heavy enemy artillery and tank use, plus firing from their own air force and artillery, led to chaos. In the repeated attacks, after the loss of upper and lower leaders, a panic-like flight to the starting position took place.

Only when the 169th Infantry Division moved in from the north to attack Salla on July 7, 1941 did the Soviet troops give up the fortress area. The losses of the SS Division "Nord" (mot.) were high. They suffered 261 dead and missing plus 307 wounded in that week. The then SS Rifleman Helmut Uphoff remembers:

> "The attack on Salla on July 6, 1941 took place on the Keskimainen; a rocky bunker position before Salla. Our company lost its chief, *SS-Obersturmführer* Herold. Finally it was even led by an SS-Sturmmann. We could withdraw only laboriously with heavy losses. Our own fighter-bombers and also artillery cut loose on us. The neighboring companies moved back and left us alone! Only 28 men came back from this attack unharmed – I had taken an infantry bullet in my right thigh and bled endlessly!"

For the *Reichsführer-SS* the failure of an SS unit was a loss of prestige. On July 14, 1941 he gave a speech before 200 replacement men in Stettin, in which he pointed out that the events before Salla put the reputation of the Waffen-SS on the line. On July 21, 1941 the Division reported, with a full strength of 12,000 men, an actual strength of 9,435 members. Aside from the fact that the leaders and lower leaders, because of their ages, were scarcely right for an active front unit, about 700 lower leaders were lacking.

Since the needed unit training at a troop training camp could not be realized, the Division was not used together any more at first. Rather it was divided among other units, some Finnish. While the units thus got acquainted with combat in the Karelian forests, the division command tried to prepare the supply units for the circumstances.

On August 1, 1941 the Finnish 3rd Division began to attack Louhi. After heavy forest and swamp fighting, the fully destroyed Kiestinki could be captured on August 7, 1941. Some 35 km before the target of Louhi the attack came to a stop in the area of Mount Gankaschvaara. On August 28, 1941 the offensive of the XXXVI. Army Corps on Alakurtti began. Here too, the further advance began in heavy enemy fire after the city was taken. When the Red Army began a counteroffensive in the Gankaschvaara area at the end of August 1941, the SS Infantry Regiment 7 moved to the III. Finnish Corps on September 1, 1941. The strengthened SS Reconnaissance Unit remained subordinated to the 169th Infantry Division in the XXXVI. Army Corps.

At the beginning of September 1941 the troop units of the Division were reunited and took over the area between the Kiestinki-Louhi road and rail lines with the III. Finnish Corps. Major Soviet attacks could be held off with heavy losses. From July 1 to September 20, 1941, 692 members of the Division had died and 1,770 were wounded. This equaled the strength of more than three battalions. To replace the losses, the strengthened SS Reconnaissance Unit "Nord" was first added to the Division on September 21, 1941; shortly afterward, so was SS Infantry Regiment 9 (mot.), having belonged administratively to the Division since June 17, 1941 and seeing service separately.

On October 30, 1941 the SS Division "Nord" (mot.) began a new advance on Louhi. In remarkably bad weather and a clever and tough enemy defense, only small success could be gained. After two weeks the III. Finnish Corps ordered a halt on further attacks, not only to protect their own forces, but also for a political decision. If the USA had tolerated the Finnish fighting to regain the lands lost in the 1940 winter war, they now expressed their opposition to further gaining of ground. Here too, the wish was surely decisive that the Murman line, on which arms deliveries of the USA ran to the Soviet Union, not be broken.

While SS Infantry Regiment 9 (mot.) withdrew completely from the group shortly thereafter and saw action before Leningrad, the remaining troop units took up their winter positions. On January 22, 1942 the Division, with a full strength of 12,716 men, reported an actual strength of 9,892 men.

In April 1942 the Red Army began an offensive to thrust at Kienstinki. In vigorous combat, the units of SS Division "Nord" and the Finnish Division "J" were able to stop the enemy about 1.5 km before the start. At the beginning of May 1942 the German and Finnish troops made a counterthrust and were able to drive the enemy back to his original positions until the end of the month. From April 1 to May 31, 1942 a total of 159 Division members had died, 790 had been wounded, and 28 were missing.

On January 15, 1942 the SS-FHA ordered the motorized Infantry Division to be reformed into the horsedrawn SS Mountain Division "Nord". This was, in fact, only begun in April 1942 with newly inducted ethnic Germans from Hungary and the involved new creations at the "Wildflecken" troop training camp. This partly involved unusually large troop units, such as seven Flak batteries. On April 20, 1942 *SS-Brigadeführer* Kleinheisterkamp took command of the new SS Mountain Division.

In Karelia at the same time, the releasing of strong groups for new formations was followed by the reducing of troop units to a regiment-strong battle group. On June 1, 1942 the two SS Mountain Rifle Regiments were given numbers

6 and 7. Three days later Hitler gave the SS Mountain Rifle Regiment 6 the name of *SS-Gruppenführer* Reinhard Heydrich who had recently been assassinated.

After the newly formed division units reached the action area in Karelia in mid-July 1942, various changes were made. The now-complete SS Mountain Division "Nord" took over the positions of the 7th Mountain Division, which in turn replaced the Finnish Division "J". At the same time, the Finnish III. Corps turned its former front sector over to the XVIII. Mountain Corps. The Finnish units were thus taken out of action. Until the Soviet offensive in April and May of 1942, there were no major battles. This also showed the losses of the division. From January 1 to December 31, 1942 "only" twelve commanders and 277 other ranks had fallen. *SS-Sturmmann* Willi Wild described the combat area in summer very vividly to his mother:

> "It is now 8:15 P.M. and the weather has changed again, so that the sun stands in the sky very splendidly. Here the sun shines until about 11 P.M. and rises again at 2 A.M. The sun rises in the east here and sets in the north. Funny, isn't it?
>
> I am still well, which I also hope you are, dear Mother! The food is better now, mainly for the following reason. Yesterday five men of us had to go back to the baggage train and unload five trucks of potatoes. Each of us now has a goodly quantity that he could take home with him. So every evening I take my butter and make fried potatoes.
>
> It may sound somewhat funny when I say that we brought the potatoes home, for home is really where you are!
>
> It is now also very nice, for we have built ourselves very good bunkers. They are real blockhouses or weekend houses, and we feel really good here. There is just one problem: the lice. But there are no longer as many as there were. …
>
> Here the gnat plague has reached its high point, and it is terrible when one has to be outdoors all day. We are even stung through the gnat net so that at night we cannot sleep from the pain when the gnats are in the bunker. Well, in six weeks this too will be all over, but then the winter will come on again gradually. …
>
> One must, dear Mother, still find vulgar things here. Three days ago one of our men went over to the Russians, and the lousy cripple betrayed a lot. Since that guy is gone, our regimental command post and other important points have received a thorough drum fire, and this has caused serious losses."

On December 31, 1942 the Division Command reported the actual strength at 21,104 men. Thus the troop units had even attained a higher strength than the full strength because of large inductions of Hungarian ethnic Germans. The year of 1943 went by like 1942. In April there were limited Soviet attacks, which were cleaned up in counterthrusts. Although in action at a small theater of war, the men naturally were aware of the developments on the other fronts. So *SS-Sturmmann* Willi Wild wrote on August 19, 1943:

> "So something simply must happen with the war or it will certainly not last much longer, since Sicily is given up now, the war is coming very close to us. For the Italians are not capable of self-defense. But we depend strongly on our Führer!"

In October 1943 the unit, in the course of renumbering the Waffen-SS, was named the 6th SS Mountain Division "Nord". The Mountain Rifle Regiments were numbered 11 "Reinhard Heydrich" and 12.

The *SS-Sturmmann* Willi Wild was transferred to the baggage train and wrote to his mother on December 2, 1943 about action in winter:

> "It is very cold here and there is quite a lot of snow. Today we measured 20 degrees of cold, and it is only the beginning of winter. But I miss one thing very much back here: the boards. You know that I am such an old ski nut, and when the scouting troops always go forward on skis, I often think oh, if I could be there. And they are such young fellows, often 17 years old, and I feel so sorry for them. I always ask them where they are going, for I know almost every tree out there. I know that I won't hold out here very long, for it is too quiet for me, and that won't do permanently!"

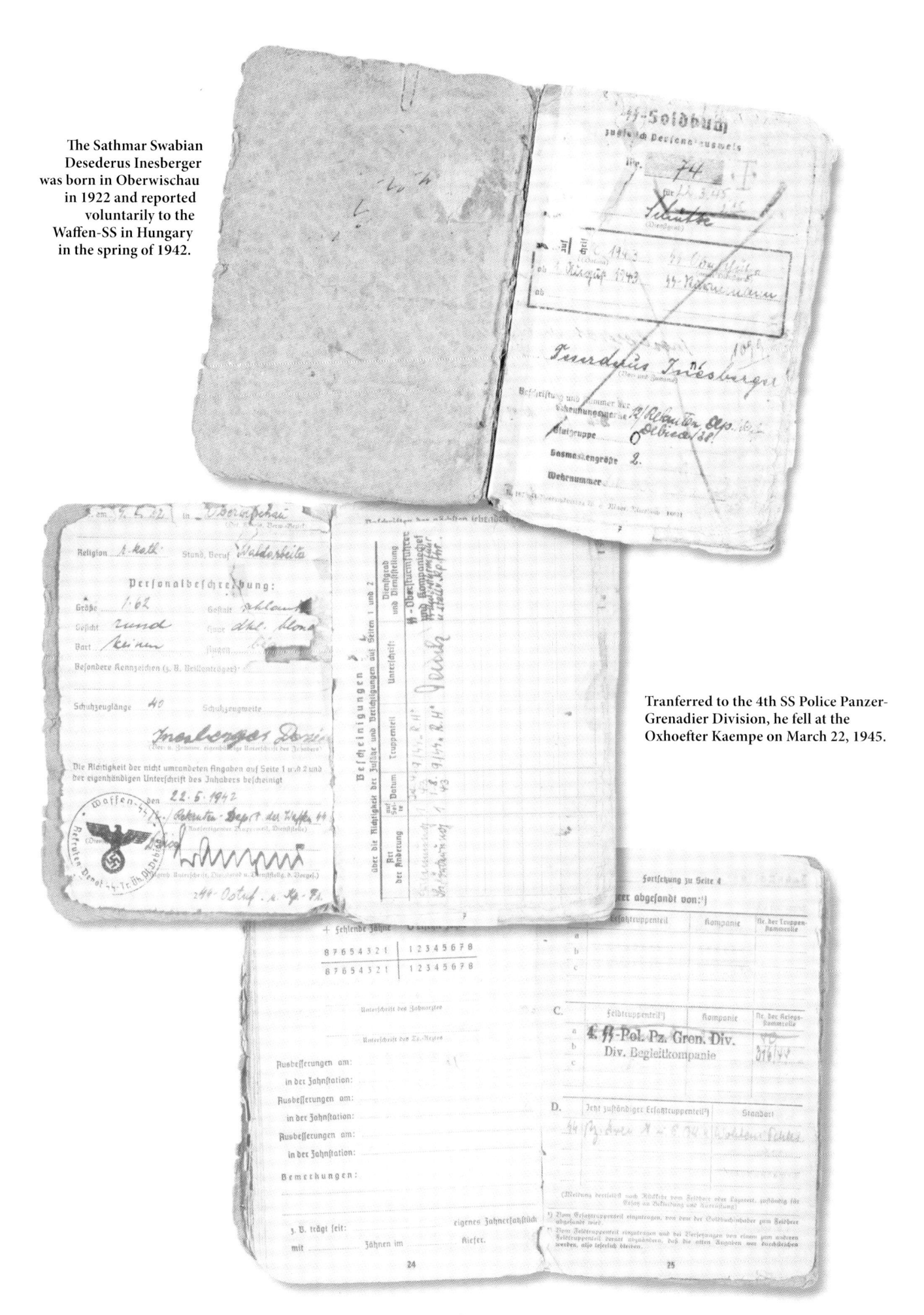

The Sathmar Swabian Desederus Inesberger was born in Oberwischau in 1922 and reported voluntarily to the Waffen-SS in Hungary in the spring of 1942.

Tranferred to the 4th SS Police Panzer-Grenadier Division, he fell at the Oxhoefter Kaempe on March 22, 1945.

71

On December 31, 1943 the Division reported a strength of 19,995 men. While the units in the central sector had been poured together to battle-group size, this SS unit, interestingly, still had almost its specified size. In January 1944 *SS-Brigadeführer* Debes took command of the Division.

In the spring of 1944 the Red Army began larger undertakings. Above all, in March 1944 there was heavy fighting, in which during just a few days, some 60 members of the SS reconnaissance Unit 6 fell. That made 20% of the men who had died in the Division in the whole year of 1942.

In April 1944 *SS-Obergruppenführer* Krüger took command of the 6th SS Mountain Division "Nord". At the same time, the unit received orders from SS-FHA to provide 5,000 lower officers and men for new units (among others, the 21st and 23rd Waffen Mountain Divisions of the SS). For them, 5000 new recruits from Hungary were to be integrated into the unit. Trained in Oulu, their addition to the combat units took place two months later.

Because of the overshadowing events on the other fronts, the Division (strength 19,255 men) was told at the end of June 1944 to find and prepare possible retreat routes and collecting places in the backland area. At the same time, Hitler gave the SS Mountain Rifle Regiment 12 the name of the Tyrolean farmer-leader Michael Gaissmair.

When the enemy was able to break into the defensive positions northeast of Kiestinki in the course of their summer offensive, there followed six weeks of the hardest fighting. At the beginning of August 1944 the attacks first calmed down, and the 6th SS Mountain Division "Nord" had held its positions.

On August 25, 1944 talks between the USSR and Finland ended, after which, on September 5, 1944, a mutual armistice began. The Finnish government, in the process of that of Germany, called for the immediate withdrawal of all troops from the country. The Operation "Birch" was arranged, in which, among others, the XVIII. Mountain Corps marched via Rovaniemi, 300 km away, in a northwesterly direction, and after another 400 km was to meet the XXXVI. And XIX. Mountain Corps in the Skibotn area.

On September 18, 1944 the 6th SS Mountain Division "Nord". With a strength of 17,041 members, reached Kuusamo, about 120 km away. From there the troops marched some 200 km to the west to Kemi and then turned north to Rovaniemi. There were fights with Finnish troops, who according to the terms of the armistice agreement had to regard their former German comrades-in-arms as enemies.

By October 16, 1944 the SS Mountain Rifle Regiment 12 "Michael Gaissmair" secured Rovaniemi and then withdrew with other remaining parts of the Division via Kittila to the north in the direction of the Norwegian border. On November 5, 1944, after a march of some 1000 km, the 6th SS Mountain Division "Nord" reached the Karesuando position on the Finnish-Norwegian border. The former *SS-Rottenführer* Willi Wild wrote on December 19, 1944:

> "Now I sit in a soldiers' home in a little hamlet in Norway, and we have reached our marching destination here. From here on we'll go farther by train at last; we have marched 1,100 km up to now, and I will never in my life forget this march.[67] We all have received no more mail since five weeks ago, and I believe we won't get any more mail in Norway. I am now very excited about where we'll spend Christmas. Maybe it will be in a cattle car, and it will be very dry too. In January we'll come home. As we here, we'll get a furlough right away. It would be nice, but with Barras we can't say. It is just hoping and waiting."

The units first traveled to Oslo by train. Since there was no coal available for the locomotives, the boilers were heated with birchwood. Since that was only a small source of energy, a motorized group rode ahead along the rail line to prepare wood depots at short intervals. After some 1,200 km the SS Mountain Rifle Regiment 12 "Michael Gaissmair" reached the Oslo area and was ordered to Denmark on December 22. The remaining units followed after Christmas of 1944. *SS-Rottenführer* Willi Wild wrote home on December 30, 1944:

> "So, dear Mother, you shall still have a letter from your youngest in the old year. After a long eight weeks I have finally received mail again at last, which I have awaited with longing. The Christmas festival is now ended,

---

67 Serving as the leader of beasts of burden, *SS-Sturmmann* Wild had the sad job of shooting sick and weak horses and mules. In part, three days of rest would have been enough to be able to march on with lame animals. Since this time was not given and the animals could not be left to the enemy alive, they were to be shot.

and the holy evening has become quite miserable for us. We did not even have bread to eat, for we arrived in Oslo on the 24th and food could not be supplied that fast. On Christmas Day it was said when the Chief went to the Army entertainment hall that the Christmas cake had run out. Now we have been in Denmark for three days and I call this country the land of paradise. Here there is everything that the heart desires, just like in Germany in peacetime. Starting with the best cakes to the finest ham, which I have now eaten in the last three days. But know, dear Mother, the money is lacking again. We received 30 Kronen of Danish money. That equals 15 Reichsmark."

On December 24, 1944 one battle group, made up primarily of SS Mountain Rifle Regiment 12, and commanded by the Regimental commander, *SS-Standartenführer* Schreiber, was sent to the 1st Army in the Palatinate. As they were being unloaded, there were losses from enemy fighter-bombers. Subordinated to the 361st Peoples Grenadier Division, the Battle Group took part in the so-called Vosges offensive to ease the Ardennes offensive.

During the fighting around Wingen, the remaining troops of the 6th SS Mountain Division had arrived in the Pirmasens area and taken over the positions of the 361st People's Grenadier Division. On January 13, 1945 they were subordinated to the LXXXX. Army Corps. This had the job within Operation "Northwind" to advance to the southeast on both sides of Bärenthal and first reach the Moder between Ingweiler and Pfaffenhofen (circa 20 km west of Hagenau). The attack that began on January 24, 1945 was called off two days later, after heavy losses. The then *Leutnant* Hans Eschenbach (III./Artillery Regiment 256) remembers:

"In January 1945 I lay in the Lower Vosges near Bärenthal as an advanced observer and shot with six light Field Howitzer 18s of the 6th and 7th Batteries. Our grenadiers were not able to storm Height 420, on which there was an American battalion. Soldiers of the 6th Mountain Division came to strengthen us but had very heavy losses. I can remember that a company had only 13 men left. Countless wounded men dragged themselves past my hole in the ground. But their attitude was exemplary! How often they told me, "Greet Hauptsturmführer Degen!"

The action of the SS on Height 420 was a tragedy in my eyes. The infantry had, as they said, come to the Reich in a land march from Finland through Norway. The heavy weapons were still on the way by ship or not yet unloaded. The boys are really bled out before we could support them with artillery!"

At the end of February 1945 came a transfer to the Reinsfeld area about 120 km to the northwest (20 km east of Trier). Within the LXXXII. Army Corps the Division was supposed to cross the Buwer on March 6, 1945 and cut off the already occupied Trier from the south. The American material superiority led to great losses and halting of the attack on the night of March 7-8, 1945. 500 Division members died or were missing. Six assault guns and five heavy antitank guns of Panzerjäger Unit 6 were lost.

Then came the march to the Boppard area. On their transfer, the SS Mountain Rifle Regiment 12, along with the II. and III./SS Artillery Regiment 6, became subordinated to the 7th Army in the Traben-Trarbach area on March 10, 1945. The rest of the Division, with a combat strength of some 3,000 men, reached the Rhine in mid-March 1945 and was subordinated to the LXXXIX. Army Corps. The LXXXIX. Army Corps ordered the establishment of two battle groups, one of which served near St. Goarshausen and the other near Eltville on the Rhine. On March 26, 1945 the rest of the Division gathered near Limburg and moved to Usingen. Surrounded by U.S. troops and constantly attacked by fighter-bombers, the men tried to reach Gelnhausen. Here the Division was shattered in the woods around Büdingen. Small units were able to get through Franconia to Bamberg, and reached Nürnberg on April 9, 1945. In the Neumarkt area they were subordinated to the 38th SS Grenadier Division "Nibelungen."

Thus the story of the division ended even before the surrender. It was set up in 1941 under Himmler's pressure to put together new SS units for the Russian campaign. The thus formed SS Division "Nord" was not ready for combat , and so its first action ended in disaster. In action on the northern front in the relatively quiet sector east of Kiestinki, the unit gave up more than 6,000 members for new formations and received Hungarian and Slovenian ethnic German recruits in exchange. In 1945 the Division was smashed on the western front by Allied aircraft and artillery.

7th SS Volunteer Mountain Division "Prinz Eugen"

On March 1, 1942 the SS-FHA ordered the creation of an SS Mountain Division "Southeast"[68] out of ethnic German volunteers from the entire southeastern area. First a division was formed completely of ethnic Germans. Four weeks later the group, to be set up northeast of Belgrade, was named the SS Volunteer Mountain Division "Prinz Eugen". The Division Commander, Artur Phleps, was born in Siebenbürgen.

Since the planned inductions in Serbia and Croatia did not at first bring the desired numbers, the full strength was reduced from 26,000 to 20,000 men. Several already existing ethnic German formations, such as the ethnic German combat squadron,[69] were taken into the Division completely. To receive a basic stock of weapons, the SS Postschutz, among others, contributed some 9,000 carbines, 1,500 pistols and 500 machine pistols.

In October 1942 the SS volunteer Mountain Division "Prinz Eugen" was transferred from the Banat into the Uzice-Cacak-Novi Pazar-Mitrovica area. In the southwestern borderland of the German Military Commander in Serbia the unit, along with the Bulgarian 9th Infantry Division, was to smash the organizational center of the Serbian partisans.

This unified first action outside the Banat contradicted the wishes of the ethnic group leader, but the transfer order into the area of the Commander of the German Troops in Croatia showed that the SS-FHA was not thinking of ethnic German service near home *"to protect house and home"*, but instead moved the whole unit away over the borders to fight partisans.

At the beginning of 1943 the Division, with a strength of 411 leaders and 19,424 other ranks was located in the area south of Zagreb (Agram). From there, large parts of the unit took part in Operation "Weiss I-III" from January 20 to March 15, 1943. Thus the High Commander "Southeast" tried to knock out the partisan movement under Tito in Croatia. Actually it only succeeded in driving away the enemy units on the Montenegran border. Then came Operation "Schwarz" from May 15 to June 15, 1943, directed against the Serbian partisans under Mihailovic in Montenegro. The Division had lost 110 dead, 424 wounded and 21 missing in these battles.

After this action the units moved for further formation to the area north and east of Sarajevo. By being supplied with 500 Machine Gun 42, 9 7.5 cm Antitank Gun 40, 9 7.5 cm Mountain Guns and 8 15 cm Heavy Field Howitzers, further troop units, already filled with personnel, could be made ready for action. In the same month came the formation of General Command V. SS Volunteer Mountain Corps. *SS-Obergruppenführer* Phleps was named commanding general and replaced in the division command by *SS-Brigadeführer* von Oberkamp.

After the change of government in Italy on July 25, 1943, the SS volunteer Mountain Division "Prinz Eugen" was ordered to move into the Mostar area of Bosnia-Herzegovina. Because of Italy's potential withdrawal from the alliance, the unit was to occupy the area between Split and Ragusa as part of the XV. Mountain Corps and secure Dalmatia from an Allied landing.

Now great tension ran through the unit via the new Division Commander. Phleps had held the native German commanders to disciplined treatment of the ethnic German Division members, but von Oberkamp showed only indifference. After the ethnic Germs had repeatedly been described as *"Gypsies,"* *"Serbs"* and *"Croatian filth"*, the situation escalated and on August 30, 1943, 173 members of the SS Volunteer Mountain Rifle Regiment 2 refused on principle to do any service.

For the ending of the "Axis" case, the disarming and interning of the Italian troops, the SS Volunteer Mountain Division was given the order on September 8, 1943. There the SS Volunteer Mountain Rifle Regiment 1 was to occupy the Split area, and the SS Volunteer Mountain Rifle Regiment 2 the Ragusa area. On the next day the I./SS Volunteer Mountain Rifle Regiment 1 was flown to the Italian airfield at Sinj (some 30 km north of Split) and occupied it without a fight. On the other hand, heavy fighting with Italian soldiers and Croatian partisans followed on the advance to Split. Only at the end of September 1943 could Split be occupied. In the fighting, the II./SS Volunteer Mountain Rifle Regiment 2, among others, was completely shattered near Sveti. SS Volunteer

---

68   The name was inspired by the SS Mountain Division "Nord", founded about nine months before.
69   The combat squadron resembled the Allgemeine-SS in Germany and was armed to fight partisans.

Mountain Rifle Regiment 2 also met heavy fighting on its way to Ragusa. On September 11-12, 1943 it stormed the city after air preparation. Only after tough street fighting did the commanding general of the Italian VI. Corps surrender.

On October 22, 1943 the Waffen-SS was renumbered. The two mountain rifle regiments in what now became the 7th Volunteer Mountain Division "Prinz Eugen" were designated SS Volunteer Mountain Rifle Regiments 13[70] and 14.

On the next day the SS Volunteer Mountain Rifle Regiment 13 began to occupy the islands of Brac, Hvar, Korkula and the Peljesac peninsula in the roughly three weeks of Operation "Herbstgewitter". The SS Volunteer Mountain Rifle Regiment 14 had to spend ten days, beginning on November 5, 1943, with Operation "Landsturm" freeing the Split area of partisans and Italian turncoats.

His inability to lead the unit brought the discharge of Division Commander *SS-Brigadeführer* von Oberkamp after barely five months.[71] Under the commissary command of *SS-Standartenführer* Schmidhuber, the Division was involved in Operation "Kugelblitz" as of December 2, 1943. The I., II. and III. Communistic Partisan Corps, which had fallen upon Serbia from the Bosnian area, were to be fought northeast of Sarajevo in cooperation with the 369th (Croatian) Infantry Division and 1. Mountain Division.[72] In the roadless area, large numbers of the partisans were able to escape through the German enclosing ring. While some of the German troops made the pocket smaller, others took part in the pursuit of the escaped enemies, beginning with Operation "Schneesturm" on December 18, 1943. At the end of December 1943 the operation ended. The partisans were beaten and had lost many weapons. The parts of the Division that had been in combat were transferred to Zenica, some 50 km northwest of Sarajevo.

The 7th SS Volunteer Mountain Division reported a strength of 21,102 members at the end of 1943. Although the unit had some 2,000 more men than its intended strength, the use of the entire Division was only possible within limits, due to the lack of over 800 commanders and lower leaders. From September 1943 to the end of December 1943, 296 men had fallen, 1170 were wounded and 215 were listed as missing.

On January 4, 1944 the Operation "Waldrausch" began. The two-week operation took the men into the area west of Travnik. The actions of fighting the partisans, in the mountains that in some cases stood 1,500 meters high, led in the winter weather to the total exhaustion of the men. The units were thus only marginally usable.

With the transfer back to Dalmatia, *SS-Oberführer* Kumm took command of the unit at the end of January 1944. He recalls in correspondence with the author:

> "The Division was in a very poor condition when I took it over. One of the two rifle regiments had even been suggested for disbanding by von Oberkamp.[73] Commanding General Phleps was so angry that he wanted to fire the Division Commander at once. He succeeded in doing that. At first I had the individual battalions appear and talked with all of them. Above all, though, I made sure that a group or battery would never again be left standing in the rain."[74]

On February 20, 1944 the regional composition of the Division was set. Accordingly, there were 8.5% native Germans and 91.5 ethnic Germans. Of the latter, 53.6% came from the Banat and Serbia, 21.3% from Romania and 11.2% from Croatia. Barely 3% were from Slovakia and around 2.5% from Hungary. In all, the strength at that point was 22,659 men.

---

[70] On November 9, 1944 the SS Volunteer Mountain Rifle Regiment 13 was given the name of the *SS-Obergruppenführer* and *General* of the Waffen-SS Artur Phleps, who had recently died in Siebenbürgen.
[71] Von Oberkamp was transferred to the SS Headquarters and finally functioned as Inspector of the Motorized Troops in Amtsgruppe C (sic!).
[72] Tito wanted to bring Serbia under his influence. As a result, there were repeated combat disputes between the nationalistic Serbian partisans under Mihailovic and the Communistic Croatian partisans under Tito.
[73] A sign that von Oberkamp was completely out of his depth with the command of such a unit.
[74] Von Oberkamp had little interest in the welfare of his subordinates.

Erwin Ellner was born on September 22, 1923 in Gross-Betschkerek, Serbiam and entered the SS Volunteer Mountain Division "Prinz Eugen" on April 25, 1942.

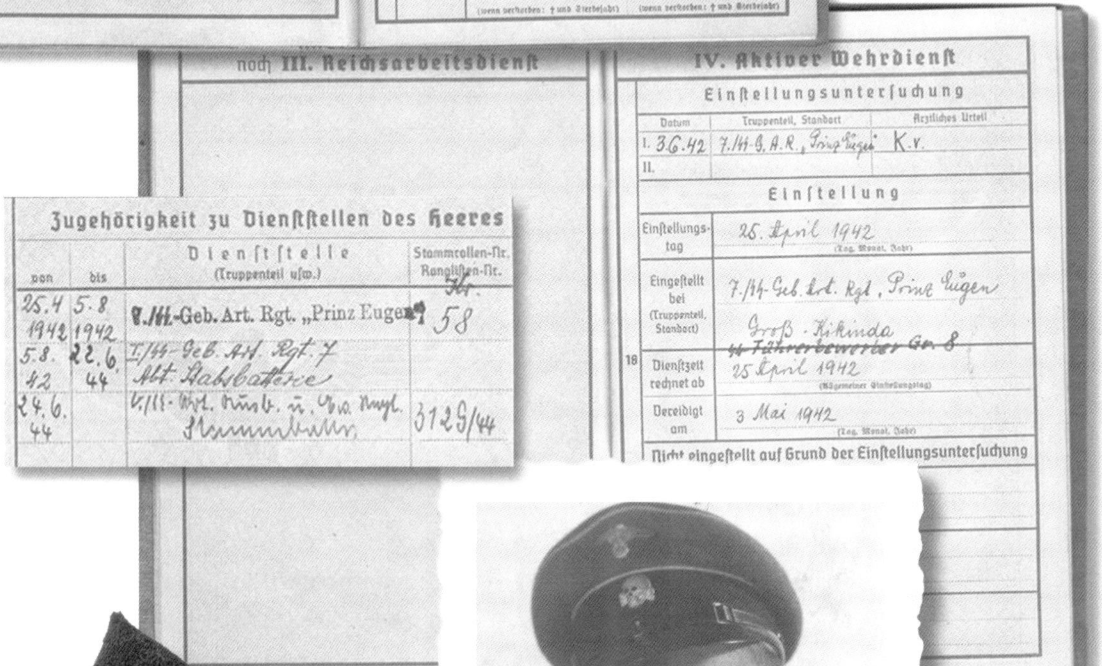

The special collar emblem of the ethnic Germans of the 7th SS Volunteer Mountain Division "Prinz Eugen" – the Odal Rune.

Wilhelm Habschmied

Along with smaller actions in the Split-Ragusa area, *SS-Oberführer* used the next four weeks mainly to make a combat-ready unit of the weakened Division. After many German troops had been transferred northward from the securing region for the planned occupation of Hungary at the beginning of March 1944, there came an order to transfer the unit back to the coast in the area around Sarajevo. The 7th SS Volunteer Mountain Division "Prinz Eugen" was divided there over a territory of about 80x200 km.

The withdrawal of German troops allowed Tito to let the II. Partisan Corps to move southward over the Lim River to Serbia on March 22-23, 1944. The low combat value of the Bulgarian occupation troops led to hasty spatial development of the offensive. Yet this brought on considerable supply difficulties for the partisans. Finally pushed into the defensive, the III. Partisan Corps was to bring relief.

As a countermeasure, the Commander "Southeast" ordered the 7th and 13th SS Volunteer Mountain Divisions and the Serbian Volunteer Corps to smash the partisan divisions in the Vlasenica area and the Drina. On April 26, 1944 the V. SS Volunteer Mountain Corps began Operation "Maibaum". Since the action area of the 7th SS Volunteer Mountain Division extended northeast to the Drina, the exit points were quickly taken. On May 10, 1944 the partially successful operation ended, after some hard fighting.

A few days later, the Division was ordered some 150 km westward over the Vrbas into the Banya-Luca-Mrkonic-Jaice line. From there it was supposed to take part with the XV. Mountain Corps in Operation "Rösselsprung" as of May 25, 1944. The attempt to capture Tito and his staff failed. The final report of the XV. Mountain Corps after the operation ended showed, though, that *SS-Oberführer* Kumm had succeeded in barely half a year in motivating the ethnic German division members again and forming a strong combat unit:

> "7. SS Division and parts of V. Mountain Corps: As the only mountain troops, the SS units have borne the burden of the operation and gained the main successes. Combat readiness, ambition, especially the company and battalion leadership, good, clear leadership and corresponding reports are to be emphasized."

From June 18 to July 9, 1944, large parts of the Division were used in Operation "*Freie Jagd*". This was a continued operation to the "Rösselsprung" southeast of the last starting position. Other troop units were gathered into a battle group and sent to the 21st Waffen Mountain Division of the SS "Skanderbeg". At the beginning of July 1944 the 7. Volunteer Mountain Division "Prinz Eugen" reported a strength of 18,835 members. Through the new ethnic German recruits, the losses could always be balanced.

After Tito's hitherto unsuccessful attempts to bring Serbia under his direct influence, he repeated this intention before the expected arrival of the Red Army in the summer of 1944. The preparations were not concealed from the Commander "Southeast", and so at the end of July 1944 he ordered Operation "Rübezahl". As of August 5, 1955 the V. SS Volunteer Mountain Corps was to wipe out the partisan divisions in the area southeast of Sarajevo. Along with the 7th SS Volunteer Mountain Division, the 13th and 21st Waffen Mountain Divisions of the SS and the 1st Mountain Division were involved. Because of the withdrawal of Romania from the pact with Germany, Operation "Rübezahl" was broken off on August 22, 1944 without any great success.

Events kept coming, for on September 8, 1944 Bulgaria also declared war on the German Reich. With the departure of Romania and Bulgaria from the former Axis pact, the Red Army could reach the Serbian border almost without fighting. The 7th SS Volunteer Mountain Division "Prinz Eugen" was ordered some 300 km eastward to the Serbian-Bulgarian border and subordinated to the "Müller" Corps Group.[75]

In the front sector, over 100 km wide, from Zayecar to Leskovac, the units of the 1st Mountain Division[76] were relieved of service. Taking over the positions was done under strong attacks by Bulgarian and Soviet troops plus partisan bands. The Wehrmacht report of October 10, 1944 stated:

---

75   This belonged to the Military Commander "Southeast", by whom on September 26, 1944 the "Serbia" Army Unit was formed.
76   The Division was supposed to turn away the Soviet advance at the Iron Gate. Suggestions from *SS-Oberführer* Kumm to divide his unit for this task were declined because of the front experience of the 1st Mountain Division.

> "In the bitter fighting in eastern Serbia, the 1st Mountain Division, under the command of Knight's Cross bearer Generalleutnant von Stettner, and the 7th SS Mountain Division Prinz Eugen, under the command of SS-Oberführer Kumm, have stood out particularly in attack and defense on difficult terrain through exemplary steadfastness and enthusiastic attacking spirit."

Without the needed support from the German Luftwaffe, heavy artillery, tanks and tank destroyers, the German support-point positions were broken through quickly again and again and could be regained only partially. The units lost connection with each other for lack or failure of communication equipment, so that orders could be passed on only by messengers.

On October 22 the battle for Kralyevo, which was the support point for the withdrawal of Army Group "E", began. There was heavy fighting. Here the Division, along with remainders of the 1. Mountain Division and the 177th Rifle Division, took over a bridgehead position over the Morava. Because of the Bulgarian advance, the German plan to keep Croatia, Montenegro, Northern Albania and Serbia in the so-called Blue Line had to be given up. Instead the Commander "Southwest" tried to hold the Drina-West Syrmia-Croatian borderline. The order to move back behind the Morava already was given on October 10, 1944.

Decimated by constant Bulgarian aircraft and tank attacks on their positions, the men were in purely infantry combat. From October 1 to 28, 1944, the 7th SS Volunteer Mountain Division lost 1,421 dead, 3,679 wounded and 2,610 missing.[77] After this loss of almost 8,000 men within four weeks and the high material losses, among others, 800 vehicles were lost, the unit was beaten despite a nominal strength of around 10,000 men.

All the same, the situation was stabilized on the Serbian-Croatian border and in Syrmia in November 1944. On November 24, 1944 the Kralyevo bridgehead was given up. Via Pozega and Uzice the Division men reached the Drina near Lyuboviya (north of Srebrenica). Again subordinated to the XXXIV. Army Corps (the renamed "Müller" Corps Group), they faced hard fights with partisan near Zvornik and Biyelina. On December 13, 1944 there was heavy fighting while crossing the Drina near Zvornik.

After the last German troops of Army Group "E" had crossed the Drina bridgehead near Visegrad on January 13, 1945, the withdrawal begun in the Aegean and Greece in September 1944 was finished. The Commander "Southeast" immediately ordered the 7. AA Volunteer Mountain Division, strengthened by the SS Division Group "Skanderbeg", and others to the Srymian front. Here they were first supposed to free the Vinkovici-Brcko line north of the Save, which had been broken by partisans.

To stabilize the Syrmian front, the Division entered the area south of the Danube between Ilok and Sid to Erevik as part of Operation "Frühlingssturm" as of January 17, 1945. At the end of the month Hitler ordered the Commander "Southeast" to destroy the Soviet south wing in Hungary. Here four divisions, including the 7th SS Volunteer Mountain Division, were supposed to move from the Esseg area northward over the Drava. But no front combat was considered. Instead, the 7th SS Volunteer Mountain Division was to fight partisans in the backline area of the front along the Drava.

At the end of January 1945, *SS-Brigadeführer* Kumm turned the division over to the former commander of the 21st Waffen Mountain Division of the SS "Skanderbeg", *SS-Brigadeführer* Schmidhuber. He first led the units into the area of the LXXXXI. Army Corps, some 100 km to the west, on February 4, 1945. Two days later Operation "Werwolf" began, in which strong partisan bands were fought in the area south of the Save near Virovitica. They formed a lengthening of the Soviet front before the 2nd Panzer Army, and could go into action to either the southeast or northwest. Barcs was supposed to be freed in the operation, and a thoroughgoing front south of the Drava was finally to be formed.

On February 10, 1945 Hitler ordered the Commander "Southeast" to prepare to secure the Croatian area on the Seny-Biohac-Banya Luka-Doboy-Syrmian Front line. To carry out this transfer movement, the 7th SS Volunteer Mountain Division was ordered back from Bosnia. For this, the unit was subordinated to the XXI. Mountain Corps in the Sarajevo area on March 1, 1945 and marched some 150 km southward to Zenica. Together

---

77 A great number of them left the troops without permission to be with their families in these difficult days.

with the 181st Rifle Division and the 369th (Croatian) Infantry Division, Operation "Feüwehr" ensued. Here parts of the Division moved over 100 km farther to the southeast and back to the Drina near Foca. On March 3, 1945 the 7th SS Mountain Division was able to build a stable front again in the Zenica-Busovaca area and reach Sarajevo. Parts of it were at Doboy. From there the Division Commander planned on March 19, 1945 to fight the numerous partisan bands in the northwest and northeast.

Two days later the evacuation of Sarajevo and transport of the approximately 1,500 wounded men there began. After Zenica was given up on April 12, 1945, the 7th SS Volunteer Mountain Division marched into the Tuzla area. Covering the withdrawal of the XXI. Army Corps, it fought partisans for a distance of almost 150 km via Maglay and Doboy to Brod. Here it crossed the Save on April 21, 1945, under enemy fire, on rubber boats. Then came the march to Agram, some 200 km away. Here the 7th SS Volunteer Mountain Division was subordinated to the LXIX. Army Corps z.b.V. on April 29, 1945 and ordered to the area of Karlstadt (some 50 cm southwest of Agram). On May 6, 1945 *SS-Brigadeführer* Schmidhuber received the order to lead his group to the Reich border. Five days later the men arrived in Steinbrück, some 75 km away in Styria.

Via Franz and Stein the group reached the Krainburg area (northwest of Laibach) almost intact. From there it marched, according to the capitulation regulations, into Yugoslavian imprisonment on May 14, 1945 with a strength of some 7,000 men. On May 22, 1945 about 2,000 ethnic German division members were murdered by partisans near Rann/Brezice in Slovenia. Confined to Yugoslavian work and concentration camps, hundreds of additional ethnic German members lost their lives.

Improvised in 1942 with ethnic Germans from the whole southeast area, the unit provided important support in the next years in fighting partisans in the Balkans. As the changing motivation of the ethnic Germans in action showed, the saying that a unit is only as good as its leadership was proved here too.

8. SS Cavalry Division "Florian Geyer"

In view of the war against the Soviet Union, Himmler ordered the combination of the two SS Totenkopf Cavalry Regiments into an SS Cavalry Brigade on February 24, 1941. On April 9, 1941 it was subordinated to the newly formed Command Staff *Reichsführer-SS* in the Lyck area of East Prussia. This was formed for *"special tasks in service of the Führer, which result from the war finally to be waged by two opposed political systems."* Among them, in particular, the persecution of Jews and Communists was to be understood.

From East Prussia the Command Staff first sent the SS Cavalry Regiment I briefly to the 87. Infantry Division on the main battle line on June 26, 1941. There was no further front action. On July 19, 1941 the Command Staff made known:

> "On order of RFSS, Kav.Rgt. 1 and 2 are in action in and around Baranovice, SS Kav.Rgt. 2 is subordinated to Standartenführer Fegelein, who retains the leadership of SS Kav.Rgt.1. When it crosses the Reich border, the SS Cavalry unit is subordinated tactically and in supplying terms to the Higher SS and Police Leader with the commander of the Backline Army Zone Center."

The restructuring of the units followed. Without changing the strength, new units were formed of the 16 available squadrons. According to the original task, the Higher SS and Police Leader "Russia Center" also used the SS Cavalry Brigade for *"pacifying"* the captured territory. Besides fighting with deserted regular Soviet troops, there were shootings of Jews and Gypsies.

From July 27 to August 11, 1941 the SS Cavalry Brigade combed through the Pripyet Swamps between Route 1 and the Pripyet. *SS-Standartenführer* Fegelein reported the shooting of 13,788 persons while losing only two of his men. Entire villages were liquidated.[78] Even if one considers that the SS leaders, particularly *SS-Standartenführer* Fegelein,[79] boastfully exaggerated the numbers, the unbelievable procedure remains essentially what it was.

From August 15 to 30 the area south of the Pripyet between Turov and Mosyr followed. From there the SS Cavalry Brigade marched into the triangular area between the Pripyet in the southwest, the Dniepr in the east and the Mosyr-Gomel rail line in the north. He Higher SS and Police Leader "Russia-Center" noted in his war diary:

> "… a gigantic area in which German troops have not been before. … On the Bobruisk-Mosyr route I flew over the marching columns of the SS Reiter Regiment 2. The troops waved enthusiastically to me, as always when I fly over them. … After I had a radio talk in Retschitzka with the commander (of the backlands army region) about the results of my investigations, I flew back over Choiniki, where the Staff and Reconnaissance Units had meanwhile arrived. Fegelein had meanwhile, with the help of assembled women and men, set up the quarters properly fantastically and provided a good supper. I lived with Fegelein and his staff in the Party House, a wooden house under old oaks, beside a brook on which wild ducks quacked. The 10th of September passed talking with the Führer, writing orders for the pacification and reconnaissance against the wooded complex between Choiniki and Retschitza. The final orders given in the evening before the Party House, while the SS men sang soldier songs around their campfire as if on maneuvers, was even recorded on records by the radio truck of the propaganda company. … Because of the good example, and because only one – Fegelein –

---

78 *SS-Brigadeführer* Gottberg reported on April 10, 1943 on the partisan fighting in White Russia. He expressed himself as follows: *"If one advances with an advance guard, communication men and then a spearhead, and if the rear guard comes marching up, then those who carry out active partisan fighting are overjoyed, and one finds old men, women and children. If one knocks them dead and burns the village, then the population says that the Germans are even wilder dogs than the Bolsheviks, and the women run to the bandits' women's battalions."*

79 *SS-Gruppenführer* von dem Bach noted in his war diary for August 14, 1941: *In the Cavalry Corps actions the Brigade had only two fatalities, who drove onto a mine. But when one hears Fegelein's reports, one must believe he is fighting the Russian campaign all alone. … The endless self-praise, the basic exaggeration and the omnipresent rattling of the advertising drum muss repel learned officers whose "old Prussian Tradition" says: "More being than seeming!"*

wanted to lead, I armed myself with a machine pistol and, thus equipped, took part in the action on the front line. The success, especially in the village of Torny, was good. I was personally able to capture 1 commissar, 2 leading partisans, 6 other partisans and 13 Russian soldiers. Trials began at once, and all who were found to carry weapons were shot at once."

During the Soviet winter offensive, the Red Army was able to cross the Volga between Seliger-See and the area north of Rshev and place the German units in a bad spot. The German XXIII. Army Corps was surrounded west of Olenino. Without winter clothing and suitable lubricants for weapons and equipment, the German troops could offer practically no resistance. Lacking supplies of food and ammunition led to catastrophic conditions.

In this situation the SS Cavalry Brigade was ordered some 500 km north to the Toropez-Cholm area at the beginning of October 1941, and finally in the direction of Rshev to support the front. The Commanding General of the XXIII. Army Corps, General of the Infantry Schubert, evaluated the achievements of the SS Cavalry Brigade after the fighting:

"The Brigade has not only ruined all the enemy's attempts in heavy warfare, sometimes costly, but always carried out with great spirit; it has also led the main attacks in the enclosing pocketing and destruction of enemy forces southwest of Rshev in day-long advances.

After the end of the Soviet winter offensive, the SS Cavalry Brigade remained in its positions west of Rshev and was used sporadically against scattered enemy forces. In mid-April 1942 the unit was moved out of the front to be built up to a division at the SS "Heidelager" troop training camp. At the main battle line there remained, under the command of *SS-Sturmbannführer* Zehender, at first only a battalion-strong battle group, which also followed to Debica at the end of July 1942.

After the agreement with Hungary to call ethnic Germans into the Waffen-SS, over 16,000 replacement men were available. To the remaining approximately 3,000 native German members, thus more than 9,000 Hungarian Germans were ordered off gradually to set up the SS Cavalry Division. After *SS-Standartenführer* Fegelein was named communication leader at the *Führer*'s Headquarters, *SS-Brigadeführer* Bittrich took command of the new division.

While the newly formed units, particularly those formed with ethnic German recruits (SS Cavalry Regiment 3, SS Flak Unit and SS Engineer Battalion), remained at the SS training camp, the division command was given orders in mid-August 1942 to return the combat-ready troop units to the 9th Army. *SS-Brigadeführer* Bittrich formed two battle groups of SS Cavalry Regiments 1 and 2, strengthened by supporting units, which were transported to the Demidow region (east of Vitebsk) until mid-September 1942.

Subordinated to the 330th Infantry Division, the units first took part in Operation "Spätlese" until September 20, 1942. This was directed against scattered Red Army men and partisans in the wooded and swampy area west of Jarzewo. After that the two battle groups marched to the front and took positions between the 197th and 330th Infantry Divisions at the seam between the XXIII. And LIX. Army Corps in the Demechi area.

In mid-October 1942 the troop units still in Debica were summoned to the unit that was now the SS Cavalry Division. The recruits, mostly ethnic Germans, thus had a sufficient six months of training behind them. On October 26, 1942, *SS-Brigadeführer* Bittrich reported a combat strength of 6,309 men. At this time the fighting strength was some 9,000 and the supplying strength some 12,000 men, approximately corresponding to the planned strength. After several small undertakings against partisans in the backland area, new action followed at the end of November 1942 with the XXX. Army Corps to close a hole in the front between Demechi and Belyi. After stabilizing the front successfully, the penetrated enemy units were fought until December 15, 1942.

On December 19, 1942, with a strength of 310 commanders and 10,569 other ranks, the unit was subordinated to the XXXXI. Panzer Corps. There scattered Red Army troops and partisans behind the front were to be fought. Under the leadership of *SS-Standartenführer* Freitag, around 3,000 SS cavalrymen took part in Operation "Sternlauf" in the Vop River area.

On February 14, 1943 the SS Cavalry Division was ordered to the Bobruisk area and again subordinated to the Higher SS and Police Leader "Russia Center". *SS-Oberführer* Freitag, commanding the Division since January 4, 1943, received a warning from Himmler on March 8, 1943 because of his obviously faulty commands.

Albert Schwenn was transferred to the 5th/SS Cavalry Regiment 1 in February 1943:

> "In 1940 I reported voluntarily to the 5th/SS Cavalry Regiment 1. Of about 50 young men, only eight were accepted. All the others did not meet the prerequisites then to be used – How this was to change later, when we received ethnic German comrades about 1.60 meters tall! Then when the long-awaited call to induction came, the disappointment was great at first. I was to go to the cavalry, though I had wanted the tanks or the motorcycle rifles. As great as my disappointment was, equally great was my father's pleasure, for he loved horses over all else and could not imagine what a difference there was between civilian and military riding. In October 1942 I was an SS rider in the SS Cavalry Replacement Unit. The training was not exactly suited for giving us young fellows enthusiasm about a soldier's life. Anyway, we were hungry from the beginning to the end of our recruit period and stole turnips from the supply depot to gobble them up raw.
>
> In February 1943 we were ordered to the field unit. We were in a former Russian cavalry barracks in Lapitchi near Ossipovici. For "partisan hunting" we got up at 4:00 A.M. and rode away at 5:00. After three kilometers we dismounted and then went five kilometers on foot, for the horses had to be rested. At 9:00 A.M. the motorized units, later broken up, caught up with us. The comrades sat comfortably leaving back in their Kfz.15 and waved kindly to us horse boys."

On February 16, 1943 the order already came to form a regiment-strength battle group. This was to serve in the Orel bend near Dmitrovsk in the XXXXVII. Panzer Corps. Here the Red Army had begun a major offensive in the course of their winter offensive and had pushed the German troops into a tight spot. After the fighting ended in mid-March 1943, the PzAOK 2 ordered, on March 24, 1943, fighting against the partisans who were strengthened by Red Army men. On April 5, 1943 the SS Battle Group "Zehender" was ordered back to Lapichi (northwest of Bobruisk).

On April 20, 1943 Himmler removed *SS-Standartenführer* Freitag from the command of the Division and temporarily put the former commander of the SS Cavalry Brigade, *SS-Oberführer* Fegelein, in as division leader. At the same time, the men of the SS Cavalry Regiment 3 were divided between the other two cavalry regiments. At the SS "Heidelager" training camp the regiment was to be filled up with ethnic Germans.

About two weeks later, action ensued in the area between the Pripyet in the southwest, the Dniepr in the east and the Mosyr-Gomel rail line in the north. Here the SS riders had already seen service from August 15 to 30, 1941. Under the command of Higher SS and Police *Führer* "Russia-South", *SS-Obergruppenführer* Prützmann, the approximately 10,000 partisans who had gone there were to be fight. Operation "Weichsel I" lasted from May 9 to June 10, 1943 and led above all to numerous requisitionings. Thus 5,675 cattle, 1,073 calves, 1,233 horses, 3,153 sheep, 1,398 pigs were stolen. A few days later Operation "Weichsel II" began; it included the area of the so-called Nassen Triangle in the Ovrutsh-Mosyr-Petrikov-Olevsk area and also led to many confiscations. The civilian population practically lost their means of living in these two actions.

Already during the failed German summer offensive, Operation "Zitadelle". The Red Army itself went on the offensive and was able to advance to Kharkov. Then the SS Cavalry Division was ordered to move some 500 km east from the Mosyr area, into the Merefa area (south of Kharkov). On August 21, 1943 the unit, with a strength of 8,792 men, reached the XXXXII. Army Corps and was placed on the seam with the LVII. Panzer Corps. It was not lacking some 30% of its specified strength, but the fact that the SS Cavalry Division in its conception was not suited for mobile large-scale combat with armored enemies, that led in the following weeks to chaotic conditions.

With nothing to oppose the material superiority of the Soviet troops, the SS riders tried to reach the Dniepr near Mischurin-Rog in costly retreat fighting. There they were subordinated to the LVII. Panzer Corps on September 25, 1943. Pushed to the southwest, the survivors drew back over the Ingulez into the Kirovgrad area. At this time the renumbering of the Waffen-SS units took place. The new names thus became 8th SS Cavalry Division and SS Cavalry Regiments 15 to 17. The Division units also received the number 8.

After the unit had been smashed in the ongoing combat, Himmler arranged with the Chief of the Wehrmacht command staff on December 8, 1943 that the 8th SS Cavalry Division should be set up anew. On December 21,

1943 about half of the men were taken out of action and sent to Syrmia (north of the Save) for new structuring. The remaining units stayed with the XXXXVII. Army Corps as the SS Battle Group "Lombard" and followed to the Esseg area in Croatia in January 1944. On December 31, 1943 the strength of the Division, without SS Cavalry Regiment 17, was 5,182 men.

The SS Cavalry Regiment 17, at the SS "Heidelager" training camp, reported an additional 1,820 members. For a planned second SS Cavalry Division, SS Cavalry Regiment 15 was also set up with ethnic Germans in November 1943. On December 31, 1943 it already had 1,581 men. For SS Artillery Regiment 8, a third unit was formed. This reported 632 members at the end of 1943.

While the Division was completed with some 3,000 ethnic Germans at Esseg, the SS Cavalry Regiment 17 at the SS "Heidelager" training camp was ordered to Kovel for action. Here the Red Army had succeeded in penetrating the main battle line to a width of 150 km between the 2nd Army and 4th Panzer Army. Although the ground was mainly swamp, there was the danger that the enemy could advance quickly through the traffic intersection of Kovel into the General Government. On January 16, 1944 the Regiment was sent to the "von dem Bach" Group and took positions southeast of the city. After the Soviet troops were able to surround Kovel in mid-March 1944, the LVI. Panzer Corps came to its relief on April 4, 1944 and was able to stabilize the front again. At the end of April the SS Cavalry Regiment 17 was taken out of action and sent to the Kisber area in Hungary. There it formed the cadre of the new 22nd SS Volunteer Cavalry Division.

Meanwhile the reforming of the 8th SS Cavalry Division with native and ethnic German replacements had been conducted. On March 12, 1944 Hitler gave the cavalry unit the name "Florian Geyer." To form a front-capable division, much stress was put on motorizing and equipping with heavy weapons. The ordered enlargement of the SS Assault Gun Battery to a regiment, though, could not be realized. One SS Assault Gun Unit 8 was not set up, and the battery was transferred to SS Panzerjäger Unit 8. The unit lacked heavy combat-supporting units for battles with the strong Soviet troops.

Until Operation "Margarethe", the occupation of Hungary, on March 19, 1944, the service in Croatia consisted of securing the area with actions against partisans and the training of reserves. During the Hungarian action the 8th SS Cavalry Division "Florian Geyer", under the command of *SS-Oberführer* Streckenbach, moved into the area along the Danube between Mohacs and Duna-Foeldvar. Not far from there were the hometowns of many ethnic German members of the Division.

While some strong combat units were quickly withdrawn from Hungary and sent to the distressed eastern front, the SS cavalry stayed in the securing area until the summer of 1944. On June 30, 1944 the Division reported a strength of 12,895 members. Thus for the first time since it was formed, the unit had not only reached its specified strength but, in pure numbers, was even stronger. It must be kept in mind, though, that it lacked some 900 commanders and lower leaders.

Because of the collapse of the front in Romania, the Division command received, on August 20, 1944, the order to transfer to Siebenbürgen. The units had been trained almost nine months and thus formed a combat-ready troop. After rail transport of about 500 km, the 8th SS Cavalry Division was subordinated to the Higher SS and Police *Führer* "Siebenbürgen" *SS-Obergruppenführer* Phleps.

The troop units that arrived at the beginning of September 1944 moved into defensive positions on the northwest bank of the Marosch in the Neumarkt (Romanian: Targu Mures) area right after unloading. On September 20, 1944, at a strength of 14,040 men, they were subordinated to the XXIX. Army Corps. Again stocked with ethnic Germans from Hungary, their actual strength was again even higher than the planned number. When the Red Army, along with Romanian units, began an offensive on October 6, 1944, the 8th SS Cavalry Division secured the withdrawal of the German-Hungarian units in a northwest direction. The Wehrmacht bulletin reported on October 9, 1944:

> "In the fighting in Siebenbürgen, the 8th SS Cavalry Division, made up overwhelmingly of Germans from the southeastern area, under the command of Knight's Cross bearer SS-Standartenführer Joachim Rumohr, struck splendidly!"

In the general German withdrawal, the SS cavalry covered about 200 km by October 13, 1944 and marched through Marghita by October 23, 1944 and another 80 km to the Nyireghyhaza area. Involved in defensive combat again and again, the unit moved westward and crossed the Theiss near Iisza-Keszi a week later. Without decently built defensive positions and defense-ready units, the river offered no hindrance to the Red Army's advance.

Then came another withdrawal of some 140 km from the Theiss. Then the 8th SS Cavalry Division, with the III. Panzer Corps, took up the Pecel-Maglod-Vesces-Gyal line in the first week of November 1944 While the units were increasingly mixed from the frequent forming and disbanding of alarm forces, General Command IX. Waffen Mountain Corps of the SS arrived at the end of November 1944 and the Balkans arrived in Budapest and took over the leadership of General Command III. Panzer Corps on December 13, 1944.

Ten days later the Red Army was able to surround the Hungarian capital. Hitler immediately ordered the 8th SS Cavalry Division to leave the eastern bridgehead and take over the defense of the strategically important Buda. The situation for the enclosed troops soon became catastrophic, what with the constant artillery fire and assault attacks, plus the lack of German supplies.

In February 1945 the 8th SS Cavalry Division lost 221 dead and 1,086 wounded.[80] After all the combat attempts had failed, the commanding General ordered *SS-Obergruppenführer* and *General* of the Police Pfeffer-Windenbruch, against Hitler's order to stop, to break out on February 11, 1945. Of some 30,000 surrounded soldiers, only 785 reached the German lines. The then *SS-Rottenführer* Helmut Schreiber reported on the days in Budapest:

> "I was born in 1924 and went to the Uhlan Garrison in Warsaw on April 15, 1942. From there I went for basic training at the SS Cavalry Replacement Unit in Cholm near Lublin, and after the recruit period to the forming of the 8th SS Cavalry Division in Debica, at the so-called Heidelager. I was assigned to the artillery and went the way of our division in that unit.
>
> On Christmas Eve of 1944 we were ordered into the interior of Budapest on a position change. Early that morning the hole in the pocket was closed by the Russians. Ince we had no more ammunition for our guns (lFH 18 1-.5 cm) anyway, we were immediately used as infantry. I was at first assigned to the unit's command post as an advanced observer. Our poor horses had already starved or been killed by bullets and aerial bombs. A help for the starving civilians. In no time the horses were cut up.
>
> From the Gellertberg I was able to observe the blowing up of the Danube bridge. At the beginning of January 1945 the rest of the battery manpower (baggage train) was set up as a small battle group for me. At my side was an assigned officer candidate and a scattered lower leader of the 2nd Battery. A reliable connection with the other groups scarcely existed any more. Every group was more or less on its own, whether for rounding up food or ammunition.
>
> I remember well an incident in a house occupied by us in the vicinity of the post office on Wiener Strasse. While looking through the house, we found a man in a bed in one apartment. He was apparently sick. There was his bed in front of a door to a pantry full of sausage, bread and other food. What were we to do? First still our own hunger and then take a washbucket full to the starving inhabitants in the cellar. I was then temporarily bandaged by two women after being wounded.
>
> On night we had god luck; our ammunition was almost running out, when the crew of a damaged SPW left us ammunition, and so we could at least defend ourselves. In this house-to-house fighting was wounded on January 30, 1945. First a bullet in the head, which fortunately did not go through my steel helmet, and ten minutes later a shot into my right collarbone. A comrade brought me to the main dressing station, which was in the underground passages of the castle. The matter was handled with a temporary bandage. The cellar vaults were full of badly wounded men, lying on the ground without beds, covered with paper. A piece of bread and a cup of tea was the food. My comrades took me out of there two days later. Their reason: If we must, we want to go to the dogs together!

---

80 The daily food ration of the more than 11,000 wounded men in the fortress was finally only fifteen grams of legumes and half a slice of bread.

"On February 10, 1945 came the order to gather all wounded who could walk in the vaults of the castle; they were apparently to be taken on by the Swedish Red Cross. Nothing came of that. On the night of February 11-12, 1945 it was said that the men still able to fight wanted to try to break out. Many walking wounded went along, but it did not last long and many came back confused. The breaking-out was more or less ruined. Then on February 12 the Russians took us out of the cellars. What happened then was hell. Whoever could not walk was shot. On the march to Budafok we could convince ourselves of the horror of the last days. Shot soldiers lay everywhere in smaller nests of resistance. Then we went across Romania and the Black Sea to Odessa. A path almost nine years long began, leading through half of Russia to the Urals."

Set up and equipped for action in the backline areas, the SS cavalrymen were repeatedly ordered to the front as the last reserve and were repeatedly able to stabilize the situation. Consisting at first of native Germans, the composition changed through the assigning of thousands of ethnic Germans from Poland, Hungary and the USSR. When the material superiority of the Red Army became too great, there came the full shattering of the Division in front action southwest of Kharkov. Because of this situation it was tried at the beginning of 1944 to make the unit capable of front use with motorized heavy combat support units. The strength of the soviet troops, plus the weakness of the German-Hungarian bands, prevented their successful use in Siebenbürgen. Finally, after losing all their heavy weapons and vehicles in infantry action in Budapest in February 1945, the units broke down. The men who went into Soviet imprisonment were punished severely for their numerous actions in backline areas. Most of them came home from the USSR only in 1955-56.

11th SS Volunteer Panzergrenadier Division "Nordland"

The Free Corps "Danmark"

After the beginning of Operation "Barbarossa" on June 22, 1941, there were talks between the German Reich and Denmark, which had been *"occupied by German troops for its own protection"* since 1940. There the question of to what extent Danes would willingly be allowed and able to take part in fighting against the Soviet Union was raised. The official sending of a Danish troop contingent was refused by Denmark m, but they allowed the reporting of volunteers for an independent unit within the German Army.

Himmler's plans to integrate the Danes into Waffen-SS units as *"Germanic"* was opposed by the German ambassador to Denmark, Renthe-Fink, who feared that scarcely a Dane would then volunteer. Many Danes, in fact, greeted the battle against the USSR, which was obviously interested in expansion, and had already fought against the Red Army in Finland in 1939-40, but the Nazi Party and particularly the SS had little understanding of them.

In any case, the *Reichsführer-SS*, after talks with the Wehrmacht, was able to arrange for the so-called *"Germanic"* volunteers to be gathered under the command of the SS Command Headquarters. The letters "SS" were not included in the unit's name, for the aforementioned reasons. It was known as of July 3, 1941 as the Volunteer Unit "Dänemark", and the Danish media announced five days later that active and discharged soldiers could report voluntarily to fight against Communism. Along with Danes, numerous so-called North Schleswigers, ethnic Germans from Denmark, also joined.

On July 19, 1941 came the departure of barely 500 volunteers in Copenhagen. They received SS ranks with the added *"Freiwilligen"*, for example, *Freiwilligen-Sturmmann*. Via Hamburg-Langenhorn the men in what was known since August 15, 1941 as the Freikorps "Danmark"[81] reached Posen-Treskau. There in the next weeks there were open confrontations between the members. While the Danes were certainly anti-Communistic not nationally Danish-inclined, the other group, made up of ethnic Germans, made polemics with National Socialistic agitation. When the Commander of the Free Corps, *Freiwilligen-Obersturmbannführer* Kryssing, had a North Schleswiger arrested for Nazi propaganda and an apparent call for mutiny, the SS Headquarters intervened and finally named the Danish National Socialist *SS-Sturmbannführer* Schalburg, serving until then in the SS Division "Wiking", as the new commander.

After about nine months of training, the Free Corps "Danmark", about 800 men strong, was flown to the surrounded Demyansk at the end of April 1942. Subordinated to the SS Totenkopf Division, the Danes took positions on the Lovat on May 20, 1942. Until they were removed from the front on July 26, 1942, the Free Corps "Danmark" had lost 346 dead and wounded in about nine weeks. Transferred to Mitau, the Danes were given their annual four-week furlough on September 7, 1942. The propagandistic success desired by the Germans was omitted. Quite the opposite, the provoking arrival of numerous members (especially members of the Danish National Socialistic Worker Party) led to much tension with the Danish population.

On October 18, 1942 they gathered again in Mitau. Then came their transfer on November 21, 1942 to Bobruisk and subordination to the 1st SS Infantry Brigade (mot.). Along with it, the Danes took part in the combat southwest of Welikiye Luki. Of the original approximately 1,100 men, 643 took positions along the Ushyza until the Usho Lake. At the end of February 1943 the Free Corps "Danmark" took part in Operation "Kugelblitz". There the partisan forces south of the Nevel-Vitebsk rail line were supposed to be smashed. On March 17, 1943 came their action in Operation "Donnerkeil", ended on March 4, 1943. There the area west of the Nevel-Vitebsk rail line around the Obol River was to be combed through. As in the first operations, great success was also denied them there. The partisans were able to move into the swamps and woodlands.

After that the Free Corps "Danmark" was ordered to the Grafenwöhr troop training camp and disbanded effective May 20, 1943. The remaining approximately 650 Danes and North Schleswigers formed the cadre for the newly formed SS Volunteer Panzergrenadier Regiment "Danmark."

---

81 After Denmark was not occupied by German troops after combat action, this *de facto* legion was a called a free corps.

The Volunteer Legion "Norwegen"

As also in Denmark, recruiting in Norway for the SS Standarte "Nordland" brought little response. Only the war with Russia made the possibility of luring volunteers reawaken. Now those who essentially had no link with Germany, but were opposed to Communism, reported.

After Hitler had authorized the formation of the Volunteer Legion "Norge" on June 29, 1941, the German Reich Commissar for Norway announced this grandly on the radio. As of August 1, 1941 the volunteers were gathered at the Fallingbostel army camp, and they took the oath on October 3, 1941. As with the Free Corps "Danmark", the official name of the unit omitted the "SS" for political reasons. The men received their ranks with the added *Freiwilligen*, for example, *Freiwilligen-Unterscharführer*.

When the Volunteer Legion "Norwegen" was ordered to the front before Leningrad at the end of February 1942, 1,218 Norwegians had volunteered freely. On March 16, 1942 the battalion reached the area of the L. Army Corps and was subordinated to the Police Battle Group "Jeckeln" north of Krassnoye Sselo. When the Red Army began a major offensive on August 24, 1942, the Volunteer Legion "Norwegen" also experienced heavy and costly defensive fighting.

At the end of November 1942 the Norwegians were placed under the command of the 2nd SS Infantry Brigade mot.) and reported a strength of 698 men on December 31, 1942. After vigorous winter fighting, the battalion was taken out of action in March 1943 and transferred to Mitau. From here the approximately 600 remaining volunteers went to the Grafenwöhr training camp. After the disbanding of the Legion on May 20, 1943, about half of them formed the cadre of the newly formed SS Volunteer Panzergrenadier Regiment "Norge". The others were released to Norway or went into other troop units.

The 11th SS Volunteer Panzergrenadier Division "Nordland"

In the course of the efforts to set up new units after the great losses in Stalingrad and Africa, the SS Volunteer Panzergrenadier Division "Nordland", among others, was formed with numerous ethnic German volunteers. For purely propagandistic reasons, the unit was named "Nordland", and thus took on the appearance of a division with Northern European volunteers. Despite taking over the Free Corps "Danmark" and the Volunteer Legion "Norwegen" plus the SS Panzergrenadier Regiment "Nordland" of the SS Panzergrenadier Division "Wiking", they made up only about 15% of the total strength. On September 15, 1943 there were 20 Norwegian commanders, 50 lower leaders and 464 men, plus 33 Danish leaders, 162 lower leaders and 1,191 men in the Division. Half of them were ethnic Germans from North Schleswig.

At the Grafenwöhr troop training camp the formation was begun in April 1943. Four months later Hitler, in view of the announced withdrawal of Italian troops from the Balkans, ordered their transfer into the developing vacuum. Along with the III. (Germanic) SS Panzer Corps, the 11th SS Volunteer Panzergrenadier Division "Nordland" moved into the area south of Sisak, some 50 km south of Agram, beginning on August 20, 1943.

Besides the formation and training of the troop units, many ethnic Germans entered only in the summer of 1943, and there was action against partisans as well as the disarming of Italian units in the Sambor and Karlovac area. The Norwegian volunteer Ingebret Lilleborge remembers the formation time:

> "Some were even released from the SS Panzergrenadier Regiment "Norge" and transferred to Finland. New replacements came from Norway and calmed the excited German commanders. I had just returned from a training session on Kostaynica and was called to my battalion commander Vogt" You stay here to become a real soldier!"
>
> The relationship to the population was very good in Croatia. Behind our positions, life went on very peacefully and normally, for we also protected them from the terror of the partisans."

In October 1943 the divisions and regiments of the Waffen-SS were renumbered. For the two Panzergrenadier regiments this meant numbers 23 and 24. After Hitler had ordered the transfer of the III. (Germanic) SS Panzer Corps to the eastern front at the end of November 1943, the 11th SS Volunteer Panzergrenadier Division "Nordland", with 12,462 men, to the Oranienburg pocket in the Kirova area during December 1943.

When the Red Army, in the course of their winter offensive, was able to break into the positions of the 9th and 10th Field divisions (L) on the eastern edge of the pocket on January 14, 1944, parts of the 11th SS volunteer Panzergrenadier Regiment were immediately sent to clean up the situation. The Soviet attacks, what with their massive superiority, led to a collapse of the German front. In remarkably costly fighting, the units tried to reach Narva, some 75 km to the southwest. The ethnic German SS volunteer Franz Bereznyak says of the fighting:

> "On January 30 we stood before Narva. Who would have thought that in the course of two weeks our proud unit would look like this?"

On February 4, 1944 the newly formed Army Unit "Narva" took command of the III. SS Panzer Corps and the XXVI. Army Corps. In mid-February 1944 the 11th SS volunteer Panzergrenadier Division "Nordland" received replacements and could fill decimated units. At the end of February 1944 the unit reported a strength of 11,134 members. Despite the addition of over 1,000 new men, the strength of the unit, in comparison with the 1943-1944 new year, had decreased by some 1,500 men. Thus in two weeks of combat action over 2,500 men had been killed, wounded or taken prisoner. The first two battalions of the Panzergrenadier Regiment were thus disbanded. They were to be formed anew at the SS "Hammerstein" troop training camp.[82] Thus the regiments had only two battalions and therefore the same strength as the Panzergrenadier divisions of the Wehrmacht.

While the positions along the Narva were being held, division units were moved to the southwest to stop the enemy troops pushing toward Vaivara and Auvere. In costly combat, the advance of the Red Army southwest of Narva could be stopped. Thus the front calmed down in the area of the Army Unit "Narva" until the summer of 1944. The 11th SS Volunteer Panzergrenadier Division "Nordland" reported its strength as 11,020 members on June 30, 1944.

The number of personnel had thus decreased somewhat again. After the Red Army was able to break through in the area north of Vilna and south of Dünaburg, on the seam between Army Groups "North" and "Center", the SS Panzer Reconnaissance Unit 11, well equipped with *Schützenpanzerwagen*, was alarmed. On July 11, 1944 they were transferred to a focal point some 500 km southwest of Dünaburg.

While the troops were still in rough combat on the Narva front, the SS Panzer Reconnaissance Unit 11 reached Lithuania via Latvia. There, in constant movement, it appeared to represent stronger German units in an area almost without troops between the two army groups.

Since the German troops were able to hold up the Soviet advance in the Latvian-Lithuanian area and restore a thoroughgoing front, the pressure of the Red Army on the Narva front led to a withdrawal on July 25, 1944 to the so-called Tannenberg position between Vaivara and Auvere. There was bitter and very costly combat in the next few days for the three strategically important hills[83] in the position.

On July 31, 1944 the SS Panzer Reconnaissance Unit 11 was taken out of service in Latvia and ordered back to the Division in the Tannenberg position near Vaivara. There were changing and heavy fights for the individual hills there until the beginning of August 1944. When the Tannenberg position finally could not be captured, the Soviet command transferred the focal point of the attack farther south. There on August 10, 1944 the Red Army succeeded in breaking through the German front south of the Pleskau Lake and reaching the area east of Voeru. Through a push to the north, the German troops were to be enclosed in the Tannenberg position.

To prevent the potential cutoff of the Army Unit "Narva", Hitler approved in mid-September 1944 the evacuation of Estonia. The 11th SS Volunteer Panzergrenadier Division "Nordland", with a strength of 10,480 soldiers, moved out of the Tannenberg position and crossed the Estonian-Latvian border near Ainazi on September 21, 1944. Ordered to the Baldone area, the Division immediately came to relieve the threatened Latvian capital. Until September 26, 1944 there was heavy fighting with tremendous losses on both sides. The Red Army halted its advance on Riga and

---

82 They did not go back under the command of the 11. SS Volunteer Panzergrenadier Vision "Nordland", but were subordinated in November 1944 to the very decimated IV. SS Panzer Corps.
83 These were Hill 69.9, the so-called Grenadier Hill and Children's Home Hill.

moved the focal point to the Dobele area. Then the 11th SS Volunteer Panzergrenadier Division was moved out of the position and transferred via Jaunpils to the new attack area. After further heavy fighting, the unit was dispersed. When the enemy troops reached the Baltic Sea near Polangen on October 14, 1944, the units in the Priekule were to be ready for a thrust to the southward.

It remained a theory, for on October 16, 1944 the first battle of Courland began. The Soviet offensive met the 11th SS Volunteer Panzergrenadier Division with its full weight. With the greatest efforts, the men were able to hold the positions. The fighting died down at first, until on October 27, 1944 the Red Army, after heavy drumfire, made another attempt to break into the positions. The second battle of Courland had begun. The offensive ended relatively without success at the beginning of November 1944. The enemy moved the focal point again.

Only on January 23, 1945 were there attacks on Priekule again as part of the fourth battle of Courland. Now the enemy troops were able to break into the positions several times. The Division received support from the 14th Panzer Division and could thus maintain the positions. For the 11th SS Volunteer Panzergrenadier Division there were its last battles in Courland. At the end of January 1945 the transfer by ship to Stettin began.

In Pomerania the Army Group "Weichsel" was just being formed to hold the area between Stettin and Danzig. The subordinated 11th Army was also newly formed; it consisted almost entirely of battle groups and parts of the Replacement Army from the mouth of the Finow Canal into the Oder to the Jastrow-Ratzebuhr-Neustettin line. The III. SS Panzer Corps, transported out of Courland, was, despite the costly combat it had gone through, the most combat-ready part of the 11th Army and took command of the Freienwalde-Neu-Wedell area as early as February 5, 1945.

Without actually having the chance to reorganize the groups, the 11th SS Volunteer Panzergrenadier Division was supposed to be refreshed for the coming German Pomerania offensive as of February 12, 1945. The SS Panzer Unit 11 was brought to regimental strength by subordinating the heavy SS Panzer Unit 503 to it. The I./SS Panzer Regiment 11 had 30 assault guns and 30 Panzer V "Panther" tanks, and the II./SS Panzer Regiment 11 had 39 Panzer VI "Tiger II" tanks. Interestingly, the unit was not renamed as the 11th SS Panzer Division "Nordland."

Just two days after the beginning of the refreshing, the Division of some 6,000 men was alarmed and moved on February 15, 1945 to the readiness area for Operation "Sonnenwende". On the next day the Pomeranian offensive began. The 11th SS Volunteer Panzergrenadier Division successfully moved out of the Reetz area to the Arnswalde, which was threatened by the Red Army.

After the troops and civilians were evacuated, the troops gave up the city. In heavy fighting the units went back to their original positions. On March 1, 1945 a Soviet offensive against the units in Pomerania began. Within hours the entire German front collapsed. Constantly in motion, the 11th SS Volunteer Panzergrenadier Division reached the area around Altdamm east of Stettin, which was planned to be an Oder bridgehead.

Since Hitler wanted to direct an offensive in the direction of Danzig (some 300 km away) from the bridgehead at a later time, the units in action here bled in the Soviet artillery and aerial bombardment. Only on March 19, 1945 did Hitler approve the evacuation of the whole senseless bridgehead over the Oder. The remaining units of the 11th SS Volunteer Panzergrenadier Division moved back into the region southwest of Stettin in the night of March 19-20, 1945.

Here, by a directive of the Inspector-General of the Panzer Troops, the unit was supposed to be restructured into a so-called Panzer Division 45. The theoretical arrangement remained. But the units were filled with replacements from the Luftwaffe, Navy and Waffen-SS. Among them were several members of the "British Free Corps."

From September 1, 1943 to the end of March 1945 there were:

	Commanders	Other Ranks	Total
Dead	102	2,837	2,939
Wounded	267	10,005	10,272
Missing	23	1,255	1,278

With a complete total of 14,489 the Division had thus lost its entire personnel number. On March 27, 1945 the unit, with the III. SS Panzer Corps, moved to the area north of Angermünde.

In the course of the Soviet *"Berlin Operation"* beginning on April 16, 1945, the 11th SS Volunteer Panzergrenadier Division was to move into the area south of Frankfurt on the Oder. For lack of vehicles and fuel, the transport first ended in the Strausberg area. Here the unit was subordinated to the LVI. Panzer Corps. Two days later it took up defensive positions before Strausberg. On the next day there was a single tank battle before the gates of Berlin. The SS Panzer Regiment 11 was able to shoot down about 100 enemy tanks near Prötzel. For this, the regimental commander, *SS-Obersturmbannführer* Kausch was awarded the 846th Oak Leaves to the Knight's Cross of the Iron Cross on April 23, 1945.

Exhausted, the soldiers moved back through Mahlsdorf to Berlin. Constantly fired on by Soviet tanks, the units crossed the Spree in Treptow on April 23, 1945 and took up a new defensive front along the rail ring between Treptow Park and Tempelhof. Two days later the commander of the 11th SS Volunteer Panzergrenadier Division, Dr. Krukenberg, was relieved. He had tried to get his men out of the Berlin combat area.

Without any cohesive front, the men fought past the Air Ministry to the Weidendamm Bridge. There they wanted to break through their narrow Soviet encirclement on the night of May 1, 1945. In several waves the last tanks tried to force a path over the bridge and through the adjoining streets. Under heavy defensive fire, all their attempts failed. The last of the 11th SS Volunteer Panzergrenadier Division was then taken prisoner by the Soviets.

With that the history of a remarkable unit ended. As opposed to the designation "Nordland", it consisted mainly of Romanian Germans, and in 1943 it already showed the difficulty of equipping the men with weapons, equipment and vehicles. In its first front action there was large-scale defensive fighting against the Soviet winter offensive in the Oranienbaum pocket. Despite high losses, the morale of the men stayed high to the war's end thanks to the Division's leadership. For the Waffen-SS, in terms of the action areas, the most Knight's Crosses were awarded to the 11th SS volunteer Panzergrenadier Division "Nordland."

17th SS Panzergrenadier Division "Götz von Berlichingen"

On September 23, 1943 Hitler ordered the formation of a central reserve of men born in 1926. They were to form 14 divisions: 10 infantry, 2 paratroop and two SS divisions. The two SS divisions were the 16th and 17th Panzergrenadier Divisions. The latter was formed as of November 15, 1943 in the Saumur/Loire-Bressuire-Parthenay-Poitiers-Chatellerault (1st Army) area.

Besides 270 members of the *SS-Unterführerschule* Posen-Treskau, 4,400 17-year-old native Germans and 2,500 ethnic Germans from Romania (born 1902 to 1922) came to the Division. Personnel transfers also came from the 10th SS Panzergrenadier Division "Frundsberg". In all, the unit, after receiving further ethnic German recruits from the USSR and Romania, already numbered over 11,147 members on December 31, 1943.

In January 1944 the Division's parts gathered at the French "Thouars" troop training camp (between Saumur and Parthenay) for their unit training. The training of some 500 drivers was finished by April 1944 on requisitioned French motor vehicles.

On April 10, 1944 *Reichsführer-SS* Himmler visited the Division, which had just finished its platoon and company training. There he gave it the name given by Hitler, "Götz von Berlichingen."[84] At the end of April 1944 the unit was kept ready by the OKW as a reserve for the expected invasion.

When the Allies landed in Normandy on June 6, 1944, the 17th SS Panzergrenadier Division "Götz von Berlichingen" was in the area south of the Loire. The unit, almost 18,000 men strong, was alarmed as its barracks and sent to the 7th Army. On the next day its march to the sector of the II. Paratroop Corps, some 210 km away, began. Except for that, the SS Panzerjäger Unit 17 and SS Flak Unit 17 were still being set up.

Via Laval, Fougeres, Avranches, Villedieu and Torigny the first units reached the Balleroy area. This was the border between the American and British landing sectors. It immediately got into combat with troops of the V. U.S. Corps. When U.S. units landed at Carenta on June 9-10, 1944, the 17th SS Panzergrenadier Division, unaccustomed to combat, was ordered into the area some 30 km to the west. In the heavy fighting from June 13 to 16, the division commander, *SS-Brigadeführer* Ostendorff, was severely wounded. The command of the unit was given to *SS-Standartenführer* Binge until June 28, 1944.

---

84 Götz von Berlichingen, the knight with the iron hand, lived from 1480 to 1562 and took command of the rebels in the Odenwald in the Peasants' War in 1525.

Under steady fire from enemy naval artillery and fighter-bombers, the units had to draw back to the area northeast of Perriers and west of St. Lô until the beginning of July 1944. On June 30, 1944 the Division reported a strength of 16,976 men. After some three weeks of combat, the unit still had over 600 men more than its planned strength. But as some 1,400 lower leaders were lacking, its readiness for action was limited.

During July 1944 the positions on the line some 5 km south of the Lessay-Perriers-St. Lô road were won back. This main battle line could be held until an American breakthrough in the direction of Granville took place on July 28, 1944. At first the troops drew back to the southwest and then tried to get away to the southeast through gaps in the front. On the congested marching routes the Division was constantly attacked by enemy fighter-bombers and lost a great deal of its equipment. After the Division, scarcely trained as a unit, had been at the focal point of the defensive fighting, the Wehrmacht report praised it on July 29, 1944:

> "In the heavy fighting in the St. Lô-Lessay area in the last few weeks, the 17th SS Panzergrenadier Division "Götz von Berlichingen", under the command of its badly wounded commander, SS-Brigadeführer Ostendorff and his deputy SS-Standartenführer Baum, have stood out particularly on defense and counterattacks."

SS-Standartenführer Baum commanded both the remainder of the 17th SS Panzergrenadier Division and the utilized parts of the 2nd SS Panzer Division in a personal union. On August 6, 1944 the units, now designated only as battle groups, reached the area northeast of Mortain. Here, despite their losses within the XXXXVII. Panzer Corps, were supposed to begin a counterthrust toward Avranches, about 34 km away. A motorized battle group was formed to do this. On the night of August 6-7, 1944 this Operation "Liege" began. Because of the continuing enemy air attacks that caused heavy losses, the Commander 'West', *General* Kluge, ordered the halting of the operation the next day and sent the troops back to their starting positions.

On August 19, 1944 the Anglo-American units were able to close the pocket of Falaise near Chambois. Around 80,000 German soldiers, including 9,000 members of the 17th SS Panzergrenadier Division, were surrounded. In the night of August 19-20, 1944 the German troops tried to break through to the east. Here apocalyptic conditions arose. On the morning of August 21, 1944 only about 20,000 soldiers reached the German lines. Among them were some 1,500 members of the 17th SS Panzergrenadier Division. The rest died or were captured.

At first the remainder marched to Laigle, about 60 km away. From there they went via Verneuil and Dreux to the Seine, which they crossed at Paris. On August 25, 1944 thee survivors were near Meaux. The 17th SS Panzergrenadier Division itself was now to be refreshed in the Saarbrücken area. For this, around 4,000 SS members, plus some 2,000 members of the Luftwaffe, were integrated into the group. After U.S. troops advanced to Lorraine at the beginning of September 1944, several groups were moved out of the gathering area near Saarbrücken to the front some 60 km away.

In the middle of the month the Division command took over its own sector within the XIII. SS Army Corps on the Moselle south of Metz. Since the unit was set up in terms of numbers but had little fighting power for lack of training and equipment, the enemy was able on September 17, 1944 to form a bridgehead in its sector. Counterattacks were unsuccessful for lack of support by heavy weapons.

Along with the Division units that were not called into the costly combat in Normandy, the group reported a strength of 14,816 members on September 20, 1944. Although the troop units were 90% filled in numbers, the total equipping of a Panzergrenadier Division was almost completely lacking.

After the front had grown quiet in October 1944, the Division Commander received the order on November 7, 1944 to remove the 17th SS Panzergrenadier Division from the front so it could be refreshed. But before this could be done, the U.S. Army went on the offensive the next day and smashed the Division units at the bridgehead. Panzergrenadier Regiment 38, which was to the north, was separated from the group, and a few days later it was subordinated to the fortress command of Metz. SS Panzergrenadier Regiment 37 moved off to Saargemünd with the other parts of the Division.

Through the withdrawal of the 17th SS Panzergrenadier Division, enemy troops were able to swing to the north and attack Metz from the south. Here SS Panzergrenadier Regiment 38 had meanwhile arrived. When U.S. units reached the edge of the city on November 18, 1944, the Regimental commander, contrary to the orders of the Fortress Commander, ordered his troops to march to the Division's new gathering place near Neunkirchen (some 16 km northeast of Saarbrücken). A court-martial case because of unilateral leaving of the fortress of Metz could no longer be initiated, since Schützeck died in the following combat.

On December 20, 1944, according to orders of November 7, 1944, the Division could be taken out of the main battle line to be refreshed in the Neunkirchen area. The rest of SS Panzergrenadier Regiment 38, coming from Metz, was incorporated into SS Panzergrenadier Regiment 37. Coming from the SS troop training camp of "Böhmen", the SS Panzer Instructional Regiment formed of ethnic Germans from the USSR formed the new SS Panzergrenadier Regiment 38.

At the new year, it was ordered to the area between Bitsch and Saargemünd. Within the XIII. SS Army Corps, the unit was to take part in Operation "Nordwind" as of January 1, 1945. The offensive was halted by the Commander of the 1st Army, *General* of the Infantry von Obstfelder, on January 3, 1945. The American superiority made the attacking goals unattainable.

When the U.S. troops were able to break into the positions of the 17th SS Panzergrenadier Division on January 6, 1945, Himmler stated in a letter to the Chief of the SS Command Headquarters, *SS-Gruppenführer* Jüttner, that the SS Panzergrenadier Instructional Regiment of Russian Germans, despite six months of training, *"ran away"* when the enemy appeared.

Finally the front sector quieted down until mid-February 1945. After the U.S. troops, with strong artillery preparation and air support, tried to advance through the positions of the 17th SS Panzergrenadier Division in the direction of Zweibrücken, the units were able to hold off the attack in costly combat in the Rimlingen area.

On February 28, 1945 the Division command reported 15,984 members. Fairly well equipped except for the lacking Schützenpanzerwagen, the 17th SS Panzergrenadier Division experienced the American "Undertone" offensive on March 15, 1945. By March 18, 1945 the lines had already been pushed backward 15 km northward to Contwig. Despite the good equipment it was clear that the unit could not stand up to the enormous pressure of the U.S. troops.

Then came the almost fleeing attempt to reach the Rhine, some 70 km away via Rodalben, Pirmasens and Landau, near Germersheim. When the Division crossed the Rhine on March 25, 1945m it hade lost most of its heavy weapons and equipment, plus almost half of its men, who had been captured. In the Wiesloch area (some 30 km east of the Rhine) the shattered Division tried to reorganize.

At the end of March 1945 came the transfer to the Neckarelz-Möckmühl area 30 km away. Here, beyond the Neckar, the Division, along with the XIII. Army Corps, took on the main task of defense. At the beginning of April 1945 the units, used purely as infantry, had to be sent farther east, and took up provisional positions between Kocher and Jagst.

While SS Panzergrenadier Regiment 38, strengthened to three battalions, mainly by Luftwaffe men, was drawn into the fighting around Nürnberg and smashed there, the remainder of the Division reached the Neumarkt region on April 16, 1945. Since the last remaining artillery unit had stayed with the XIII. Army Corps because of transport problems, it was assigned the two artillery units brought in for the 38th SS Grenadier Division.

On April 18, 1945 the unit had to withdraw to the south because of enemy pressure. Three days later the units were in the Berching area, and on April 25-26, 1945 they reached the Danube near Neustadt. There the Division command reported a strength of only 6,710 men.

Ordered into the Dürnbuch Forest as Army reserve, the simultaneous command of the 38th SS Grenadier Division was given to its commander. By assembling all the men used as infantry and the remaining troops who broke out of Nürnberg, the SS Panzergrenadier Regiment 38 was set up anew.

On April 27, 1945 the unit was ordered to transfer to the XIII. Army Corps in the Augsburg area. The swift advance of the American armored troops forced the units, involved in combat again and again, back toward Austria. There was heavy fighting in the Dachau area on April 28, 1945 and near Penzberg the next day.

In twelve days the Division, under constant combat and air attacks, had covered around 180 km to the south. At the beginning of May 1945 what was left of the Division was in the Bad Tölz-Tegernsee-Lenggries area and marched farther from there toward Achensee. At the capitulation the SS Panzergrenadier Regiment 37 was north of Kreuth and SS Panzergrenadier Regiment 38 near Jenbach.

There the nine-month combat action of the 17th SS Panzergrenadier Division "Götz von Berlichingen" ended. Because of the Allied material superiority, the inexperienced Division was already hit hard during its first action. Until the war ended, it lacked a chance to be completely refreshed and integrate the differently motivated replacements of ethnic Germans and Luftwaffe members into the group well. In action the Division lost its repeatedly supplied heavy weapons and equipment several times.

Otto Kalmbach was born on April 26, 1923 in Bessarabia and moved to West Prussia in September 1940.

In 1942 he reported to the Waffen-SS and served in the SS Vehicle Driver and Replacement Regiment. At the beginning of 1945 he was transferred to the 17th SS Panzergrenadier Division "Götz von Berlichingen."

Christian Kreter was born on December 10, 1900 in Ceschka, Croatia. After the Balkan campaign the area belonged to Hungary. He reported voluntarily to the Waffen-SS there at the beginning of 1942 and was inducted on May 7, 1942 into the Recruit Depot of the Waffen-SS in Debica.

Serving for a short time at the Field Recruit Depot of the 1st SS Infantry Brigade, he was transferred to the SS Radio Protection Battalion. In February 1945 Kreter was on duty in Danzig, and died on March 31, 1945 after being wounded in combat in the Danzig-Gotenhofen area.

18th SS Volunteer Panzergrenadier Division "Horst Wessel"

The 1st SS Infantry Brigade (mot.)

In the course of preparations for action in the Soviet Union, effective on April 24, 1941, the SS Totenkopf Standarten 8 and 10 – then called SS Infantry Regiments (mot.) 8 and 10 – were combined into SS Brigade 1 (mot.). The I./SS Infantry Regiment 10 was made up entirely of ethnic Germans from Romania. First under the command of *SS-Brigadeführer* Demelhuber, it was taken over on May 25, 1941 by *SS-Brigadeführer* Krüger. On June 21, 1941 the brigade was subordinated to the Command Staff *Reichsführer-SS*, and four days later the command over both regiments was given to *SS-Brigadeführer* Hermann.

Gathered at the beginning of July at the SS "Debica" troop training camp (some 30 km east of Tarnow), training in forest and town fighting for combing the occupied area began. On July 22, 1941 the Brigades sent to the Higher SS and Police Leader "South" in the Rovno area, about 350 km to the east. Three days later, parts of the Brigade were sent to locate scattered enemy troops and Jews between Ostrog and Schepetovka. About 800 of the latter were shot *"for favoring Bolshevism)* (sic!).

After this first action, the SS Brigade 1 (mot.), along with the 56th Infantry Division, was subordinated to the Commander of the Backline Army District "South". On August 4, 1941, parts of SS Infantry Regiment 120 (mot.) shot 1,385 Jewish civilians in Ostrow, Hrycov and Kunev. The district court director Otto Albert explained under oath on March 29, 1947:

> "During my tenure as a military law officer to Field Command 787, our unit was in Ostrog in August 1941 right on the then Polish-Russian border.
>
> One day an SS battalion arrived in Ostrog and began to pull all the Jews out of the houses and drive them out of town.
>
> The major on the staff of the Field Command, Major z.V. Karl Behr, came and made sure that it was intended to shoot the 6- to 7,000 head of the Jewish population.
>
> Herr Behr became extraordinarily excited, sat down with me in my capacity as military law officer, and went with me at once to the gathering place, to prevent the shooting if possible.
>
> At the gathering place we found the commander of the SS regiment, an Oberstleutnant, with whom we had a very spirited disagreement. Herr Behr referred to the impossibility of the process and explained that it was "an obvious murder."
>
> Then the SS commander explained that the matter was very unpleasant to him. But there was an order from "the highest place" that he had to obey.
>
> After further negotiating he finally said he was ready to release all the Jews employed by the Field Command and their adherents, whom we were to name.
>
> When we then gave him a very extensive list, he explained that the whole action would then have no great value any more. He kept sticking to his agreement, so that the greater part of the unfortunate Jews could return to their homes, which had meanwhile been plundered by the population. To my knowledge, on that day, as a result of our intervention, only 400 to 500 Jews are said to have been shot."

Two days later the unit marched farther to the northeast and combed through the area south of Ovrutsch. In the wooded areas there, some 300 Jews were shot in the process. While parts of the SS Infantry Regiment 8 were in combat with regular Soviet troops as of August 20, 1941, the SS Infantry Regiment 10 was again ordered to actions in the *"fight between outlooks on life"*. Here, for example, 280 Jews were shot on August 24, 1941. Assigned to search the area north of the Korosten-Belokorovici road, there followed until September 12, 1941 the shooting of over 1,000 Jews and scattered Red Army men.

On September 20, 1941 the unit, now called the 1st SS Infantry Brigade (mot.), moved into the area around Konotop, over 300 km away, and, among other things, took over the guarding of Soviet prisoners of war. Because of the Soviet winter offensive, the march through Orel into the area south of Verkhovye (some 75 km east of Orel) took place on December 12, 1941. Within the XXXIV. Army Corps, the Brigade was again subordinated to the 56th Infantry Division. Heavy fighting ensued, in which, among others, the Commander of the Brigade, *SS-Brigadeführer* Hermann, was killed. When the Red Army was able to break through at the Trudy bend, the 2nd Army made the leadership of the SS Infantry Regiment serving there responsible for it.

As the combat went on, the 1st SS Infantry Brigade was subordinated to the 299th Infantry Division. For around eight months the Brigade was in its new position. During this time an exchange of men was undertaken. Native German personnel were taken out and replaced by 2,300 ethnic Germans from Hungary on May 26, 1942. The commander of the 2nd Army released the Brigade at the beginning of August 1942:

"Originally intended for securing tasks in backline areas, in decisive days called to service at the front, the Brigade developed into a proved combat troop."

There followed the subordination under the Higher SS and Police Leader "Ostland", *SS-Obergruppenführer* Jeckeln, and transfer into the area around Minsk, about 700 km away. Here it was again used in backline areas against partisans. As of September 1, 1942 the units were thus in service in the Nalibocki Forest (some 70 km southwest of Minsk). On September 13, 1942 the Operation "Sumpffieber" began in the area south of Baranovici (about 130 km southwest of Minsk). In the one week of action, as in the summer of 1941, there were repeated murders of suspected partisans or Jewish inhabitants. There were 389 partisans and 1,274 civilians shot, plus 8,350 Jews and 1,217 suspected partisans deported to work camps.

On October 11, 1942 Operation "Karlsbad" began. For it, the units moved into the Borissov-Orscha area. Along with other German and foreign units, it was tried under the command of *SS-Gruppenführer* von dem Bach to end the almost daily blowing up of the rail lines. Here more than 1,000 suspected partisans and civilians were shot. As of November 5, 1942 the five-day Operation "Frieda" took place in the swamps south of Borissov, and from November 22 to 26, 1942 Operation "Nürnberg" in the area north of Postavy (some 140 km northwest of Minsk). Here too, 715 civilians were shot as suspected partisans, with the loss of four of their own dead and one slightly wounded.

At the end of the month, the 1st SS Infantry Brigade (mot.) was alarmed and prepared for action near Welikiye Luki. Here the Free Corps "Danmark" was added to it. On December 2, 1942 the units already reached the Gorodok area 150 km away (about 50 km northwest of Vitebsk and from there on were subordinated to the General of the Infantry von der Chevallerie to be sent to the city. Under Soviet pressure, the city could not be freed. Instead, the 1st SS Infantry Brigade (mot.) and others also had to move to positions in the rear. On December 31, 1942 the unit reported a strength of 6,135 members. When a final relief attempt was shattered under heavy defensive fire, the last German defenders broke out of the city on January 16, 1943. Of the former 7,000 soldiers, 200 reached their own lines.

Until February 1, 1943 the 1st SS Infantry Brigade (mot.), along with the subordinated Free Corps "Danmark", was with the LIX. Army Corps at the front. Under the command of the 201st Securing Division, the units took part in Operation "Kugelblitz" from February 22 to March 8, 1943, and Operation "Donnerkeil" from March 31 to April 2, 1943. There the backline area of Vitebsk-Gorodok-Senniza Lake was to be freed of partisans.

After another brief move to a sector of the main battle line, the unit was transferred to Borissov (some 75 km northeast of Minsk) at the beginning of July 1943. From there the 1st SS Infantry Brigade (mot.), under the command of the Higher SS and Police Leader "Russia-Center" in the Mir-Koidanov-Rakov-Rubiezewicze area (southwest of Minsk), took part in Operation "Hermann". Whole regions were depopulated, suspected partisans put into work service, the cattle given to German agricultural leaders and the non-suspected population settled in so-called closed villages. At that time the strength of the 1st SS Infantry Brigade was 6,395 men.

When the Red Army attacked the seam between the 4th Army and 3rd Panzer Army on August 13, 1943, the Brigade was alarmed at the end of the month and transferred into the Yekyna area (some 75 km northeast of Smolensk). From there it marched into the Yarzevo area (circa 45 km northeast of Smolensk) and was subordinated to the 25th Panzergrenadier Division. There was heavy fighting there in the area before Smolensk as of September 14, 1943. On September 24, 1943 the Brigade marched away through burning Smolensk in the direction of Orsha.

During the month the unit had lost 215 dead, 1,173 wounded and 77 missing. After further heavy fighting in the area west of Smolensk, it was named in a Wehrmacht report on October 15, 1943:

> "West of Kritschev (ca. 100 km east of Mogilev, author's note) and especially westward of Smolensk, strong Soviet attempts to break through were stopped. Just in the combat area southwest of Smolensk, 46 Soviet tanks were destroyed. In the last three days the enemy, in seven vain attempts, lost a total of 354 tanks and 233 airplanes… In the heavy defensive combat in the central front sector, the 1st SS Volunteer Grenadier Brigade (mot.) has stood out particularly."

On October 22, 1943 the units of the Waffen-SS were numbered systematically. The brigade units were given number 51 and the SS grenadier regiments numbers 39 and 50, to support the heavily pressured front between the Dniepr and Beresina, the Brigade formed a battle group that saw action before Bobruisk in mid-November 1943. After costly front actions the SS Battle Group "Wiedemann" was taken out of action and was to secure the bridgehead over the Beresina near Paritchi (ca. 40 km south of Bobruisk). Here it again came into heavy fighting with Soviet partisans.

While the Commander of the Brigade, *SS-Standartenführer* Trabandt, came out of action with the mass of the unit to be refreshed at the Stablack troop training camp near Königsberg, the SS Battle Group "Wiedemann" was withdrawn from the front only at the end of December 1943.

The 18th SS Volunteer Panzergrenadier Division "Horst Wessel"

Through the large numbers of ethnic Germans inducted in 1943-44, not only could the high losses of the existing SS divisions made up for, but small bands could be strengthened into division size. Thus the SS Command Headquarters made known on January 25, 1944 that what remained of the 18th SS Panzergrenadier Division should be restocked. To be set up in the Slovenian Cilli-Gurkfeld-Rann area, it could also give that area security against the Tito partisans there. On January 30, 1944 Hitler gave the Division the name of the *SA-Sturmführer* "Horst Wessel."[85]

At the beginning of February 1944 the transfer of the rest of the 1st SS Infantry Brigade from East Prussia into the southeast region began. There it was subordinated to the LXIX. Mountain Corps. When the Chief of the General Staff of Army Group "F", *Generalleutnant* Förtsch, arranged the setting up of a battle group of the 18th SS Panzergrenadier Division in view of the occupation of Hungary, the unit still reported a strength of 4,111 members. But there were scarcely weapons or equipment available even for them.

From May 5 to 7, 1944 units took part in Operation "Schneeschmelze". The partisans in the formation area were to be fought. Finally the SS Panzer Reconnaissance Unit 18 was strengthened for the occupation of Hungary and marched with the LXIX. Mountain Corps from the area east of Agram to Nagykanisza. After numerous units had to be given up after being transferred to the front, the 18th SS Panzergrenadier Division, just being formed, was ordered to transfer to Hungary at the beginning of April 1944. When it had to give up 200 Volkswagens and 300 trucks to the 3rd SS Panzer Division "Totenkopf" there in the Batschka, it was as good as immobile.

On June 6, 1944 *SS-Standartenführer* Trabandt received the order to set up a battle group again, this time for front service. This unit of 3,000 men was formed to a great degree from former members of the 1st SS Infantry Brigade (mot.). At that time the Division had grown to a strength of 8,530 men. On July 11, 1944 the SS Battle Group "Schäfer" was sent to the Army Group "North Ukraine" and relieved parts of the 371st Infantry Division in the area east of Podhayce on the Strypa on July 17, 1944. At once involved in backline fighting through the Soviet summer offensive, the units reached the Dniestr via Rohatyn west of Chodorov on July 27, 1944.

To strengthen the seriously threatened left wing of the 1st Panzer Army, the SS Battle Group "Schäfer" moved at the beginning of August 1944 into the Sanok area (some 50 km southwest of Przemysl). Here it was strengthened by a battle group of the French Waffen-Grenadier Brigade of the SS "Charlemagne". Despite heavy fighting, the German troops were not able to make connections with the neighboring 17th Army at first. This was only possible when the Front was moved backward.

---

85 Horst Wessel wrote the words of the SA song: *"Die Fahne hoch, die Reihen fest geschlossen…"*

Stefan Lutz was born on August 11, 1921 in Csatalya near Nagybaracka, Batschka, and reported to the Waffen-SS voluntarily as a Hungarian ethnic German in the spring of 1942.

At first serving in the SS Cavalry Division "Florian Geyer". He was transferred on May 22, 1944 to the SS Volunteer Panzergrenadier Division "Horst Wessel."

Lutz died at Hatvan, Northern Hungary, on November 18, 1944.

The collar emblem with the SA rune for the ethnic Germans of the 18th SS Volunteer Panzergrenadier Division "Horst Wessel."

On August 16, 1944 the SS Battle Group "Schäfer" received the order to move through Krosno to Radomysl-Wielky (ca. 25 km northeast of Tarnow) to the LIX. Army Corps. There it took up defensive positions on the Wisloka south of Mielec. When the Red Army launched an offensive after two hours of drumfire on August 20, 1944, the units had to draw back. On August 22, 1944 the SS Battle Group "Schäfer", already reduced to two German and one French battalion, was in the area south of Dabrova (ca. 20 km north of Tarnow).

After fighting that swung back and forth, the Battle Group was removed from the main battle line shortly thereafter. It was separated and returned to its own units. For the members of what was now the 18th SS Volunteer Panzergrenadier Division, this meant a transfer to Hungary. In fact, the two remaining battalions were gathered in Skrzyzow near Tarnow and, were ordered by the Army Group "North Ukraine" into eastern Slovakia on August 31, 1944. Here the Slovakian national uprising had broken out, and the SS Battle Group "Schäfer" was to advance through Käsmark and Deutschendorf (Poprad) into the Rosenberg area. On September 6, 1944 the Battle Group took Rosenberg and turned to the southwest.

While the Battle Group was active in Slovakia, the forming of the 18th SS Volunteer Panzergrenadier Division went on in Hungary. On September 20, 1944 the division command reported a strength of 10,063 members. After the rebellion in Slovakia could not be put down by the German troops engaged to that time, and the Red Army moved forward steadily, the *Reichsführer-SS* released further contingents of the Waffen-SS on October 5, 1944. This included the 18th SS Volunteer Panzergrenadier Division, which was moved forward from the Batschka to the Hungarian-Slovakian border in the Rimavska Sobota-Aggtelek area.

After the Battle Group returned to the Division command, the unit was supposed to advance into central Slovakia as of October 18, 1944. The SS Volunteer Panzergrenadier Regiment 40 advanced via Muran to Tisovec, where it met the SS Panzer Reconnaissance Unit 18, which was advancing from Rimavska Sobota. The units faced only weak opposition. Even before the official end of the Slovakian national uprising, the Army Group "South" authorized the release of the 18th SS Volunteer Panzergrenadier Division "Horst Wessel". Although in formation since January 1944, the unit, after its slow outfitting with weapons and equipment and shortages in training, was still, after ten months, far from being a division that could be used at the front. Therefore the unit was subordinated to the 4th SS Police Panzergrenadier Division and took up defensive positions in the Jasz-Ladany area (ca. 20 km north of Szolnok). When the Red Army went on the offensive on November 9, 1944, there was a disaster for the involved units of the 18th SS Volunteer Panzergrenadier Division. The war diary of the Army Grioup "South" showed on that day:

> "In the LVII. Panzer Corps in Sector of the 4th SS Police Division, parts of the 18th SS Division have fully failed, let themselves be rolled over, and surrendered."

The reasons for the failure were faulty leadership, training and lack of motivation of the ethnic Germans, some of whom were forced to enlist. By November 13, 1944 the troop units had been pushed back to the Jasz-Bereny area. Two days later the units occupied parts of the so-called Karola position before Budapest. Fighting near Aszrod ensued, followed until Noievmber 25, 1944 by a withdrawal into the Ecseg area some 30 km to the north.

When the Red Army began the operation against Budapest on December 5, 1944, the 18th SS Volunteer Panzergrenadier Division "Horst Wessel" joined the 4th SS Police Panzergrenadier Division under the IV. Panzer Corps. In the initial hard fights, the units left their positions again and threw most of their weapons away. On December 16, 1944 the removal of the Division from action was begun, so that it could be reorganized in the Schemnitz-Karpfen area of Slovakia. At the beginning of January 1945 it was ordered to move to the Marburg-Ciolli area for new formation.

The combat-strong 1./SS Volunteer Panzergrenadier Regiment 40 was not transferred with it, but taken into the 4th SS Police Panzergrenadier Division with many heavy weapons.[86] On January 13, 1945 the Wehrmacht report said of this battalion:

---

86   The Battalion remained with the 4th SS Police Panzergrenadier Division and then moved to Pomerania with it.

> "In seven days of defensive battle south of the Slovakian border, SS-Sturmbannführer Riepe in an SS Volunteer Panzergrenadier Division … has beaten off all attacks of the superior enemy under heavy losses for the enemy and held the town of Czesani (ca. 16 km east of Balassa-Gyarmat, author's note) unshakingly as a pillar of the German front."

In Lower Styria the 18th SS Volunteer Panzergrenadier Division "Horst Wessel" was to be newly equipped with lacking equipment and, by adding native German personnel, have its combat power increased. The High Command of Army Group "South" said of the unit on January 18, 1945:

> "Combat Value IV. Consists mainly of ethnic Germans from Hungary. Not ready for crisis situations. Only remaining parts on hand. Leadership not stiff enough. Change of leader already ordered by Reichsführer-SS."

In the course of the change of commanders, *SS-Standartenführer* Bochmann took over what remained of the Division. By adding men from the Luftwaffe the relation between native and ethnic Germans was to be equaled. But since the former Luftwaffe personnel – which was added, among others, in the lower and middle leader levels – brought little experience in infantry ground combat, the desired increase of combat power remained only a theory.

Just two weeks later, the Division was taken out of the Maribor area and sent 440 km north to Märisch-Ostrau because of the situation in Silesia. Subordinated to the XI. Army Corps, the regiments had positions to occupy south of the Soviet Oder bridgehead near Cosel in the first weeks of February. On February 16, 1945 the Red Army began an offensive from the Cosel bridgehead. In the combat, which lasted until February 23, 1945, the 18th SS Volunteer Panzergrenadier Division was able to hold its positions. When the XI. Army Corps, on March 8, 1845, arranged the unsuccessful attack on the enemy bridgehead, parts of the 18th SS Volunteer Panzergrenadier Division saw action. A week later the Red Army launched a major offensive and was able to smash the entire defensive front in Silesia. The Soviet troops were able to surround large parts of the Corps Group "Schlesien" and the XI. Army Corps in the area west of Oppeln to Cosel.

On March 19, 1945 the surrounded German troops tried to break out to the west. While the last assault guns of SS Panzer Unit 18 should have made the breakthrough possible, the two Panzergrenadier regiments had the outbreak to the east to cover. On the morning of the next day the soldiers reached the German lines near Hotzenplotz. The breakout succeeded despite high losses of personnel and materials.

By March 21, 1945 the rest of the Division gathered in the Obersdorf area. From there, small battle groups saw much action, until on March 26, 1945 the order to transfer to the Karlsbrunn area (ca. 28 km south of Ziegenhals) ensued. The Division, which now reported only 5,212 men, was to be reorganized.

While the I. and II./SS Volunteer Panzergrenadier Regiment 39 and the I. and II./SS Volunteer Artillery Regiment 18 were to be restructured at the SS "Böhmen und Mähren" troop training camp, the remaining battalions and added infantry forces with combat-supporting weapons were to be formed into a battle group. Under the command of *SS-Sturmbannführer* Schumacher, they reached the Ratibor area and were again subordinated to the XI. Army Corps. In the heavy fighting in and around Ratibor, the units were hit hard and finally, subordinated to the 371st Infantry Division, were taken prisoner.

On April 10, 1945 the last parts of the 18th SS Volunteer Panzergrenadier Division, with 6 Assault Gun III, 7 Antitank Cannon 7.5 cm (mot./Sfl.) and one Antitank Gun 8.8 cm (mot.), were sent to the front. Parts of the two SS Panzergrenadier regiments and SS Panzer Reconnaissance Unit 18, with the VIII. Army Corps, then took positions in the Zobten area on the Bober (ca. 6 km southeast of Löwenberg). Since the focal point of the battles was on the right wing of the Soviet army group, there were no more large battles in the Hirschberg area until the capitulation.

On May 7, 1945 the Division Leader, *SS-Standartenführer* Petersen, was ordered by the VIII. Army Corps to separate from the enemy and march to the demarcation line. At first the units moved smoothly into the Reichenberg area and tried to reach the Elbe in small groups. Many Division members were killed by Czech partisans on the way.

This unit, planned as a Panzergrenadier Division, reached its full strength and usefulness in a short time. Despite ten months of training of the ethnic German recruits, the first front action was a fiasco. Faulty leadership and training, plus the lack of heavy weapons, prevented the Division from being ready for action. Shortages in the German armament industry also led to the unit, officially a Panzergrenadier Division, lacking some 900 trucks even when it had 700 of them. Thus only battle groups of regimental size were ready for action.

22nd SS Volunteer Cavalry Division

In the autumn of 1943 the SS-FHA planned to set up a second SS cavalry division with ethnic Germans from Hungary. Thus in November 1943 the formation of a fourth SS cavalry regiment was arranged, to serve at first with the 8th SS Cavalry Division. This SS Cavalry Regiment 18 had over 1,581 members as of December 31, 1943.

At this time over 22,000 ethnic Germans from Hungary had been inducted into the Waffen-SS. Through a further agreement between the countries, this total was to rise considerably again. In the process of the government change in Budapest, the treaty was quickly ratified.

On April 29, 1944 the SS-FHA, in view of this potential, ordered the already planned formation of an SS Volunteer Cavalry Division in Hungary. The name of the unit with "Maria Theresia" is not provable in official documents. For the formation, which was to be completed by October 30, 1944 in the area between Kisber (ca.70 km west of Budapest) and Gyoer (ca.95 km northwest of Budapest), the Commander of the Waffen-SS in Hungary, *SS-Obergruppenführer* Keppler, was responsible. As the cadre of the Division, instead of the originally planned SS Cavalry Regiment 18, SS Cavalry Regiment 17, which had just taken part in the combat around Kowel, was chosen.

After eight weeks the Division Commander, *SS-Brigadeführer* Zehender, reported a strength of 4,914 men. By September 20, 1944 the unit, known since July 1944 as the 22nd SS volunteer Cavalry Division, reached a strength of 12,453 soldiers. Though the specified strength was nominally almost attained, the Division was not ready for action, what with the lack of some 2,000 upper and lower leaders and the lacking training and equipping with heavy weapons. After urgent requests from the Commander of the Army Group "South", *Generaloberst* Friessner, only a battle group of battalion strength could be formed and sent to the hard-fighting front.

Under the command of the Leader of SS volunteer Cavalry Regiment 52, *SS-Sturmbannführer* Wiedemann, about 1,000 members of his regiment and combat-supporting units went into action. After Wiedemann's death, *SS-Hauptsturmführer* Ameiser took over the battle group, which finally bore his name. Moved to the LVII. Panzer Corps in the Hungarian-Romanian border area near Sarkad, the SS battle group saw action with the Hungarian 4th Infantry Division. After the Hungarian units showed almost no opposition to the Soviet attack, the SS riders were surrounded on October 2, 1944. After four days, *SS-Hauptsturmführer* Ameiser ordered a breakthrough to the German lines. In an adventurous flight, some of the men were able to cross the Koeroes and Theiss Rivers and reach the LVII. Panzer Corps at the end of October 1944. From there they were sent on to the formation area of the 22nd SS Volunteer Cavalry Division west of Budapest for refreshing. After the SS riders variously succeeded in causing the enemy considerable losses of men and material, Ameiser was promoted to *SS-Sturmbannführer* and decorated with the Knight's Cross of the Iron Cross.

While the SS Battle Group "Ameiser" was in action some 200 km from the Hungarian capital, other parts of the 22nd SS Volunteer Cavalry Division were alarmed in mid-October 1944. After the Hungarian Regent, Admiral von Horthy, prepared to remove his country from the war at once, Hitler planned to depose Horthy. Under the command of *SS-Sturmbannführer* Skorzeny, Operation "Panzerfaust" was carried out on October 16, 1944. The 22nd SS Volunteer Cavalry Division was given the task of placing an outer barrage belt around the government area, the Budapest Castle, and occupying the railroad stations and other strategically important establishments. Without much attention, the takeover of the government by the right-wing Pfeilkreuzler Party under Szalasi took place. On October 22, 1944 the involved parts of the 22nd SS Volunteer Cavalry Division marched back to their barracks west of the capital.

Just a week later the group was alarmed again and subordinated to the III. Panzer Corps. Without the units of the shattered SS Battle Group "Ameiser", *SS-Brigadeführer* Zehender moved, withy some 4,000 division members, to the front southeast of Budapest.[87] In almost pure infantry action, the Division members occupied the area of the "Carola opposition" between Csepel Island and Vecses. As of November 1, 1944 the young, inexperienced SS riders

---

87 Of the barely 12,500 Division members (September 1944), around 6,000 men had been inducted only in August and September 1944. Most of them were not sent into front action, but remained with all the horses at the formation area at first, and in February 1945 they formed the basis of the 37th SS Volunteer Cavalry Division.

Ethnic German members of the
22nd SS Volunteer Cavalry Division.

The cornflower, instead of the Sig-runes, decorated the
collar emblems of the ethnic Germans from Hungary.

were in heavy defensive fighting, which grew more intense after November 8, 1944. At the beginning of December the positions on the Csepel Island were extended. At first there was no more heavy fighting, since the focal point of the Soviet operations was north of Budapest.

After the successful enclosing of the Hungarian capital at Christmas 1944, the strategic focal point moved to the part of Buda west of the Danube. For this, the 8th SS Cavalry Division and large parts of the 22nd SS volunteer Cavalry Division were transferred from the so-called east bridgehead of Pest to Buda. On January 17, 1945 Pest was given up after the last bridges were blown up, and fighting continued only in Buda.

Here an apocalyptic situation developed. Without any food or medical treatment, increasing apathy spread under the constant enemy artillery fire. When the Commanding General of the IX. Waffen Mountain Corps of the SS ordered a breakthrough from Budapest on February 11, 1945, not even 100 members of the 22nd SS Volunteer Cavalry Division reached the German lines. The combat-ready part of the SS unit had thus been wiped out in ten weeks of combat. The then *SS-Unterscharführer* Walter Sass describes his time in the Division very vividly:

> "My company, the Radio Company of the 22nd SS Volunteer Cavalry Division, was n Hungary for new formation and the training of the new recruits (mostly ethnic Germans from Hungary). We were stationed in Bia-Torbacy. Our radio-technical training took place under primitive conditions: we lacked training equipment. Thus much value was placed on infantry training. As we learned later, that had its reason. At the beginning of October 1944 part of our company was ordered into action to prevent a swing in Hungary, as we were told. I myself saw action on the nearby roads to Budapest Castle, and later inside the castle grounds. After six days we returned to Bia, fortunately without losses. On October 31, 1944, in the late evening hours, came the order to march to east of Budapest. On November 2, 1944 we already made enemy contact. We were used as infantry, and in the morning hours of November 8, 1944 the Russians began the already expected large attack before our positions. At first we had to give up our village, gathered at the edge of town and then made a concentrated counterattack in the morning hours. Te Russians had to get out again. In the stubborn house-to-house fighting we lost contact with our neighbors to the right. Then I was given the order to reestablish contact. In attempting to do this, I was wounded in the knee. Rescued by my platoon leader and two comrades, I reached a garden that served as our main dressing station. My right knee was shattered, and I was taken to Budapest in an ambulance. There they told me that my leg could not be saved and had to be amputated. Completely in despair and depressed, I went to Prague on a hospital train."

After only a part of the Division was ordered into infantry action in the "Carola position", the rest, along with more Hungarian (ethnic German) volunteers, formed the 37th SS Volunteer Cavalry Division in February 1945.

Thus the Division was quickly disbanded before it had ever seen service as a complete unit. The rapid worsening of the war situation meant that more and more troops, without full training and equipment, went to the front as battle groups and were quickly shattered there.

23rd SS Volunteer Panzergrenadier Division "Nederland"

(Netherlands No.1)

The 4th SS volunteer Panzergrenadier Brigade "Nederland"

With the increasing induction of ethnic Germans from Romania in the spring of 1943, the enlarging of smaller SS units could begin. For propagandistic purposes, there were also plans to form a *Netherlands* division with the help of ethnic Germans. Ordered to be set up on July 19, 1943, its strength was still limited to that of a brigade on October 23, 1943. In the former Volunteer Legion "Niederland" there were only some 2,200 volunteers, and large volunteering from the Netherlands was not to be expected.

The Volunteer Legion "Niederland", existing since November 1941, was first transferred from the eastern front to the "Mielau" troop training camp. From there it was ordered to Thuringia in the Sonneberg-Hildburghausen-Schleusingen area for the establishment of the 4th SS Volunteer Panzergrenadier Brigade "Nederland". In the summer of 1943 it was sent to the Balkans to strengthen the German forces at least numerically in view of the expected withdrawal of Italy from the Axis alliance.

At the end of August and beginning of September 1943, the rail transports reached the area north of the Save and were to finish the formation of the SS Volunteer Panzergrenadier Regiments 48 and 49 and the brigade units, such as the SS Panzerjäger Unit 54,[88] as well as securing the area from partisans. There were repeated actions against Tito's partisans, because of which the Commander of the Brigade, *SS-Brigadeführer* Wagner, was executed in Belgrade on April 5, 1947.

After Hitler ordered on November 21, 1943 that the III. (Germanic) SS Panzer Corps be moved to the eastern front along with the 11th SS Volunteer Panzergrenadier Division "Nordland" and the 4th SS Volunteer Panzergrenadier Brigade "Nederland", the transport of the troops began in mid-December 1943. At the end of December 1943 the brigade reported a strength of 5,426 men. Of them, only about 2,200 were Netherlanders. Some 1,000 native Germans were assigned as cadre personnel and about 2,200 Romanian Germans brought the brigade almost to its specified strength. Thus only 40% were volunteers from the Netherlands. Later this percentage sank to below 10%. The supply of heavy weapons and equipment was very meager. For a long time the artillery regiment had only one unit and the Panzerjäger unit at first had only 12 heavy 7.5 cm antitank guns. Only at the eastern front were 10 assault guns supplied to it.

When the 4th Volunteer Panzergrenadier Brigade "Nederland" arrived at the front near the Oranienbaum pocket in the sector of the 18th Army, it first relieved the battle group of the 4. SS Police Panzergrenadier Division in the Kernova area. For reasons of camouflage, the Commanding General of the III. (Germanic) SS Panzer Corps ordered on January 14, 1944 that the brigade be called SS Volunteer Panzergrenadier Division "Nederland".

When the Red Army began into winter offensive against the left wing of the 18th Army near Oranienbaum on the same day, there was heavy fighting the next day with troops of the 4th SS Volunteer Panzergrenadier Brigade.[89] After Soviet troops had been able to surround parts of the 9th and 10th Field Division (L), battle groups of the brigade and others were able to open the pocket and let the enclosed German troops flow out.

On January 26, 1944 the Brigade received the order to move into the so-called Panther position along the Narva. After heavy defensive fighting, they marched via Krikkolo at the beginning of February 1944 and took an intermediate position near Jamburg on the Luga. When the troops finally moved into the Narva bridgehead, the front remained quiet for a few days. Thus ended their first action after about two weeks of heavy fighting and a withdrawal of almost 100 kilometers.

After several small fights, heavy attacks on the whole main battle line began as of March 11, 1944. There the SS Volunteer Panzergrenadier Regiment 48 served in the northern area of Narva and the SS Volunteer Panzergrenadier Regiment 49 at the eastern bridgehead of the border city. On March 15, 1944 the Wehrmacht report praised them:

---

88 The Brigade units all received number 54.
89 The official usage, as a brigade, is continued here.

> "In the battles o the last days, the Netherlands SS Volunteer Panzergrenadier Regiment "General Seyffardt", under the command of SS-Obersturmbannführer Jörchel, has proved itself very well in the northern sector of the eastern front."

On the next day the formerly subordinated III./SS Police Artillery Regiment was moved intact to the SS Volunteer Artillery Regiment 54. Thus the Regiment had at least two light units. From January 1 to March 31, 1944 the Brigade lad lost 651 men dead, 2,277 wounded and 478 missing. In the first two weeks of April 1944 another 322 dead, wounded and missing were lost. Thus in fourteen weeks of action, the unit had lost 3,728 men and almost had to be regarded as shattered.

On the front before Narva it had meanwhile become quiet, and except for opposing scouting-troop operations in the area of the eastern Narva bridgehead, there was no more major combat. After the arrival of numerous replacements, especially more ethnic Germans from Romania, the brigade reported on June 30, 1944 a strength of 6,714 men. Even before the Army Unit "Narva" and then also the strengthened 4th SS Volunteer Panzergrenadier Brigade "Nederland" were attacked again, there was an attempt on Hitler's life on July 20, 1944. *SS-Brigadeführer* Walter expressed himself like a demagogue in his daily orders:

> "SS men of the Brigade 'Nederland'!
> Since I was assigned to lead you as Netherlanders, ethnic Germans from Siebenbürgen and native Germans, I have always emphasized to you that the hardest fight will come at the time of decision.
> Now it has come!
> Surrounded by enemies in total superiority, a vulgar clique of traitors tries to murder the German people and thus Europe for the second time. The indication of Divine leadership that was given to us today in preserving the life of our Führer gives up the increased power to fulfill that which one man has devoted his entire life, and who is our Führer.
> As an old SS man, I call to you, in this difficult hour that has struck all of us, the words that the National Socialistic concept has always brought us to the high point of our accomplishments in the hardest years of war: Now indeed! Our lives belong to the Führer – we stay true to him!"

In the large Soviet offensive, first parts of the Brigade left the front on July 24, 1944 to form a new battle line in the so-called "Tannenberg position". On the night of July 25, 1944, SS Volunteer Panzergrenadier Regiment 48, put in as a rear-guard, left its positions. The I. Battalion was surrounded by Soviet troops in the forests southwest of Lagna and completely shattered.

After the German troops had taken the new position, the front ran from the Gulf of Finland some three kilometers to the south to the Narva-Peryatse road. Here the so-called Blue Hills and the Children's Home Hill in the east and the Grenadier Hill just to the west, plus Hill 69.9, formed the crux of the defense. From the 4th SS Volunteer Panzergrenadier Brigade, the SS Volunteer Panzergrenadier Regiment 49 "de Ruyter" (Netherlands No.2) and the SS Engineer Battalion 54 were sent into the main battle line. On July 26, 1944 the Red Army was ale to occupy the Children's Home Hill. There was also heavy fighting on the Grenadier Hill and Hill 69.9.

With the movement of the Soviet focal point to the southern limits of the Army Unit "Narva", the front calmed down in front of the Tannenberg position. After taking over a battle group for the threatened Dorpat area, *SS-Brigadeführer* Wagner was replaced by the Adjutant of the Army Unit "Narva", *Oberst* Friedrich, from command of the rest of the 4th SS Volunteer Panzergrenadier Brigade. On September 9, 1944 *SS-Brigadeführer* Wagner again took command of the remainder of his brigade. After the situation developed in southern Estonia, indicating an enclosure of the German troops in northern Estonia, including those in the Tannenberg position, Army Group "North" ordered the evacuation of Estonia on September 18, 1944. On that same evening the departure from the positions and march to the Pernau began.

On September 21, 1944 the III. SS Panzer Corps ordered the new formation of the SS Volunteer Panzergrenadier Regiment 48 at the Pomeranian troop training camp of "Hammerstein". At the end of September 1944 the Brigade reported a strength of 6,530 soldiers. The numerical strength had scarcely changed in comparison with June 30, 1944 through the transfer of Navy men, despite the heavy combat losses. The percentage of Netherlanders in the 4th SS Volunteer Panzergrenadier Brigade "Nederland", with about 1,000 men, now was around 15% of the personnel.

After the unit reached Latvia from Estonia, it was subordinated to the L. Army Corps and used first as a corps reserve. After a total of 300 km, the troops reached the area south of Doblen on September 28, 1944 and were immediately involved in heavy defensive fighting. At the beginning of October 1944 the Red Army was able to encircle the Army Group "North" in Courland. The SS Volunteer Panzergrenadier Brigade "Nederland", as it was now officially known again, was then ordered to the area south of Libau, some 150 km away, on October 12, 1944.

Within the III. (Germanic) SS Panzer Corps, the breakthrough to the main battle line, running to East Prussia, was planned. Strong Soviet troops prevented the undertaking. Instead the Brigade was subordinated to the 11th Infantry Division two days later. Here enemy troops that broke through were to be fought in the woodlands north of the Tirs-Purvs swamp. On October 17, 1944 the unit, despite strong enemy attacks, was taken out of action and sent back to the III. SS Panzer Corps in the area 10 km south of Prekuln. In the fighting that ensued here, the Brigade's positions were broken through repeatedly, and had to be recaptured in the area 15 km southwest of Prekuln.

On November 1, 1944 the Brigade moved off to the line a bit west of Skuodas-Prekuln. There followed the occupation of the so-called Kriemhild position, which was held until 1945. After relatively quiet days, the Red Army made a large attack on the entire front on January 21, 1945. After heavy fighting in Kaleti, the SS Volunteer Panzergrenadier Brigade "Nederland" was taken out of the main line and subordinated to the X. Army Corps. On January 26, 1945 *SS-Brigadeführer* Wagner reported on the remaining combat units:

> "SS Volunteer Panzergrenadier Regiment 49: The Regiment has no combat value any more since its removal. The infantry combat strength amounts to some 10 to 20 men. The heavy weapons are almost all gone, and the operating crews are scarcely still available, since they have been used strictly as infantry since the breakdown of the weapons.
>
> SS Artillery Regiment 54: The Regiment's personnel strength has decreased more. It had considerable losses in its infantry combat by alarm units. Although personnel refreshing for its full combat readiness is necessary, it can be regarded as ready for action.
>
> SS Engineer Battalion 54: The Engineer Battalion has no more combat value. Aside from the Adjutant and one company chief, it has no more engineer leaders or lower leaders. Its combat strength is only about 10 to 15 men. The backline parts are essentially still preserved."

On January 28, 1945 what remained of the unit was shipped from Libau to Stettin. Unloaded here as of February 2, 1945, it was renumbered as the 23rd SS Volunteer Panzergrenadier Division "Nederland" (Netherlands No.1). Other than the fact that it lacked at least 5,000 men of the prescribed strength of an infantry division, its designation as a Netherlands SS volunteer unit was paradoxical. The Netherlands formed only the strength of a battalion. The specified structure could not come anywhere near being reached. Above all, united action was not at all possible, what with the separation of the two Panzergrenadier Regiments.

The first unit to see action was the SS Volunteer Regiment 48 "General Seyffardt", which had been restructured at the "Hammerstein" troop training camp since October 1944. The I. Battalion had been reformed with remaining men of the original regiment, and the II. Battalion arose from transfers from the SS Panzergrenadier Instructional Regiment from Neweklau. While in the I. Battalion, above all, ethnic Germans from Siebenbürgen served, the II. Battalion consisted mainly of former Navy artillerymen. There were scarcely any Netherlanders in the Regiment any more, despite its *"Netherlands No.1"* name.

When in mid-January 1945 the Red Army advanced westward from the Vistula bridgeheads on both sides of Warsaw, the Regiment was alarmed and subordinated to the XVI. SS Army Corps. On February 1, 1945, enclosed in the defense of Schneidemühl, the rest of it broke out to the German lines on February 14, 1945. Subordinated to the XVIII. Mountain Corps, it was then ordered to Group "Ax". This had no heavy weapons and was in strictly infantry use. Carbines, machine guns and antitank weapons stood against the Soviet aircraft, artillery and tanks.

Scarcely able to oppose the further Red Army advances, the group was pushed to Hammerstein on February 26, 1945. There it was subordinated to the Corps Group "Tettau", which formed the left wing of the 3rd Panzer Army to the Baltic Sea. First pushed back to Belgard, the corps was almost surrounded. In trying to make connections with the German lines, it came into chaotic conditions. Without strict leadership of the units, the Commanding General of the Corps Group, *Generalleutnant* von Tettau, saw no alternative to ordering all the remaining heavy weapons and vehicles destroyed. The men were to fight their way westward in small groups.

Via Croessin and Zedlin what was left of the SS Volunteer Panzergrenadier Regiment 48 set up the Dievenow bridgehead on March 11, 1945. Combat-ready parts were subordinated to the Corps Group "Munzel" for service in the bridgehead position. On March 19, 1945 the men left the bridgehead and moved to the Heinersdorf area (ca. 5 km northwest of Schwedt) for restructuring. To this area, several days later, there came the troops of the 23rd SS Volunteer Panzergrenadier Division that had been in Pomerania.

The bulk of the Division, with SS Volunteer Panzergrenadier Regiment 49 "de Ruyter", was immediately subordinated to the III SS Panzer Corps of the 11th Army after being evacuated from Courland. As replacements for the SS Volunteer Panzergrenadier Regiment 48 "General Seyffardt", the Division was subordinated to the SS Panzergrenadier Regiment "Klotz", composed of ethnic German recruits, at the SS Panzergrenadier School in Kienschlag.

The SS Reconnaissance Company 54 and the SS Flak Company 54 were disbanded, effective on February 5, 1945. The SS Engineer Battalion 23 received two instructional companies from the SS Engineer School in Hradischko. In the entire 23rd SS Volunteer Panzergrenadier Division "Nederland" (some 6,000 men) the percentage of Netherlanders had meanwhile fallen below 10%. For lack of a tank unit, Schützenpanzerwagen or motorized artillery, its structure was nothing like that of an SS Panzergrenadier division.

On February 15, 1945 *SS-Brigadeführer* Wagner was ordered to gather his units in the Ravenstein-Jacobshagen area for the forthcoming German Pomeranian offensive.[90] On the next day, the 23rd SS Volunteer Panzergrenadier Division was already in action to recover Reetz. Until the offensive was suddenly halted, the Division was in heavy, changing combat in the Reetz area. The material and personnel superiority of the Red Army prevented any success.

After a few days of rest at the front, the enemy went on the offensive in Pomerania on March 1, 1945 and was able to make a gap 15 km wide on the seam between the X. SS and III. SS Panzer Corps. With nothing to oppose the massive attack, the 23rd SS Volunteer Panzergrenadier Division had to draw back. Via Freienwalde and Daarz, the units reached the Gollnow area (ca. 25 km northeast of Stettin) on March 7, 1945. Then it occupied the northern Lübzin position area in Hornskrug at the Stettin-Altdamm bridgehead.

In the fight for this German bridgehead, which was supposed to serve as the starting point for an offensive against Danzig, the German units were almost destroyed. On March 20, 1945 the bridgehead was given up. Gathered in the area west of Stettin, the commander of the 3rd Panzer Army evaluated the unit's combat value a week later:

> "The Division is practically just a strengthened regiment. Combat strength is almost shattered at this time, needs a complete new formation. Time for the end of refreshing is not visible at this time, therefore only suitable for defense, combat value IV."

From March 1 to 31m 1945 the Division, with 2,014 men in all, had lost the strength of almost four battalions. The high number of missing men resulted from the circumstance that the quickly assembled units had no togetherness and consisted to a considerable part of soldiers who had little enthusiasm and quickly departed or surrendered as prisoners.

From September 1, 1943 to February 28, 1945 the unit had the following losses:

	Leaders	Other Ranks	Total
Dead	55	2,487	2,542
Wounded	141	5,448	5,889
Missing	42	1,609	1,651

---

90   Compare Chapter 11, SS Volunteer Panzergrenadier Division "Nordland".

With a total of some 12,000 dead, wounded or missing – from its formation in Croatia to April 1, 1945 – the unit had twice been totally wiped out numerically. The number of some 2,400 missing is notable. They included a number of ethnic Germans who left the troops to go to their families.

Transferred to the area southwest of Gartz, the remainder of the Division was at first subordinated to the 547th People's Grenadier Division. The SS Volunteer Panzergrenadier Regiment 48 was reformed in the Heinersdorf area at that time with three battalions of Waffen-SS, Luftwaffe and Navy men, and then sent into the Garz area. In the ensuing last battles, the Division was again used separately. When the Red Army launched an offensive from the bridgeheads on the Oder on April 16, 1945, the Commander of the 9th Army called for the release of the men of the 11th and 23rd SS Volunteer Panzergrenadier Divisions then being refreshed. Intended for the area of Frankfurt on the Oder, both groups, because of transport difficulties, were first subordinated to the LVI. Panzer Corps in the Weiezen-Seelow area, also involved in the heaviest defensive fighting.

The I./SS Volunteer Panzergrenadier Regiment 49, for lack of fuel, could not be moved and took positions with the XXXXVI. Panzer Corps east of Gramzow (ca.15 cm southeast of Prenzlow). Under the command of the 3rd Panzer Army, the remaining battalion finally tried to reach the demarcation line and thus marched through Roebel toward Parchim.

The rest of the Division, with the SS Volunteer Panzergrenadier Regiment 48, newly restocked with men, was supplied with fuel and reached the area of the XI. SS Army Corps on April 18, 1945. There it went immediately into combat in the Marxdorf-Falkenhagen area and withdrew in the direction of Königswusterhausen and Mittenwalde.

When the Red Army was able to form a pocket on April 25, 1945, what remained of the 23rd SS Volunteer Panzergrenadier Division "Nederland" (ca.4,000 men), along with large parts of the 9th Army, were surrounded. Without supplies, the days in the pocket at Halbe led to the complete collapse of leadership and cohesion of the units. Using woodland roads, the men tried to avoid any enemy contact and finally reach Märkisch-Buchholz. From there the columns moved in the direction of Halbe, trying to break out to the 12th Army. In the breakthrough fighting as of April 28, 1945, countless soldiers and civilians lost their lives. Those who got through the inferno gathered at the SS facility in Redekin, northwest of Genthin. There the so-called SS Battle Group "Wagner" went into American captivity.

Thus ended the history of the 23rd SS Volunteer Panzergrenadier Division "Nederland" (Netherlands No.1). Of the 8.2 million Netherlanders, only some 6,000 men served in the ranks of the Volunteer Legion, Brigade and finally the nominal Division. As of the summer of 1944, more than 6,000 Romanian ethnic Germans served in the unit. The Division never actually reached its full strength. As also with the 11th SS Volunteer Panzergrenadier Division "Nordland", the name did not match the facts.

24th Waffen Mountain (Karstjäger) Division of the SS

The SS Karstwehr Battalion

On July 10, 1942 Himmler ordered the formation of a special mountain unit in the SS garrison of Dachau. First formed at the strength of a company, the order came on November 19, 1942 to enlarge it to a battalion with four companies. The Commander was the chalk and cave researcher, *SS-Sturmbannführer* Dr. Hans Brand. Subordinated to the newly formed SS General Command (Pz.), the unit was supposed to be trained to serve when needed in the Karst regions of the Caucasus. After its first training in the medium mountain area of Pottenstein (Upper Franconia), the SS Karstwehr Battalion was to receive further training in the high mountain area of the Triglav region in Slovenia.

To bring the troop units to their specified strength, members of the SS Mountain Rifle Replacement Battalion from Trautenau were ordered to the SS Karstwehr Battalion in March and April of 1943, as were ethnic Germans from Romania in June.

The developing situation in the Soviet Union and Italy, though, led to a different use of the small unit. Following the arrest of Mussolini on July 25, 1943, the SS Karstwehr Battalion was also ordered to move into the region around Villach. Subordinated to the 71st Infantry Division, it was to disarm the Italian troops in northern Italy if needed.

Through the half-hearted behavior of the Italian government, Hitler was able to bring about the transfer of numerous German units to Italy.[91] For the SS Karstwehr Battalion, this meant crossing the border near Tarvis on August 26, 1943 and marching to the Camporosso-Boscoverde region. Here it was greeted happily by the local ethnic Germans and took over the protection of the Villach-Gemona rail line.

On September 9, 1843 the SS Karstwehr Battalion took part in disarming the Italian armed forces at Pontebba, Uggowitza and Raibel. Since various Italian officers were following the King's order and regarded the former German allies as new enemies, there was fighting. Sixteen members of the SS Battalion died and 50 were wounded. The then SS man Emil Leininger wrote to his fiancée on September 12, 1943 about the typical attitude at that time:

> "As you have heard already on the radio, Italy has capitulated, and the Italians were urged to lay down their arms. At many places there was shooting, in which the Macaroni Soldiers got the short end of it. The SS never retreats…"

After the interning of the Italian soldiers there came combat with Italian and Slovenian partisans in the Julian Alps. From November 15 to 20, 1943, for example, they took part in Operation "Traufe". On November 26, 1943 the battalion was briefly subordinated to the Highest SS and Police Leader in Italy, *SS-Obergruppenführer* Wolff. In December 1943 it was already moved to the Görz area and subordinated to the Higher SS and Police Leader "Adriatic Coastland", *SS-Gruppenführer* Globocnik. From December 12 to 14, 1943 he ordered, among others, Operation "Blumendraht". At the end of December 1943 the battalion, with a strength of 946 men, was housed in a garrison in Gradisca. Along with the three existing rifle companies and one heavy company, an artillery battalion was set up and armed with captured Italian 7.5 cm mountain cannons. With only eight leaders, the entire battalion was scarcely ready for combat at that time.

Almost every day, parts of the battalion made small attacks on partisans. These often lasted from two to four days. For example, Operation "Zypresse", from March 3 to 5, 1944. At the end of March 1944, the large-scale two-week Operation "Osterglocke" began. In April 1944 the unit, along with the SS Mountain Rifle Training and Replacement Battalion 7, also took over rail securing between Laibach and Trieste. From April 26 to May 6, 1944 came Operation "Braunschweig". It was the last large action under *SS-Standartenführer* Dr. Brand. On May 13, 1944 *SS-Sturmbannführer* Berschneider took command of the SS Karstwehr Battalion. The former commander – more scientist than soldier – had repeated disagreements with the Higher SS and Police Leader "Adriatic Coastland", and because he was 65 years old, he was no longer suited to lead the unit. From May 22 to 24, 1944 the men took part in Operation 'Liane". And from June 7 to 16 in Operation "Annemarie."

---

91 After the capture of Mussolini, the Italian King made known that he would fight to the final victory at Germany's side. Actually, talks about capitulation had already been going on with the Western Allies for a long time.

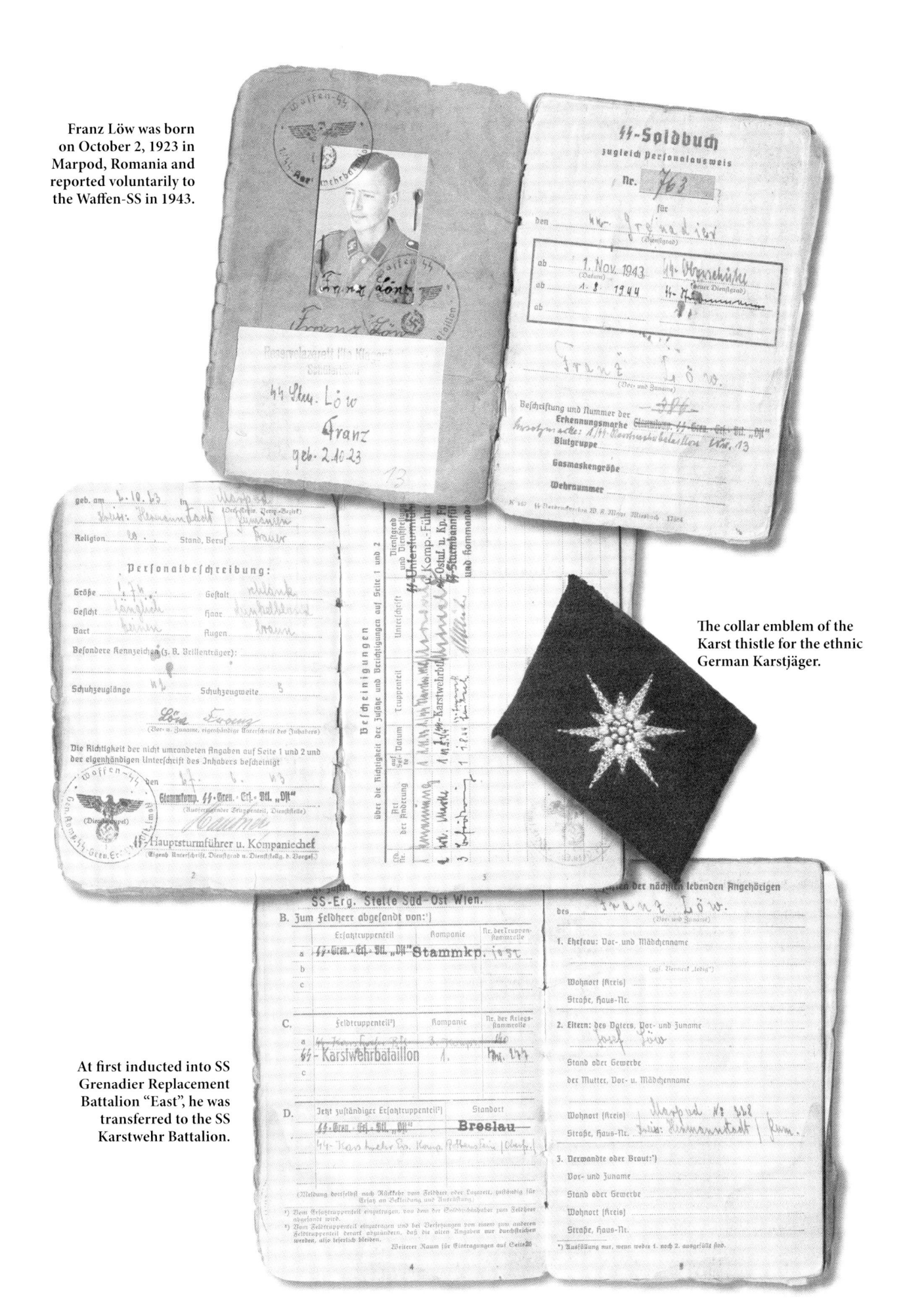

Franz Löw was born on October 2, 1923 in Marpod, Romania and reported voluntarily to the Waffen-SS in 1943.

The collar emblem of the Karst thistle for the ethnic German Karstjäger.

At first inducted into SS Grenadier Replacement Battalion "East", he was transferred to the SS Karstwehr Battalion.

The 24th Waffen Mountain (Karstjäger) Division of the SS

After military service was introduced in the Adriatic coastland, Himmler ordered, on July 18, 1944, the formation of an SS division of inhabitants from there. The SS Karstwehr Battalion of some 1,000 men served as a cadre. *SS-Sturmbannführer* Hahn was named the leader of the foundation staff of the division.

Although the military duty had already been proclaimed at the end of 1943, the forced mobilization was not begun. Rebellions were probably feared. Only in the spring of 1944 were those born in 1923 to 1925 inducted, and the obligated men had the choice of joining the Fascist Italian Army or German units. Of the few who volunteered freely, only an insignificant number could be inducted as capable. The plan of the SS-FHA was thus not to be realized. Interestingly, no other ethnic Germans from Romania or Hungary were ordered to join.

Instead of that, some 500 South Tyroleans from the SS training camps of Uggowitza and Malborghette were inducted into the division, which was to be set up in the Aupa-Pontebba-Malborghetto-Moggio area. In April and May they were already sent to Sterzing and Schlanders and trained by members of the SS Karstwehr battalion. They formed the II./Waffen Mountain (Karstjäger) Regiment of the SS 59.

In September 1944, another 300 eligible men from northern Italy, and firefly, a company of Spanish volunteers,[92] were ordered to the 24th Waffen Mountain (Karstjäger) Division of the SS. On September 20, 1944 the group reported a strength of 1,989 members. After it became obvious that not enough volunteers of the Adriatic coastland would strengthen the unit, the specified strength was already reduced to the one brigade. With a lack of some 120 leaders and lower leaders, the usability of the troops was very limited.

While the newly inducted recruits were used mainly in the foundation area for small actions (for example, along the Cereschiatis Pass), the I./Waffen Mountain (Karstjäger) Regiment of the SS 59, formed from the Karstwehr Battalion, took part in larger actions of the Higher SS and Police Leader "Adriatic Coastland" in the area north of Udine in September 1944.

On December 5, 1944 the unit, already internally commanded as a brigade, officially was renamed the Waffen Mountain (Karstjäger) Brigade of the SS. Since the strength was practically not over 2,500 men, it was merely a strengthened regiment.

At the same time came the order to transfer to the Grado-Lignano area by the lagoon of Marano. In the Province of Venetia the unit was supposed to secure the backlands against the strongly Communistic partisan bands in view of a possible landing of Allied troops. There were numerous fights there. For reasons of camouflage, Himmler ordered on February 10, 1945 to rename the brigade as the 24th Waffen Mountain (Karstjäger) Division of the SS.

At the end of March and beginning of April 1945 it came, with parts of the 1st SS Cossack Division, under the SS and *Polizeiführer* "Adria-West", into a last large undertaking in the Basischizza Plateau-Trnover Forest area (northeast of Görz). A little later the units were given the task of freeing the important withdrawal connections from Latisana to Villach in the Osoppo-Gemona-Venmzone area from partisans.

On May 2, 1945 the Karstjäger were subordinated to the SS Battle Group "Harmel", which were supposed to keep the Karawanken passes near Villach and Klagenfurt open for German bands fleeing back. There was a partisan attack near Avasinis in which a nearby village was burned down and some fifty inhabitants shot.

Shortly thereafter, the units were taken prisoner by the British. Planned and formed as a special mountain troop, its composition and tasks were changed by the war. Suffering not only from higher and lower leaders, but also lacking equipment, it is interesting that even an enlargement of the SS Karstwehr Battalion to brigade or division strength could be achieved. This is unusual, since there basically would have been possibilities to assign ethnic Germans or Luftwaffe or Navy men to it.

---

92 This was presumably a company of the Spanish SS Volunteer Legion which was then in service with the 3rd Mountain Division.

31st SS Volunteer Grenadier Division

On September 24, 1944 the SS-FHA halted the formation of a second Moslem SS division because of the unreliability of the Bosniaks. On October 4, 1944 it was already decided in Berlin to set up a division out of which originally the 23rd Waffen Mountain Division of the SS "Kama" (Croatian No.2) was to be brought to specified strength with some 10,000 ethnic Germans from Hungary from the SS Recruit Depot "Sombor".

But before the formation of the units could be started, the previous foundation staffs were ordered to the Mohacs area. In the transfer, in initiative of the Commander of the new 31st SS Volunteer Grenadier Division, some 80,000 ethnic Germans were evacuated from the Batschka.[93] In emptying the area, there were often fights with partisans.

On November 1, 1944 the men inducted in the summer of 1944 were ordered to the front and took a second position in the Mohacs-Battaszeko area. A week later, the Red Army began and offensive in this sector, and two days later it was able to form the first bridgeheads over the Danube. The 31st SS Volunteer Grenadier Division was alarmed, and on November 12, 1944 it was subordinated to the LXVIII, Army Corps (2nd Panzer Army).

Heavy fighting followed, in which the men suffered great losses for lack of heavy weapons and poor training and leadership. The LXVIII. Army Corps understandably classified the 31st SS Volunteer Grenadier Division as *"not fireproof."* When the Red Army moved out of the bridgeheads on a large offensive on November 27, 1944, the combat units of the 31st SS Volunteer Grenadier Division were thoroughly shattered in the area between Battaszeko and Kaposvar. After the enemy reached the south shore of the Plattensee on December 7, 1944, the units were taken out of action. On December 21, 1944 the Division was ordered to finish its formation the Cilli-Bonobitz-Windisch-Feistritz-Marburg area (Defense Zone XVIII).

Subordinated to the Higher SS and Police Leader "Alpenland, *SS-Obergruppenführer* and *General* of the Police Rösener, to fight partisans in the Bacher Mountains, a combat-ready front unit was supposed to be formed here. Without supplies of heavy weapons and training at division level at the troop training camp, though, this was not possible. On January 16, 1945 the specified structure was compared to that of an Infantry Division 45.

Shortly after that, the unit was already transported to the Görlitz area, around 500 km away, to the Army Group "Center", and at the end of February 1945 it was unloaded southwest of Hirschberg in Bad Warmbrunn. Out of the two SS Volunteer Grenadier Regiments 78 and 79, a battle group was formed and subordinated to the XXXXVIII. Panzer Corps (17th Army).

At the same time, the SS Fusilier Battalion 31 was to be formed with Hungarian SS volunteers, as well as the SS Volunteer Grenadier Regiment 80 out of the SS Police Regiment "Brixen". The latter followed the battle group of the 31st SS Volunteer Grenadier Division into the Striegau area (south of Jauer) on March 6, 1945 and replaced a regiment of the neighboring 208th Infantry Division. When the Red Army began an offensive there on March 15, 1945, the front-inexperienced SS Volunteer Grenadier Regiment 80 was shattered immediately. On April 6, 1945 the Division Battle Group took over the positions of the 100th Rifle Division near Strehlen, some 70 km farther to the east. Thus it came under the command of the XVII. Army Corps. Meanwhile the first heavy weapons had arrived: several artillery guns, 14 Pursuit Tank 38 "Hetzer" and several 7.5 cm antitank guns.

While there were no large battles on the front until May 6, 1945, the withdrawal led to dramatic scenes. *SS-Oberführer* Lombard gave the order to get away from the enemy and, while avoiding Prague, reach the Pilsen area more than 300 km away. Here the units were to be captured by the Americans. In countless columns, mixed with civilians and Wehrmacht men, the members of the 31st SS Volunteer Grenadier Division tried to reach Königgrätz at first via Braunau, Nachod ad Josefstadt. Others marched through Trautenau westward to Paka. In these marches there were constant incidents with Czech partisans. The then *SS-Unterscharführer* Gensicke recalls:

> "The Czechs raged at the unarmed German population and us soldiers. We were then gathered on a sport field. Here lone SS members were forced to their knees, pulled over the cinder track on their faces, and then shot! On the way to Teplitz everybody was shot who stepped out of the column to drink or relieve himself. It was horrible!"

---

93   See page 14.

Like most groups that were set up in the Waffen-SS in 1944, it was mainly a mixture of available personnel resources. Training in a large form was to happen if possible, but was usually omitted by the overly hasty orders to fight at the front. In neither quantity nor quality could the divisions be used in infantry combat as battle groups.

37th SS Volunteer Cavalry Division

On February 8, 1945 the SS-FHA ordered the formation of the 33rd SS Cavalry Division.

The numbering was changed, so that the Field Command Office of the *Reichsführer-SS* already spoke of a 37th SS Volunteer Cavalry Division on February 19, 1945. It was to be formed: *from remainders of the 8th SS Cavalry Division "Florian Geyer" and the 22nd SS volunteer Cavalry Division wiped out in Budapest, plus … Hungarian ethnic Germans and Hungarian volunteers."*

Above all, the ethnic Germans inducted into the 22nd SS Volunteer Cavalry Division in August and September 1944, who had not gone off to the front, plus the SS Cavalry Regiment 17 that was being reformed, served as the cadre. They were transferred to the Senec area (north of Pressburg), where the SS Field Recruit Depot 8 was also located. Replacements came from, among others, the SS Cavalry Training and Replacement Regiment in Beneschau. Named as the commander of the new division was the man intended to be the Instructional Group Commander at the SS Cavalry School in Göttingen since January 8, 1945, *SS-Obersturmbannführer* Gesele.

The 37th SS Volunteer Cavalry Division was to be formed at the "Kleine Karpaten" troop training camp in the Gajary-Malacky-Stupava area east of the March. The structure of the division was based on an Infantry Division 45 in shortened form, with a strength of some 6,000 men.

While two battle groups ("Ameiser" and "Keitel") saw service at various front sectors, the formation staffs of the individual troop units were transferred to the Znaim area in mid-March 1945. From there, on April 4,1945, the first units being set up were sent to the 8th Army. In the area between Marchegg and the mouth of the March in the Danube, the hole by the neighboring 6th SS Panzer Army was to be filled with subordinated Army units. On the next day the 96th Infantry Division with the subordinated SS Battle Group "Ameiser" crossed the March and took up the defensive area north of it. The SS Battle Group "Keitel", on the other hand, no longer went back under the command of the 37th SS Volunteer Cavalry Division. It will be reported on later.

The strengthened Grenadier Regiment 284 of the 96th Infantry Division, the Panzer-Grenadier Replacement and Training Battalion 82 of the 232nd Panzer Division and People's Assault Battalions were now subordinated to the Division staff. The mixing of units between the 96th Infantry and 37th SS Volunteer Cavalry Divisions clearly shows the situation at that time. Shattered troop units, like the 96th Infantry Division, had to maintain the defense as *"corset bones."*

The troop units from the staff of the 37th SS Volunteer Cavalry Division then fought in the Russbach-Aspern area near Vienna. A short time later Grenadier Regiment 284 came back under the 96th Infantry Division. On April 15, 1945 *SS-Standartenführer* Gesele took command of the remaining units in a sector northeast of Vienna. Three days later the division staff was taken back out of the front and transferred to the Pisek-Tabor area for the further formation of the division. The SS Battle Group "Ameiser" stayed in action, just as the SS Battle Group "Keitel" did.

SS-Sturmbannführer Ameiser, who had been decorated with the Knight's Cross of the Iron Cross in November 1944 as leader of a battle group of the 22nd SS Volunteer Cavalry Division, was given command of SS Volunteer Cavalry Regiment 92 in February 1945. His former battle group staff "Ameiser" served in the Senec area as the SS Formation Staff "Ameiser". On February 25, 1945 he already received the order to form a new battle group, which was to be sent to the Army Group "Balck" in view of the forthcoming German offensive "Frühlingserwachen". With a strength of some 1,400 men, the SS Battle Group "Ameiser" was subordinated to the 96th Infantry Division (VIII. Hungarian Army Corps and, on March 5, 1945, took positions in the Bicske area. On March 16, 1945 the Red Army, after the failure of the German Operation "Frühlingserwachen", opened its own offensive. Three days later the enemy was able to break through between the units of the 96th Infantry Division and the 1st Hungarian Panzer Division. The troops to the north finally formed the German Gran bridgehead.

The XXXXIII. Army Corps was entrusted with the securing of the oil refineries not far away east of Komorn, and took over the leadership of the German forces at the bridgehead. With the 96th Infantry Division, the SS Battle Group "Ameiser", successfully beating off six Soviet attacks on March 24, 1945 alone and making the evacuation of heavy weapons from the north side of the Danube possible. After the Red Army was able to cross the Gran to the north, came the order to give up the bridgehead.

On March 26, 1945 the enemy launched an offensive from his own Gran bridgehead, whereby the SS Battle Group "Ameiser" was push back over the Neutra in the area north of Pressburg. On April 5, 1945, along with the 96th Infantry Division, it crossed the March and took over from the retreating staff of the 37th SS Volunteer Cavalry Division the securing sector of the Danube-March triangle as far as Marchegg. There the SS Battle Group "Ameiser" remained as a reserve of the 96th Infantry Division, while the Grenadier Regiment 284 was subordinated to the 37th SS Volunteer Division.

From April 7 to 9, 1945 the SS Battle Group "Ameiser" was in action with Grenadier Regiment 287 in the Stopfenreuth-Engelhartstetten area. After the enemy had crossed the March, there were two days of battle near Markgrafneusiedl. There the SS riders left their position under the 96th Infantry Division and went back under the command of the 37th SS Volunteer Cavalry Division.

In the combat it was clear that the young units quickly lost defensive ability. Again and again, alarmed units were formed with little combat-ready personnel, such as Viennese policemen, and which, without training and equipment, had enormous losses. There was combat until April 18, 1945 in the Kreuztal-Hautzendorf area under their own division command. After the latter was taken out of the front to reform the division, more combat ensued under the 96th Infantry Division. Finally the SS Battle Group "Ameiser" was also taken out of action and marched via Znaim to the Freistadt area. There it at first secured the area in connection with the 3rd SS Panzer Division, and then surrendered to American troops.

One month after the formation of the SS Battle Group "Ameiser", *SS-Standartenführer* Gesele was ordered on March 26, 1945 to assemble another battle group for front action. Subordinated to the 6th SS Panzer Army, it was supposed to help stop the Red Army's advance from the Oedenburg/Sopron area. Under the command of the Leader of the SS Volunteer Cavalry Regiment 93, *SS-Sturmbannführer* Keitel,[94] the battle group of some 1,600 men was subordinated to the I. SS Panzer Corps in the Wiener-Neustadt area as of April 1, 1945. On the next day the battle group prevented the enemy from entering the Siering Valley west of Ternitz, and later occupied positions in the Grünbach-Puchberg area. In the hilly country with few roads usable by heavy vehicles, the German troops were able to hold up the enemy advance. Here too, the SS Battle Group "Keitel" was able to assert itself in partially heavy fighting.

On May 7, 1945 what remained of the SS Battle Group "Keitel" left their positions and marched via Schwarzau to Altenmarkt. Since the Enns formed the demarcation line between the U.S. troops and the Red Army, they tried to go into American imprisonment. A connection with the command of the 37th SS Volunteer Cavalry Division, whose staff was in Beching/Bechyne (south of Prague), could no longer be made, so the troops went into imprisonment separately.

The then *SS-Untersturmführer* Simon recalls:

> "I was sent on February 11, 1945, as an SS-Standarten-Oberjunker, from the SS Cavalry School in Göttingen to the newly formed 37th SS Cavalry Division and took quarters in Deutschwagram for the 8th Squadron. At the end of the month came the son of old Keitel as Regimental Leader of the SS Cavalry Regiment 93. The Regiment Staff was 18 miles from us in Obersiebenbrunn in a castle in which Keitel's introduction also took place. The people arrived gradually, just Hungarians 16 to 18 years old, moderately enthusiastic, and were supposed to free their homeland from the Russians. The cadre personnel were left from the 8th SS Cavalry Division and came from Pecs, Hungary. The command language was German, translated into Hungarian by interpreters. The equipment was still comparatively good, likewise the horses from Hungary and East Horse Hospital. In two months it was tried to teach the men a soldier's basic concepts plus discipline, steadfastness and above all, handling weapons. In view of the short time, it was somewhat successful.

---

94 The son of Field Marshal Keitel, as Leader of the SS Volunteer Cavalry Regiment 17 of the 22nd SS Volunteer Cavalry Division, was awarded the German Cross in Gold on February 6, 1945.

From March 26 to 30, 1945, I was sent to Untersiebenbrunn as a loading officer. The unloading goal was Wiener Neustadt.

Then, because of the advancing Russians, we went toward Pottenstein, north into the Wienerwald via Heiligenkreuz and Grub to Klausenleopoldsdorf. We dug in at the Schoepflgitter – to our right were parts of the 12th SS Division, to the left the 1st Panzer Division. Here there were many losses. The battles moved over the Schoepfl, which the Russians unfortunately occupied before us and could not be removed from, since they only needed to through hand grenades down. An attempt by our unit commander with leaders also failed.

Graduates of the Combat School in Wiener Neustadt replaced us. In the first night, not knowing the Russian combat tactics, they left the thick underbrush and, instead of guarding, took a nap and lost 15 dead with cutthroats. The old colonel whom I greeted the previous evening, and who wanted to know the Russians better, was nearly hysterical.

In a motorized march we went into the Paxtal to the still-standing Gasthaus Hutbauer. There the command post of the II./SS Battle Group "Keitel" was also set up. My post was the Hutbauer Chapel. Here one could wash himself with 4711 if necessary and change clothes – there was still snow everywhere!

On the evening of May 8, 1945 in a talk with the unit command post the moving of our unit was ordered, for which the greatest caution was recommended. We had not yet heard of the war's end; we were just going toward Mariazell. There we learned when we stopped that the war was over and that we were supposed to cross the Enns at Altenmarkt and turn our weapons over to the Americans.

Nobody can imagine what happened there. Soldiers came from all over, everybody hurried toward Altenmarkt. Convoys came toward us with Honveds with women and children who wanted to get back to Hungary. What was in the way and did not move at once, or did not want to, was pushed down the left slope. Many motor vehicles were abandoned, out of fuel.

On May 10, 1945 we reached the rescuing bridge and surrendered our weapons to the Americans (the so-called Rainbow Division) on the other side."

Thus the history of the 37th SS Volunteer Cavalry Division ended after three months. Like other units, and what with the war situation then, it never attained either the specified strength of personnel or equipment. In any case, two regiment-size battle groups were formed and sent into action. Composed mainly of ethnic Germans inducted in August and September 1944 with at least six months of training behind them, the battle groups were usable as infantry.

The Ethnic Germans in the Ordnungspolizei

While the Wehrmacht and Waffen-SS recruited ethnic Germans mainly from the neighboring areas, resettlement camps and allied countries, the Ordnungspolizei also recruited ethnic Germans to a large extent from the USSR. The total of foreign Germans who served in the Ordnungspolizei during World War II is thus hard to determine. Numerous formations, such as the Selbstschutz or Ordnungsdienst, were *de jure* subordinated to the civil administrations (such as ethnic-group leaders) but were directed and utilized by the Ordnungspolizei. In part, they were also used in the Security Police, for example, in Transnistria, where they ordered the ethnic German Selbstschutz to shoot Romanian Jews.

In all, there were presumably circa 70,000 ethnic Germans in service with the Ordnungspolizei between 1940 and 1945. Of them, approximately:

    1,000 came from Belgium (Eupen-Malmedy)
    8,000 from France (Alsace-Lorraine)
  17,000 from Italy (South Tyrol, Trentino, Kanaltal and Belluno)
    5,000 from Croatia
    1,000 from Luxembourg
    5,000 from Poland
    5,000 from Serbia
    5,000 from Slovenia
  20,000 from the USSR[95]
    3,000 from Hungary.

Some of them were inducted into police battalions and SS police regiments, but most served only in the cities and counties of the annexed, occupied and allied countries. Not rarely, as already noted, they belonged to the Selbstschutz or Ordnungsdienst. Between 5,000 and 10,000 ethnic Germans were also used to guard some 1,000 ghettos and numerous, hard-to-count Jewish work camps, either in Germany or, mainly, in the occupied eastern regions, including the General Government. At first separate from the Waffen-SS concentration camps, in 1943-44 most of the inductees served in them or the so-called Outside Camps. For example, around 170 work camps were run in Silesia, in which, in part, over 50,000 Jewish forced laborers were kept. In 1943 they were administratively subordinated to the Auschwitz and Gross-Risen concentration camps.

The following list of closed formations in which ethnic Germans were placed in large numbers is arranged chronologically. We begin with the units into which the first ethnic Germans were inducted. In the process of locating ethnic Germans in Europe, it happened in the course of the war that more and more troop units were included. At the same time, more ethnic German replacements were naturally inducted from the appropriate defense zones.

---

95   These included men from the old settlement areas in the Ukraine and the Caucasus who were not deported to Siberia in 1941. The first were subordinate to the commander of the Ordnungspolizei under the Highest SS and Police Leader "Ukraine", with the:

Commander of the Ordnungspolizei and Commander of the Gendarmery "Luzk"
Commander of the Ordnungspolizei and Commander of the Gendarmery "Schitomir"
Commander of the Ordnungspolizei and Commander of the Gendarmery "Kiev"
Commander of the Ordnungspolizei and Commander of the Gendarmery "Dnyepropetrovsk"
Commander of the Ordnungspolizei and Commander of the Gendarmery "Tschernikov"
Commander of the Ordnungspolizei and Commander of the Gendarmery "Kharkov"
Commander of the National police and commander of the Gendarmery "Stalino"
Commander of the National police and commander of the Gendarmery "Rostov" and the Commander of the Ordnungspolizei "Black Sea"
Commander of the Ordnungspolizei and Commander of the Gendarmery "Simferopol"
Commander of the Ordnungspolizei and Commander of the Gendarmery "Nikolaiev"

At the end of 1942 there were, in all, 4,228 Germans and ethnic Germans plus 15,665 Ukrainians under the Commanders of the Ordnungspolizei and 5,966 Germans and ethnic Germans plus 55,094 Ukrainians under the Commanders of the Gendarmery. One can see from this that there were some 6,000 ethnic Germans involved, most of them recruited directly from the Ukraine.
The Commander of the Ordnungspolizei "Caucasia" was set up for the Caucasus, with over 2,000 men serving in Gendarmery action commands. Here too, about half consisted of ethnic German volunteers.

1939-1940

As 1939 turned to 1940, the first 6,000 ethnic Germans were inducted into the Ordnungspolizei. It had received some 32,000 new recruits from the Wehrmacht to replace the Field Gendarmery units and the newly forming Police Division. Among them were 6,000 ethnic Germans from Poland and resettlers from the USSR. According to a note from the Chief of the National police of August 20, 1940, 25% of them formed three ethnic German battalions, so that of the 101 existing police battalions, 60 consisted of police reserve men, 3 of ethnic Germans and 38 battalions of native German recruits of the 26,000-man formations. The remaining approximately 4,500 ethnic Germans of this first ethnic German contingent were used mostly in the new formations of the Ordnungspolizei in Defense Zones I, II, III and VIII.

Defense Zone I (Königsberg)

The **Reserve Police Battalion 11** was formed at the end of September 1939 and was in Putulsk in the autumn of 1939. In November 1939 it saw service in Ostrow, ca. 40 km away, in the shooting of Polish civilians. During the Russian campaign beginning in July 1941, it was subordinated to the Higher SS and Police Leader "Russia-North" and guarded, among others, the ghetto in Kauen. In mid-October 1941 parts of the battalion, along with Lithuanian Auxiliary Police, moved into Smolevici, about 280 km away (ca. 40 km east of Minsk). Here, on orders from the 707th Infantry Division, it closed off the area in which the Lithuanian volunteers executed all the city's Jews. The same thing happened on October 27, 1941 in Sluzk (ca. 100 km south of Minsk) along with an action command of the Security Police. There some 300 Jews were shot. Until December 1941, strengthened by the Lithuanian auxiliary police, they murdered Jews, prisoners of war and suspected partisans in, among others, Minsk, Rudensk (ca. 40 km southeast of Minsk), Uzyany (ca. 130 km northeast of Kauen) and Ssmilovici (ca. 40 km southeast of Minsk). In January 1942 two companies saw front service in the Velikiye Luki-Nevel area and Toropez, while the third company remained stationed in Kauen as before. United in Kauen again in May, the battalion formed the **I./Police Regiment 2** in Tilsit in July of 1942.

The **Reserve Police Battalion 12** was formed in September 1939, but disbanded shortly for the formation of the Police Division.

The **Reserve Police Battalion 13** was formed in Schröttersburg at the beginning of 1940 and used, until the Russian campaign began, in Defense Zone XX (Danzig-West Prussia) in the formerly Polish districts – among other things, to guard the ghetto in Plock – and took part in the shooting of numerous Jews and Poles. In July 1941, assigned to the Higher SS and Police Leader "Russia-North", parts of it took part in mass executions of Jews and Communists as of July 22 in the Libau-Priekule-Aizpute-Skeden-Ventspils area. In July 1942 it formed the **II./Police Regiment 2 in Tilsit.**

The **Police Battalion 254** was formed in Königsberg in 1940 and prepared for action in the Netherlands in the autumn of that year. In 1941 the battalion moved to Norway and was integrated into the SS Police Division as a reserve at the end of 1941.

The **Police Battalion 323** was formed in Tilsit in 1940 and marched to the Kovno area in the summer of 1941. There it was used for, among other things, the guarding of the ghetto there. In December 1941 cam front service in the Orsha area against Red Army paratroops. The battalion commander, *Major* Griese, was honored with the Knight's Cross of the Iron Cross. In March 1942 the battalion was in Yelnya, and was then transferred first to Tilsit and from there to Paris as the **II./Police Regiment 4.**

Defense Zone II (Stettin)

The **Police Battalion 21** was formed at the end of September 1939 and used for a time in the General Government. Assigned to the Higher SS as Police Leader (Russia-North) in July 1941 the battalion took part in the shooting of presumably some 25,000 Jews in the woods at Rumbuli, near Riga, Latvia in December 1941. The battalion was then disbanded.

The **Reserve Police Battalion 22** was formed at the end of September 1939 and was located in the General Government in the autumn of 1939. In 1940 it was used to guard the camp near Thorn, which held as many as 20,000 prisoners at times. There were shootings of Jews and Poles there. Ordered back to Stettin, the battalion was subordinated to the Police Regiment "Nord" in view of the Russian campaign. There the three companies were used completely detached from each other. The 1st Company was in Frauenburg and Goldingen, Latvia for a time, while the 2nd Company was used in Riga and the 3rd Company in Mitau. In December 1941 the battalion was reunited in Riga to close off extensive mass executions. In January 1941, again with the Police Regiment "Nord" – subordinated to the 81st Infantry Division in the X. Army Corps – it saw front service between Lake Ilmen and Staraya-Russa. In July 1942 it became the **III./Police Regiment 2.**

Defense Zone III (Berlin)

The **Police Battalion 1** was created in Poland at the end of September 1939 by renaming Police Battalion I/5. It was ordered to the Police Division and disbanded in the autumn of 1939.

The **Reserve Police Battalion 2** was formed in Poland at the end of September 1939 by renaming the Police Battalion I/6. In June 1940 the battalion was moved to Kongsvinger, Norway and stayed there until May 1942. In the restructuring of the Ordnungspolizei into police regiments, the battalion was sent to the Higher SS and Police Leader "Russia-North" in July 1942 and formed the **I./Police Regiment 1.**

The **Police Battalion 3** was formed in Poland at the end of September 1939 by renaming Police Battalion II/6. In May 1940 the battalion was sent to Trondheim, Norway and replaced Reserve Police Battalion 9 in the action groups of the Security Police in the Soviet Union in April 1942. Here the 1st Company of Action Group B, the 2nd Company of Action Group C, the 3rd Company of Action Group D and the 4th Company of Action Group A were subordinated and took part in the numerous mass executions in the Soviet Union. Effective July 9, 1942 the battalion became the **II./Police Regiment 1.**

The **Police Battalion 4** was formed in Poland at the end of September 1939 by renaming Police Battalion III./6. Used to set up the Police Division, it was disbanded already in the autumn of 1939.

The **Police Battalion 5** was also in Poland at the end of September 1939 and was ordered to the Police Division and disbanded in the autumn of 1939.

The **Police Battalion 6** was formed in Poland in September 1939 by renaming Police Battalion II/5.[96] From November 1939 to the late summer of 1940 it was used as Police Battalion "Warsaw I" of Police Regiment "Warsaw". Returned to its home post in Berlin, it was ordered back to the General Government and to the Radom area. Sent to the Higher SS and Police Leader "Russia-Center", it was later subordinated to Police Regiment "Center". In July 1942 it became the **I./Police Regiment 13.**

The **Police Battalion 7** was never set up.

---

96 At the beginning of September 1939 it had already shot Poles and Jews in Bromberg on orders from the Security Police.

The **Police Battalion 8** was formed at the end of September 1939 and, in November 1939, formed Police Battalion "Warsaw II" of the Police Regiment "Warsaw" in the General Government. In the autumn of 1940 it was transferred back to its home post in Berlin and from there, in the summer of 1941, to Upper Carniola. In mid-April 1942 the battalion was disbanded and divided among other police battalions.

The **Reserve Police Battalion 9** was formed at the end of September 1939 and located in Oslo from June 1940 to April 1941. In view of the Russian campaign, a fourth company was formed and the battalion was divided in the action groups of the Security Police: The 1st Company went to Action Group "A" (Army Group "North"), the 2nd Company to Action Group "B" (Army Group "Center"), the 3rd Company to Action Group "C" (Army Group "South"), and the 4th Company to Action Group "D" (11th Army). The 1st Company was used mainly in the Baltic lands and took part in, among others, mass executions of Hochwald/Bikernieki near Riga, Latvia in July and August 1941 and in Krasnogwardeisk (Russia-North) in September 1941. The 2nd company was in White Russia – subordinated to the 221st Securing Division – and took part in shootings in Mogilev, Minsk, Rudnya and Kauen, among others. The 3rd Company was used in, among others, Krivoy Rog, Deiepropetrovsk and Saporosye, and the 4th Company was used in the Caucasus. In April 1942 Reserve police Battalion 9 gathered and moved via Mogilev, Zamosc and Zakopane to Iglau. In July 1942 it was ordered from there back to Norway to guard the Norwegian-Swedish border. Here it also formed the **III./Police Regiment 27.**

The **Police Battalion 10** was formed at the end of September 1939 and was in Warsaw as of December 1939. Effective March 1, 1942 the battalion was first ordered back to Berlin and, a short time later, to Upper Carniola, to the area between Laibach and Kranj. There the battalion formed the **III./SS Police Regiment 1** in July 1942.

The **Reserve Police Battalion 31** was formed at the beginning of 1940 and was in Litzmannstadt for a short time – among other things, to guard the ghetto there. But it was disbanded later in 1940.

The **Reserve Police Battalion 32** was formed at the beginning of 1940 and was in the Protectorate of "Bohemia and Moravia" as of the spring of 1941, subordinated to the Police Regiment "Bohemia" as Police Battalion "Klattau". In the summer of 1941 it was moved to the General Government for forthcoming action in the Russian campaign, then subordinated for a time to Police Regiment "Center". In September 1941 it took part in executions in Lemberg and, at the end of December 1941, marched to the Minsk area. In July 1942 it former the **I./Police Regiment 21/**

Defense Zone VIII (Breslau)

The **Police Battalion 81** was formed at the end of September 1939 in Poland by renaming Police Battalion IV/1 (stationed in Beuthen), and was subordinated to Police Regiment "Warsaw." From 1940 to its disbanding in 1942 the battalion was at first still n Beuthen, Silesia, and was then transferred to Olmütz and Brünn in the Protectorate of "Bohemia and Moravia."

The **Reserve Police Battalion 82** was formed in Kattowitz at the end of September 1939 and was used in the spring of 1940 to arrest Polish intellectuals (such as teachers, officials and doctors). In December 1940 the battalion took part in the deportation of Polish forced laborers to Germany from the Trzebina area (ca. 20 km northeast of Auschwitz). Then it guarded a Jewish ghetto in Chrzanov (ca. 30 km northeast of Auschwitz). In April 1941 it was under the Inspector of the Ordnungspolizei in Breslau, and in July 1941 it was subordinated with Police Regiment 'South" to the 454th Securing Division in the Schitomir area. At the end of August 1941 there were shootings of the male Jewish population there. In September 1941 the battalion was used to locate scattered Red Army men. Via Kiev the battalion marched first to Bryansk and then to Tula, some 280 km away. At the end of 1941 it was sent to Korück 532, and was often used with Police Battalion 309 in the Maloye

Polpins area. From March 1 to 10, 1942 the unit took part again, in the Shukovka-Stary Lavschinia area in the Bryansk region, in Operation "Anton" On April 2, 1942 it was in combat with partisans near Kolozovka, where 15 partisans were shot and eight houses burned down. As of mid-July 1942 the battalion was used in the Gremyach area (ca. 120 km southwest of Bryansk). There it formed the **I./Police Regiment 6.**

The **Reserve Police Battalion 83** was formed in Gleiwitz in the autumn of 1939 and was still subordinated to the Commander of the Ordnungspolizei in Breslau in October 1941. Moved to the General Government, it formed the **I./Police Regiment 24** at Lemberg in July 1942.

The **Reserve Police Battalion 84** was formed in Beuthen in the spring of 1940 with ethnic Germans from Silesia, and was subordinated to the Commander of the Ordnungspolizei in Prag as of April 1941. As Police Battalion "Holleschau" it was subordinated to the Police Regiment "Moravia". In January 1942 the battalion belonged to the Commander of the Ordnungspolizei in Cracow, and at the end of April 1942 it was flown to Krassnogvardeysk. Then came action with the SS Police Division via Lyuban to Volkov. In mid-June 1942 the battalion was disbanded and the men were added to the SS Police Division.

The **Reserve Police Battalion 85** was formed in Kattowicz in the spring of 1940 and used in the General Government until the beginning of 1942. Subordinated to Police Regiment "Center", the battalion moved to the Smolensk area. Back in Kattowitz briefly in July 1942, it was renamed the **II./Police Regiment 13.**

After the western campaign, compulsory military service was introduced in Eupen-Malmedy in the summer of 1940. Here older men were inducted into the police battalions of Defense Zone VI:

Defense Zone VI (Münster)

The **Reserve Police Battalion 61** was formed in Poland at the end of September 1939 out of Police Battalion I/4 (home base Dortmund). Used to guard the Warsaw Ghetto, it was involved in repeated shootings. It was also used in the resettling of Polish families in the General Government. In the spring of 1941 the battalion was returned to its home post, and only in December 1941 was it ordered back to the General Government. There were shootings of 110 Jews in June 1942 as revenge for the murder of German police and soldiers. Then the battalion served under the Higher SS and Police Leader "Russia-North". Relieved a police battalion in Police Regiment "North" and, in July 1942, formed the **I./Police Regiment 9.**

The **Reserve Police Battalion 62** was formed in Poland at the end of September 1939 out of Police Battalion V/1 (home base Essen), and was subordinated to the Commander of the Ordnungspolizei in Cracow. From February to September 1940 the battalion was in Königshütte. Then it was sent to the Lorient area in France, where it was used to protect the Todt Organization on the Atlantic Wall. In Dieppe in July 1942 it formed the **I./Police Regiment 28 "Todt".** In August 1942 the battalion was used in Dieppe in the defense against the Allied command operation.

The **Reserve Police Battalion 63** was formed in Poland in September 1939 out of Police Battalion II/1 (home base Wuppertal). In December 1939 it was integrated into Police Regiment "Cracow". At the beginning of August 1940 the battalion moved to Lorraine and to the Higher SS and Police Leader "West" in the Calais-Lille-Douai-Arras area in northern France, then in September 1940 to Metz.[97] Ordered to Essen in August 1941, it was under the Commander of the Ordnungspolizei in Münster. In March 1942 it was transferred to The Hague. There it formed the **III./Police Regiment 14** in July 1942.

---

97 Here it saw service with Field Command 670, among others.

The **Reserve Police Battalion 64** was formed in Essen at the end of September 1939 and sent to Leslau in October 1939 after a fourth company was formed. There the battalion was briefly separated. The 1st and 3rd Companies were ordered to Gotenhafen and subordinated to the Commander of the Ordnungspolizei in Danzig. In November 1939 the battalion gathered in Graudenz and took part in the resettling of Poles in the General Government. At the end of May 1940 the battalion was ordered to its home base, Essen, and was used in air-raid and patrol service. At the end of June 1941 it was ordered to Belgrade and subordinated for a time to Action Group "E". Then came actions against the Serbian Chetniks in the Uzice-Sabac-Klenac-Skela-Semlin area. There was also action against Jews; the battalion took part in the shooting of some 6,000 Jews on September 26, 1941 in retaliation for the murder of German soldiers in Saymiste. In July 1942 it formed the **I./Police Regiment 5.**

The **Reserve Police Battalion 65 "Cholm"** was formed in Recklinghausen in the autumn of 1939 and transferred to the Netherlands in May 1940. As of November 1940 it served in Assen, the battalion was ordered back to its home base in December. At the end of May 1941 it was ordered to Heilsberg, East Prussia, from where it marched via Tilsit into the Baltic States on June 22, 1941 with Police Regiment "North", subordinated to the 285th Securing Division. Four days later the units took quarters in Kauen and Schaulen, and took part in the Lithuanian pogroms, initiated by the Germans, in Kauen, Schaulen and Raseinen, and later in Pskov. During the German advance the battalion reached Luga in September 1941, and guarded a Soviet prisoner-of-war camp there. During the Soviet winter offensive the battalion saw front service with the Battle Group "Scherer" near Cholm from January to March 1942. At the beginning of June 1942 the battalion was sent via Luga to Brunovici near Cracow. Then came action to empty the Cracow Ghetto as part of Action "Reinhard" and to escort the Jewish transports to Auschwitz and Belzec. In the Lublin area it formed the **I./Police Regiment 25.**

The **Reserve Police Battalion 66** was formed in Cologne at the beginning of 1940 and transferred to Lorraine at the end of June 1940. At the beginning of August 1940 it was ordered to Tilburg in the Netherlands, and in December 1940 back to its home base. In May 1942 it was sent back to the Netherlands, and in The Hague it formed the **I./Police Regiment 3.**

The **Reserve Police Battalion 67** was formed in Essen in May 1940 and ordered to The Hague in the Netherlands. In February 1942 the battalion was ordered back to Essen, and from there to Lublin at the end of May 1942 as the **II./Police Regiment 25.**

The **Reserve Police Battalion 68** was formed in Cologne in June 1940 and sent to the Commander of the Ordnungspolizei in The Hague. From December 15, 1940 to April 23, 1941 the battalion was in Assen. Until July 10, 1941 it was used in Rotterdam, and then in Amsterdam until the war's end. In July 1942 it formed the **II./Police Regiment 3** there.

The **Reserve Police Battalion 69** was formed in Cologne in the summer of 1940 and transferred to The Hague in June 1940. In the spring of 1941 it was ordered to the General Government for the coming eastern campaign and enlarged to five companies. In September 1941 they were used separately (partly subordinated to action groups) in Army Groups "South", "Center" and "North". In July 1942 it formed the **III./Police Regiment 17.**

Alexander Zaharov reported voluntarily to the Police Battalion "Ostland" at a Main-Franconian resettlement camp for ethnic Germans from Estonia. At Frankfurt on the Oder in August 1941, it was then renamed Reserve Police Battalion 33 in October 1941.

1941

Another police battalion composed solely of resettlers from the USSR (Baltic Germans) was formed in Defense Zone III and called "Ostland". In October 1941 it was numbered **Reserve Police Battalion 33** of the Ordnungspolizei. In the spring of 1942 it was transferred to the General Commissariat "Ukraine" and used in the Rovno area. Here the battalion was used to guard the ghetto there. After being used in Kiev, it was disbanded in the summer of 1942.

Alexander Zaharov, then a battalion member, recalls:

"I was born on October 26, 1916, the son of a Russian officer and a German mother, and lived in Estonia. Following the Hitler-Stalin pact I was suddenly taken in custody during my work at the trust company and, in a night-and-fog action, taken out of Estonia as an ethnic German! Then I lived at first in a refugee or resettlement camp in Mainfranken and, with other ethnic Germans, reported for military service in July 1941. We had been assured we would be used in Estonia to fight the remaining Red Army troops. In August 1941 we went to the Police Battalion "Ostland" at Frankfurt on the Oder. Against our wishes, we were then not sent to Estonia, but to the Kiev area in October 1941. Here we were divided among various police districts – I went to the 5th District. Here we did normal police work: for example, we once received a notice that a Ukrainian family was always selling clothing at the market, presumably from deceased and already buried people. That's how it was then. In July 1942 the battalion was disbanded and most of us were sent to the Estonian Ss Legion."

In the summer of 1941, the forming of ethnic German auxiliary police companies also began. They grew until the end of 1941 with Serbian volunteers to five Police Volunteer Regiments (1-3 "Serbia" plus "Montenegro" and "Sandjak") with some 15,000 men. In the first three regiments, at least until the forming of the SS volunteer Mountain Division "Prinz Eugen", many ethnic Germans served. As of the autumn of 1942, mainly older men were still in the regiments. An ethnic German from Ernsthausen[98] (the Gross-Betschkerek region) remembers in his dialect-flavored writing style:[99]

"In September 1941 those born in 1919 and 1920 were mustered in the county seat, Gross-Betschkerek, and those men who were found fit to serve were inducted into the police on 10/20/1941 and had to report in Gross-Betschkerek on the named day. We took positions in rows of five, and each row was then made a company. We were divided among the following cities in the Banat: Werschetz, Weisskirchen, Pantschova, Kikinda and Betschkerek.

I went to Werschetz. On the evening of the same day we went to Werschetz and arrived at the station shortly after midnight. We were greeted by our future instructors and escorted to the garrison. We gathered according to our hometowns and occupied our assigned night quarters. At 7:00 A.M. we were awakened, at 8:00 we fell in and were then greeted by our future Company Chief (Hauptmann G., a Viennese). After his greeting we were divided by size, and the company then divided into three platoons and numbered well over 100 men. Within two weeks we received two pairs of uniforms. Now the training began.

At our first session it was made clear to us that we belonged to the SS Police and were subordinated to the SS and Higher Police Leader Dalige. Now, though, there was not much enthusiasm among us; most of us didn't want to do it and pretended to be sick. Then the matter came to Hauptmann G's ears. G assigned six doctors and had the whole company thoroughly examined, after which 12 men were released because of illness. Then they said, You are all good healthy men, and now we want to get on with the training without any hindrance.

The training was tough, and the instructors were ruthless in their work. The many lessons that we had were very educational, also for later civilian life. The instruction was given mostly by Oberleutnant G., who was an active German police officer and came from central Germany. G was an exemplary German police officer and treated us as if we were his children. In my whole military time I never again met such an officer.

---

98 Banatski Despotovac.
99 Documented by the Center Against Expulsion, Wiesbaden.

After six weeks of training we were sworn in. Our battalion commander from Belgrade appeared, Major J. When J. arrived, all the preparations for swearing in were made. J. gave a speech first about the sense and purpose of the oath and added that after taking the oath nothing more was to be thought about staying by one's mother's or wife's apron. Now J asked who believed he could not live up to the oath: Hands up. About 60 men held their hands up. First he asked a man named Bischof why he could not live up to the oath. B. answered: For economic reasons. J. answered: You'll have a servant. Now about 30 of the 60 hands were still raised. The next one was asked. I see badly. Answer: You'll get glasses. There was only one hand up. Question: What do have? Answer: Flat feet. Answer: You'll get insoles. And we took the oath and were then led to the office to sign an oath declaration. A great many did not want to sign the declaration and were removed from the office. They had to catch up the next day and were ridiculed by the instructor: stuffed shirts, traitors, etc. – Now there were nice, well-organized comradeship evenings during our training, the officers went from man to man and table to table. As for furloughs: Every 3 to 4 weeks a short furlough, married men first.

Now the training was finished in February 1942. We were then distributed among larger police stations in the Banat and subordinated to the appropriate government offices: Modosch, Werschetz City and Country. Through this distribution the company was broken up, and we were then released from the SS Police, and our uniforms were taken; in place of them we received black uniforms with boots. Then those born in 1917=-1918 was inducted after us. Our police chief in Modosch was Loch from Sartscha, Banat. I was then in Modosch until May 1, 1942 and was released from police service on that day. On May 15, 1942 I was called into the volunteer SSDivision "Prinz Eugen", Commanded by SS-Obergruppenführer Artur Phleps. I went to the 1st Regiment in Werschetz.

When I was directed by the regiment to report to the 7th Company, I was introduced to the company chief, was immediately made an instructor and given a group, as were all my comrades; all who came from the police became instructors, since they were short of instructors. The space in the workers' home where the company was housed were so cramped that we lay man to man. Then our battalion, after about ten weeks, was transferred to Karlsdorf in the sandy region, where we were again housed in crowded guesthouses. Again we had to swear an oath to the Führer. Furthermore, I would like to add that we were forbidden to wear the SS emblems in the SS Volunteer Division "Prinz Eugen"; we wore the Odalsrune (Respect and Ground); only the native Germans wore the SS emblems.

As far as I can remember, the division began to transfer to Serbia in August 1942. The division staff came to Kralyevo; our battalion, which was in Karlsdorf had rail-line watching to Kubin on the Danube, where the troops were ferried across to Mitrovica. We went as the last in October 1942. We came to Uzice, where the [staff] of the 1st Regiment was, plus the engineer battalion. Before we got to Uzice we had to go right into action at Kralyevo and were in the hills and forests two weeks, where we met by plan with Bulgarian troops on a stony hill.

I was not present for the further action in Croatia etc. In 1943 I went to the military hospital in Belgrade, then recovery company; in 1944 I was transferred to Prague and was there until the war ended. I also experienced the uprising in Prague physically, imprisonment, etc."

1942

In addition, there was a battalion for SS Police Regiment 5 formed at first of ethnic Germans, and finally ethnic Germans were sent to the whole regiment until the war ended.

SS Police Regiment 5

The regiment was formed in July 1942 of Police Battalions 64, 322 and one new III. Battalion formed in Serbia with ethnic Germans from the Banat. Subordinated to the Commander of the Ordnungspolizei in Belgrade, it was usually separated into battalions, and took part in the following actions, among others:

Many ethnic Germans from the old Austro-Hungarian regions, mostly participants on World War I, were inducted into the national police. For lack of numbers, they often received Austrian equipment or weapons, for example here, Mannlicher rifles.

6/28/42	Operation "Enzian" in Slovenia
1/4/43	Fighting partisans in Mitrovica (Kapaonik Mountains) with Bulgarian 24th Division Serbian Volunteer Corps
4/00/43	Operations "Adam" and "Baycetina-Gledic"
7/00/43	Operation "Morgenluft"
8/10-18/43	Operation "Stiefelknecht" in Jastrebac Mountains northwest of Nis
8/19/43	Move from Kragujcvac (ca. 50 km northwest of Nis) to Arandelovac (ca. 50 km south of Belgrade)
9/00/43	Action southwest of Krusevac and northwest of Prokuplye. Area between Mitrovica and Krusevac. Three battalions under Higher SS and Police Leader "Serbia", located in Topola, Kraguyevic and Krusevac.
10/3-8/43	Operation "Maiskolben" in area between Valyevo and Cacak with Bulgarian 24th Division, Serbian Volunteer Corps, among others.
10/10-20/43	Operatrion "Krumm" in Cacak-Uzice-Bayina Basta area on the Drina, to capture partisans fleeing toward eastern Bosnia.
10/31-11/5/43	Operation "Hammelbraten" west of Uzice (south of Cacak)
11/0-12/0/43	Quarters in Topola and Pozega
2/16-3/5/44	Operation "Treibjagd" in Arandelovac area with: III/4. Regiment "Brandenburg" Serbian Volunteer Corps Bulgarian 70th Infantry Regiment
3/19-5/12/44	Operation "Margarethe" (Occupation of Hungary) with XXII. Mountain Corps
5/13/44	Return via Esseg to Serbia in Cacak-Usce-Kralyevo area
6/18-7/3/44	Operation "Endlich" with XXI. Mountain Corps in Albanian-Montenegrin Borderlands with parts of 21st Waffen Mountain Division of SS "Skanderbeg"
6/00/44	Operation "Trumpf" in western Morave Mountains area with Bulgarian 27th Division
7/16-28/44	Operation "Draufgänger" in Berane area, Montenegro, with 21st Waffen Mountain Division of SS "Skanderbeg" SS Volunteer Mountain Rifle Regiment 14
8/5-22/44	Operation "Rübezahl" in area southeast of Sarajevo with 7th SS Volunteer Mountain Division "Prinz Eugen" 13th Waffen Mountain Division of SS "Handschar" 21st Waffen Mountain Division of SS "Skanderbeg"

Because of the tense situation, the regiment was sent to the LXIX. Army Corps in the Valyevo area and moved into the area south of Belgrade at the beginning of October 1944. Until mid-October 1944 the regiment was in heavy defensive fighting there and, by the beginning of November 1944, drew back via Mitrovica and Semlin to the area south of Sid. It was under the Battle Group z.b.V "Stephan", which consisted mainly of remainders of the shattered German troops from the Belgrade area. Serving in the XXXIV. Army Corps or the Corps Group "Kübler", the regiment was in the area northwest of Vinkovici in mid-December 1944. Until the beginning of April 1945 the unit moved into the Kopreinitz area on the Drava and marched at the end of the month via Legrad in the direction of the old Reich border to Austrian going into Western Allied imprisonment there.

In August 1942 compulsory military service was introduced in Alsace and Lorraine as well as Luxembourg. Here too, all the older men were called into the National police of Defense Zones V (Alsace) and XII (Lorraine and Luxembourg). Some of them saw service with the police battalions of the defense zones.

Defense Zone 5 (Stuttgart)

The **Reserve Police Battalion 51** was formed in September 1939 and first sent to the General Government to Pionki near Radom, in the autumn of 1939. In the summer of 1940 it marched into Alsace in the Saverne area (northwest of Strasbourg). In 1941 it saw action in the Protectorate of "Bohemia and Moravia", and at the beginning of 1942 it was ordered to Alsace. Transferred at the end of April 1942 to Reichshof (Rzeszov) in the General Government, it was ordered on May 8, 1942 to the Commander of the Higher SS and Police Leader "Russia-Center". After battles with partisans along the Mogilev-Bobruisk road, the battalion was renamed **I./Police Regiment 14** in July 1942.

The **Reserve Police Battalion 52** was formed in Karlsruhe in September 1939, but ordered shortly after to set up the Police division and disbanded.

The **Reserve Police Battalion 53** was formed in September 1939 and sent to the Protectorate of "Bohemia and Moravia". In the summer of 1941 it formed the I./Police Regiment 'Nord' and went into front service with the X. Army Corps

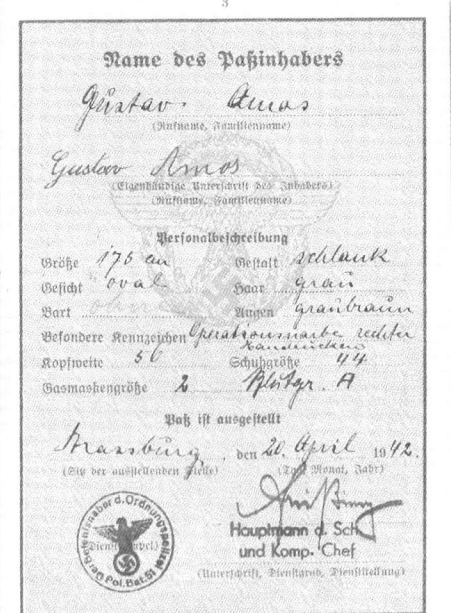

Gustav Amos was born on January 28, 1907 in Wolfskirchen, Alsace and entered Reserve Police Battalion 51 in Strasbourg on February 11, 1942.

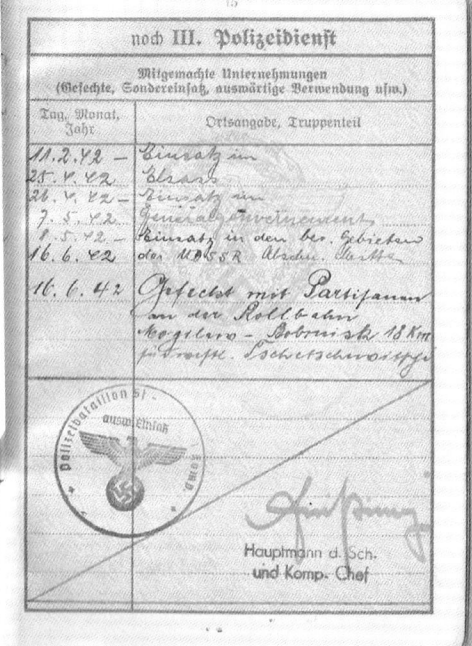

Ordered to the USSR on May 8, 1942, he died just five weeks later in combat with partisans.

near Starya Russa south of Lake Ilmen in January 1942. In July 1942 the battalion became the **III./Police Regiment 22** and stayed on the main battle line before Demyansk until transferred to Warsaw in September 1942.

The **Police Battalion 54** was formed in September 1939. Transferred to Strasbourg in Alsace in June 1940, it was disbanded shortly thereafter.

The **Police Battalion 55** was formed in September 1939 and transferred to Colmar. Like Battalion 54, it was already disbanded in the summer of 1940.

The **Reserve Police Battalion 56** was formed at the beginning of 1940 and sent to the Commander of the Ordnungspolizei in Prague. At the end of February 1942 the battalion was flown to the "Jeckeln" Police Battle Group, which was to release the 58th Infantry Division from the siege ring near Pushkin before Leningrad. Effective July 9, 1942 the battalion was renamed the **I./Police Regiment 16** there.

Defense Zone XII (Koblenz)

The **Reserve Police Battalion 121** was set up in September 1939 and transferred to the Diedenhofen area in Lorraine at the beginning of 1941. In January 1942 it was under the Commander of the Ordnungspolizei in Saarbrücken, and a month later it was ordered to the Police Battle Group "Jeckeln" in the siege ring before Leningrad. Here it formed the **IV./Police Regiment 16** in July 1942.

The **Reserve Police Battalion 122** was formed in Mannheim in the autumn of 1939 and transferred in June 1940 to the Metz area in Lorraine, just recaptured in the western campaign. During the eastern campaign it was sent to the Higher SS and Police Leader "Russia-Center" and formed the **II./Police Regiment 14** there in July 1942.

The **Reserve Police Battalion 123** was formed in Wiesbaden in the autumn of 1939 and transferred to the General Government. At the beginning of 1941 it was ordered to Luxembourg, and in the summer of 1941 to the Cilli-Krsko (German "Gurkfeld") area in Slovenia. Ordered to Hallendorf (Salzgitter) in the autumn of 1941, it served in Norway as of June 1942. In the Narvik area it formed the **III./Police Regiment 7** in July 1942.

1943

In the spring of 1943, in the process of the Stalingrad debacle, an exchange of non-serving and trained men took place as at the war's beginning. The Wehrmacht and Waffen-SS turned over the total of 7,500 ethnic German recruits and received the same number of trained men from the Ordnungspolizei, at least for outside police service. In all, they were combined into 12 Police Training Battalions and, after their training, used to fill out SS police regiments.

In Croatia the forming of a German-Croatian Police began as of July 15, 1943 to strengthen the internal safety. The office of the Commander of the Ordnungspolizei "Croatia" was set up in Esseg. Under him were the five Commanders of the Ordnungspolizei[100] in Agram, Esseg, Sarajevo, Banya-Luka and Knim. There were also five Police Volunteer Regiments[101] (1st to 5th "Croatian") formed, with a total of 15 battalions which were supposed to be made up of Croats and older ethnic Germans from Croatia. They were used mainly in fighting against partisans, but some were briefly in action against the Red Army in 1944.

In the "Alpine Foreland" and "Adriatic Coastland" operation zones, compulsory military service was introduced in November 1943. As a result, four police regiments could be set up.

---

100 At the same time, they functioned as district leaders.
101 The designation as a police volunteer regiment corresponded to that of the Waffen-SS volunteer regiment, and was in fact supposed to document that the men were foreign volunteers. Actually, and not merely in the Police, the men were recruited forcibly rather than being solicited as volunteers.

Ethnic German members of the national police in Slovenia.

SS Police Regiment "Bozen"

Effective October 1, 1943, a first police regiment of some 2,000 ethnic Germans from South Tyrol (born 1900 to 1912) was formed by the Commander of the Ordnungspolizei "Bozen" and first called "South Tyrol". After a few days it was renamed as the Police Regiment "Bozen", and on April 16 the letters "SS" were added. At the beginning of March 1944 the 1st Battalion moved from Meran to Fiume, and in May 1944 to Abbazia (west of Fiume). In April 1945 it was transferred to Gorizia, and in May 1945 it surrendered to U.S. troops in Tarvisio.

The II. Battalion remained in Bozen and moved to Belluno in February 1944. Along with the High Mountain School of the Waffen-SS in Predazzo and parts of the "Hermann Göring" Division, it shot 44 suspected partisans and destroyed 245 dwelling houses in the Valle del Biois area in August 1944 (sic!), In September 1944 two companies were moved back to Bozen and took part, among other things, in a retribution action near Travazzo (south of Bozen) in March 1945.

The III. Battalion moved to Rome and, serving the Commander of the Security Police in Rome, took part in the deportation of some 900 Italian Jews on October 18, 1943. On March 22, 1944 Italian partisans carried out an assassination on the II. Company, in which seven policemen died. On the next day, in another attack, 26 policemen lost their lives. In retribution, at first 270 Italian hostages were shot, and then another 335 in the Adriatic caves. The III. Battalion was briefly in action against the 36th US Infantry Division and drew back to Lecco in June 1944. In September 1944 the command followed to Bologna, and in December 1944 to San Stefano di Cadore (Piemonte). At the beginning of 1945 the II. and III. Battalions were joined in Bozen and marched in the direction of the Schluderbach, some 60 km northeast, as the war ended.

A IV. Battalion was set up in Gossensass in April 1944 and was already sent to form the I./Police Regiment "Alpine Foreland" in May 1944.

Police Regiment "Alpine Foreland"

As the second regiment of ethnic Germans from South Tyrol, the Police Regiment "Alpine Foreland" was created in May 1944 by taking over the VI./Police Regiment "Bozen" as its I. Battalion in Gossensass, plus further members of the South Tyrolean Ordnungsdienst in Schlanders. In October 1944 the training ended with a move to the Edolo-(ca. 70 km west of Trient)-Feltre-(ca. 60 km east of Trient)-Belluno (ca. 80 km west of Trient) area and participation in Operation "Monte Grappa" (1779 meters, south of Feltre). The I. Battalion was shattered in combat with partisans in 1945. According to an announcement on January 29, 1945, the regiment was to be renamed **SS Police Regiment 9.**

SS Police Regiment "Brixen"

In October 1944 what remained of SS Police Regiment 26 and South Tyrolean recruits from Bozen, Belluno and Trento formed the Police Regiment "Brixen". On January 1945 the regiment, located in the Brixen area, received the added "**SS**" and was sent to the 31st SS Volunteer Grenadier Division in the Striegau area (south of Jauer) at the end of February 1945. As SS Volunteer Grenadier Regiment 80 it was taken over by the Waffen-SS. In front service as of mid-March 1945, the unprepared regiment was shattered by the Red Army within a few days. A former South Tyrolean member remembers and documents how meager the regiment members' motivation was:

> "In November 1944 I was inducted into the Police Regiment "Brixen". In Brixen we were also trained. When Gauleiter Hofer appeared for our swearing-in at the end of February 1945, many said something to themselves, such as: "I do NOT swear." On the next day we were loaded onto the train and sent to Upper Silesia. Because of the air raids, the train had to stop again and again, and finally we had to leave the train and march on foot. We reached the Schneekoppe area, and I can still remember the villages of Arnsdorf (near Liegnitz) and Boehmisch Leipa. Housed at first in private quarters, we were then supposed to relieve the Wehrmacht on the front for two weeks. In the kilometer-long marches, many got blisters on their feet. Despite the specific order not to open them ourselves, I did that to myself, and then my foot swelled up so much that I was no longer front-capable. That was my great good fortune! In the process of the capitulation, I set out alone

on a woman's bicycle, as a pretended Italian tank-trap builder, toward home, which I reached in May 1945. At the town hall I was then, with other returned men, released from military service."

SS Police Regiment "Schlanders"

In October 1944 the Police Regiment "Schlanders" was formed of members of the South Tyrol Ordenungsdienst. On January 29, 1945 it received the "SS" letters in Schlanders and was moved to the 80x80x80 km Trient-Belluno-Vicenza triangle. Used mainly to protect objects and guard Italian prisoners of war, the regiment marched in mid-April 1945, first to the Cortina d'Ampezzo area some 80 km to the north, and then became Allied prisoners west of there, near Bozen.

1944

In March 1944 Hungary was occupied by German troops. In April 1944 came the general mobilization of the ethnic Germans. Around 5,000 men were inducted into the Ordnungspolizei and, among others, integrated into the SS Police Regiments 1, 6 and 8.

SS Police Regiment 1

The regimental staff was formed in Berlin in July 1942 for Police Battalions 2, 3 and 10, but the battalions were used separately of each other. Thus the:

    I. Battalion with the Higher SS and Police Leader "Russia-North"
    II. Battalion with the Security Police in the East
    III. Battalion in Upper Carniola in the Laibach-Kramberg (Kranj)-Stein (Kamnik) area.

From July 13 until August 1942 the III. Battalion took part in Operation "Enzian" in the Laibach securing area, and in November 1942 it was used in a larger operation in the Franz (Vransko) area. In the spring of 1943 the I. and III. Battalions were transferred to the Marseille area of France for the new formation of Police Regiment 14 which had been shattered on the eastern front.[102] The II. Battalion, then in the territory of the Higher SS and Police Leader "Russia Center and White Ruthenia", formed the I./Police Rifle Regiment 36 in June 1943.

    In August 1944, after almost a year and a half, SS Police Regiment 1 was reformed of men from the II./SS Police Regiment 12, II./SS Police Regiment 20 and III./SS Police Regiment 21. But in October 1944 the II. and III. Battalions were used to form SS Police Regiment 6, so that the regiment at first had only the I. Battalion. In Budapest a new II. Battalion was formed of Ordnungspolizei members and ethnic Germans, and the regiment was transferred to Lausitz before the enclosure of Budapest by the Red Army. Here it was first subordinated to the Division Staff 608 z.b.V. Effective March 12, 1945 the regiment was disbanded. The remaining men were taken into the newly formed SS Police Regiment 29 of the Police Brigade "Wirth", the later 35th SS Police Division.[103]

SS Police Regiment 6

The regimental staff was formed for Police Battalions 82, 311 and 318 at Korück 103 (Army Group "South") in July 1942 and ordered to the Kiev area. At first the battalions were used separately with Police Regiment "South" in the three Army securing divisions:

    Police Battalion   82 with 454th Securing Division
    Police Battalion 311 with 444th Securing Division
    Police Battalion 318 with 213th Securing Division

---
102 The regiment was temporarily known as Police Regiment "Griese" or "Marseille."
103 Compare Michaelis, Rolf, *Die Waffen-SS: Mythos und Wirklichkeit*, Berlin 2006.

As a result of the Soviet winter offensive in the Don, the I. and II. Battalions were ordered to the front in mid-December 1942 and, within a few days, shattered south of Voronesh near Ivanovka at the small Don bend. The remainders (including those of the III. Battalion serving with the 213th Securing Division) were moved to Adlershof (West Prussia) and disbanded there.

After the Hungarian Regent, Admiral von Horthy, planned Hungary's withdrawal from the war, in the course of many German countermeasures, SS Police Regiment 6 was reformed in Hungary by taking over the II. and III./SS Police Regiment 1 as the I. and II. Battalions. A III. and a IV. Battalion were formed with ethnic German recruits. On January 29, 1945 the Army Group "South" requested the release of the four battalions to a quiet front sector in the region of the 2nd Panzer Army. In March and April 1945, three battalions were at the front with the XXII. Mountain Corps (subordinated first to the "Steyrer" Group, then to the 16th SS Panzergrenadier Division). At the end of April 1945 the regiment belonged to the Corps Group Rösener in the Maribor-Dravograd area, and was taken prisoner there.

SS Police Regiment 8

The regimental staff was formed for Police Battalions 91, 111 and 134 at Korück 102 (Army Group "Center") in July 1942. At first the battalions were still used separately with Police Regiment "Center" in the three securing areas of the Army:

Police Battalion   91 with 221st Securing Division
Police Battalion 111 with 403rd Securing Division
Police Battalion 134 with 286th Securing Division

In August 1942 the battalions were in Gomel, and in September 1942 they moved to the Ostrov-Welikiye Luki, almost 200 km wide. In December 1942, resulting from the Soviet winter offensive, came front service on the Don. The regiment was shattered south of Voronesh in January 1943 during the withdrawal to the Donetz, and then disbanded. The remainder formed the I. Battalion of the new Police Rifle Regiment 38 in the spring of 1943.

In October 1944 the police Rifle Regiment 38 was revived and strengthened with Hungarian and Slovakian personnel; the SS Police Regiment 8 was set up anew. There the I./Police Rifle Regiment 38 formed the II. Battalion and ethnic Germans from Hungary and Slovakia formed the I., III. and IV. Battalions, the last two being formed only conditionally. At the end of the month, parts of the regiment reached the LXXII. Army Corps for front service on the Danube in the area north of Paks. On November 13, 1944 the regiment was in Dunavoeldvar, and at the beginning of December 1944 it was subordinated to the 271st People's Grenadier Division. In January 1945 the remainder was taken out of action, transferred to the Protectorate of "Bohemia and Moravia" for restructuring, and finally ordered to Army Group "Weichsel". Along with the newly formed Police Regiment 50, it formed the 1. Police Rifle Brigade, with only three battalions, and was subordinated to Division 610 z.b.V. in the Wilhelmshöhe area southwest of Stettin on the Oder.

On April 20, 1945 the Soviet 65th Army was able to cross the Oder south of Stettin and form a bridgehead near Wilhelmshöhe in the region of SS Police Regiment 8. The 3rd Panzer Army noted in their daily report of April 21, 1945:

> "Resulting from the failure of Police Brigade I, the enemy got a foothold east and north of Pargow and extended the bridgehead on both sides of the Autobahn by attacks with artillery and fighter plane support in the direction of Kolbitzow, Hohenzahden and Kurow."

At this time the fighting ability and morale of many Wehrmacht units had declined, and the SS Police Regiment 8 had no more action capability, not least because of its combination with forcibly inducted ethnic Germans from Hungary and Slovakia. The regiment was coming apart and had to be seen as shattered as of the end of April 1945.

Appendix

Highly Decorated Ethnic Germans

Holders of the Knight's Cross of the Iron Cross

The following 112 ethnic Germans were decorated with the Knight's Cross of the Iron Cross. Those so-called borderland and foreign Germans were included who held foreign nationality, at least by birth. For the sake of completeness, those soldiers born in Czechoslovakia are also included who generally held the status of Sudeten Germans. They were not explicitly dealt with in this book, since they had already been taken back into the German Reich before World War II and thuds n longer called ethnic Germans. For the Baltic Germans it is to be remembered that Estonia and Latvia belonged to Russia until 1918. Thus their nationality in these cases is listed as "Russia"; for example, *Kapitänleutnant* Bätge, who was born in Tallinn (Reval), the capital of Estonia, and was thus a Baltic German.

Abraham, Erich	11/16/21 in Krappitz, Upper Silesia	*Leutnant*, 2./Pz.Gren.Rgt.13	1/20/44
Adolph, Walter	6/11/13 in Fontanelle, Romania	*Hauptmann*, II./JG 26	11/13/40
Adrario, Friedrich	11/29/18 in Piedicollo, Slovenia	*Hauptmann*, II./JG 26	12/26/44
Bätge, Niels	4/19/13 in Tallinn, Russia	*Kapitänleutnant*, 4. S-Flotille	1/4/42
Barth, Eitel-Albert	4/20/15 in Bucharest, Romania	*Oberleutnant*, 4./KG 55	3/24/43
Barz, Herbert	3/16/16 in Grünfelde, Wolhynia	*Unteroffizier*, 3./Pz.Jäg.Abt.519	7/18/44
Behr, Heinrich Baron von	2/26/02 in Renda, Latvia	*Oberst*, Gren.Rgt.200	2/23/44,
		Oberst, Pz.Gren.Rgt.200, Oak Leaves	1/9/45
Bialetzki, Alfons	9/29/19 in Bogutschütz, Poland	*Leutnant*, 1./Gren.Rgt.333	9/17/44
Buck, Friedrich	1/30/22 in Friedensthal, Romania	*SS-Oberscharführer*, SS Kavallerie Regiment 15	1/27/45
Burian, Ewald	7/12/96 in Tschernoqitz, Romania	*Oberst*, Gren.Rgt.980	10/4/44
Dettke, Oskar	1/1/13 in Dimitrovgrad, Russia	*Hauptmann*, 9./KG 55	4/7/45
Ekesparre, Arthur von	1/8/13 in Ennenküll, *Estonia*	*Oberstleutnant*, 13.Pz.Div.	1/15/45
Enssle, Alfred	6/18/12 in Minischtal, Hungary	*Hauptmann*, 3./KG 76	12/31/43
Erasmus, Dr. Johannes	10/24/13 in Atmagea, Romania	*Major*, XXXXVIII. Pz.Korps	4/13/44
Ermoneit, Helmut	1/15/19 in Wielkieten, Lithania	*Oberleutnant*, KG 4	8/8/44
Fiedler, Alex	8/10/22 in Huszt, CSR	*Leutnant*, 3./Gren.Rgt.200	10/16/44
Fölkersam, Adrian von	12/20/14 in St. Petersburg, Russia	*Leutnant*, I./Lehr-Rgt.Z.b.V.800	9/14/42
Frieb, Erwin	7/13/24 in Mährisch-Ostrau, CSR	*Leutnant*, 1./Art.Rgt.1558	2/19/45
Fröhlich, Stefan	10/7/89 in Orsova, Hungary	*Generalmajor*, JG 76	7/4/40
Göttler, Waldemar	12/12/15 in Sumy, Ukraine	*Feldwebel*, Frontaufkl.Kdo.201	8/2/43
Goldbruch, Kurt	8/13/19 in Tetschen, CSR	*Oberleutnant*, 8./Schlachtgeschw.1	1/28/45
Grohmann, Franz	10/16/19 in Noxdorf, CSR	*SS-Obersturmführer*, 1./SS PGR 3	8/23/44
Grüner, Rudolf	1/18/23 in Brünn, CSR	*SS-Unterscharführer*, Rgt.Mohr	3/10/45
Harden, Alfred	5/30/16 in Libau, Russia	*Hauptmann*, II./Pz.Gren.Rgt.29	2/10/45
Heidrich, Kurt	11/12/19 in Schladnig, CSR	*Oberleutnant*, 5./FlakAbt.314	10/24/44
Hillebrand, Franz	12/19/20 in Bozen, Italy,	*Oberjäger*, 1./Geb.Jäg.Btl.94	4/5/44
Hintz, Erwin	7/7/23 in Willkowischken, Lithania	*Obergefreiter*, 8./Pz.Gren.Rgt. 6	3/11/45
Hoffer-Sulmthal, Herbert	1/18/20 in Karlsbad, CSR	*Leutnant*, II./Schlachtgeschw.77	8/8/44
Holtzy, Theodor	9/15/20 in Waltrowitz, CSR	*Wachtmeister*, Aufkl.Abt.7	6/9/44
Hrdlicka, Franz	1/15/20 in Maxdorf, CSR	*Hauptmann*. II./JG 77	10/18/44
Hübner, Ekhard	5/30/20 in Hohenstadt, CSR	*Leutnant*, 7./JG 3,	5/3/42
Hulha, Alois	10/2/21 in Hostomitz, CSR	*Oberleutnant*, 6./KG 53	3/17/45

Name	Birth	Rank/Unit	Date
Jäckel, Egbert	10/16/19 in Raspenau, CSR	*Leutnant*, 3./Stuka-Geschw.2	5/14/42
Jürgensen, Justus	8/14/97 in Tashkent, Russia	*Engineer*, 5./Eng.Ers.&Ausb.Btl.3	2/5/45
Kamski, Johann	10/23/22 in Janow, Poland	*Obergefreiter*, 14./Grcn.Rgt.z.b.V.,	4/30/45
Keussler, Friedrich von	1/25/07 in St. Petersburg, Russia	*Oberst*, Gren. Rgt. 1	2/23/44
Klimek, Robert	4/1/20 in Kattowitz, Poland	*Oberfeldwebel*, 14./Kampfgeschwader 27	6/9/44
Köhler, Georg	7/24/17 in Nizhni Petropalovska, Russia	*Leutnant*, 3./Pz.Gren.Rgt.26	1/3/43
Köllner, Jürgen	1/16/18 in Welikiye Ustug, Russia	*Hauptmann*, II./Gren.Rgt.671	5/4/44
Kohlhaas, Karl	1/13/05 in St. Petersburg, Russia	*Major*, III,.Füs.Rgt."G.D."	11/21/42
Kral, Ruprecht	12/18/19 in Nispitz, CSR	*Unteroffizier*, 14./Gren.Rgt.19	5/15/44
Kreuzinger, Othmar	9/9/19 in Römerstadt, CSR	*Oberleutnant*, 4./Pz.Aufkl.Abt.19	5/14/44
		625th Oak leaves	10/18/44
Krombholz, Franz-Josef	8/13/20 in Oberpolitz, CSR	*SS-Hauptsturmführer*, III./SS Frw.Geb.Jäg.Rgt.14	3/28/45
Kursell, Hans	4/6/10 in Reval, Russia	*Hauptmann*, Gren. Rgt. 3,	10/17/44
Langer, Albert	9/5/24 in Kunzendorf, CSR	*Gefreiter*, I./Gren.Rgt.51	4/7/44
Lehmann, Waldemar	4/29/13 in Pallasovka, Russia	*Hauptmann*, II./Gren.Rgt.3	8/19/44
Liebisch, Franz	2/5/21 in Georgswalde, CSR	*SS-Obersturmführer*, 8.SSKav.Div."Florian Geyer"	2/9/45
Lipinski, Hans, Dr.	2/20/16 in Czernowitz, Romania	*SS-Obersturmführer*. 1./SS Flak.Abt.18	1/2/45
Lüth, Wolfgang	10/15/13 in Riga, Russia	*Oberleutnant* U 138	10/24/40
		142nd Oak Leaves	11/13/42
		29th Swords *Kapitänleutnant*, U 181	4/15/43
		7th Diamonds *Korvettenkapitän*, U 181	8/9/43
Mühlen, Hans-Heinrich von	8/5/12 in Dorpat, Russia	*Oberleutnant*, 2./JG 3	2/28/45
Münster, Leopold	12/13/20 in Pohorsch, CSR	*Feldwebel*, II./JG 3, 12/21/42	5/12/44
		471st Oak Leaves, *Leutnant*, 5./JG 3	
Neumann, Rudolf	9/24/20 in Raspenau, CSR	*Hauptmann*, 2./Schlachtgeschw.1	4/17/45
Nitsch, Hermann	9/13/21 in Podszuhnen, Lithuania	*Obergefreiter*, 6./Art.Rgt.11	3/23/45
Nossek, Rainer	5/5/20 in Huttendorf, CSR	*Fahnenjunker-Feldwebel*,, 20./Schlachtgeschw.3	10/29/44
Nottenbeck, Jürgen von	4/20/17 in Pernau, Russia	*Hauptmann*, I./Gren.Rgt.94	1/21/45
Obschil, Alois	11/21/19 in Langendorf, CSR	*SS-Untersturmführer*, 2./Grenadier Rgt.1126	3/28/45
Öhrn, Victor	10/21/07 in Kedabek, Russia	*Kapitänleutnant*, U 37	10/21/40
Pape, Walter	12/20/14 in Balagansk, Russia	*Unteroffizier*, 5./Inf.Rgt.211	3/7/41
Paschke, Werner	9/17/20 in Tarnowitz, Poland	*Oberleutnant*, 3./Gren.Rgt.161	8/19/44
Phleps, Artur	11/29/81 in Birthaelm, Romania	*SS-Grupperführer*, 7./SSFreiw.Geb.Div."Prinz Eugen",	7/4/43
		670th Oak Leaves, V.SS Gebirgs-Korps,	11/24/44
Phoenix, Harry	1/3/13 in Szagarren, Russia,	*SS-Hauptsturmführer*, II./SS Art.Rgt.8	2/21/45
Piechulla, Alois	6/21/21 in Weidenmoor, Poland	*Gefreiter*, 2./Pz.Gren.Rgt.33	4/14/43
Pirhofer, Ernst	1/12/22 in Meran, Italy	*Obergefreiter*, 7./FlakRgt.43	5/4/44
Pollak, Johann	6/7/22 in Lindenau, CSR	*Obergefreiter*, I./Gren.Rgt.434,	5/4/44
Preussler, Wilhelm	12/3/19 in Antoniwald, CSR	*Oberfeldwebel*, 12./Gren.Rgt.12	6/9/44
Renteln, Ewert von	4/11/93 in Bremerfeld, Russia	*Oberstleutnant*, Kos.Gren.Rgt.360	1/13/45,
Richter, Bruno	11/23/14 in Bechtcice, Russia	*Rittmeister*, Div.Aufkl.Abt.24	11/26/44
		825th Oak Leaves	4/8/45
Richter, Franz	10/1/22 in Petersdorf, CSR	*Gefreiter*, 1./Pz.Gren.Rgt.114	5/14/44
Richter, Walther	5/30/19 in Radau, CSR	*Oberfeldwebel*, 5./KG 53	2/28/45
Riedel, Franz	12/2/21 in Teschen, CSR	*SS-Obersturmführer*, 7./SS Panzer Regiment 10	3/28/45
Riedel, Walter	4/6/19 in Alt Harzdorf, CSR	*Leutnant*, 3./Pz.Gren.Rgt.73	4/14/43

Name	Birth	Rank/Unit	Date
Riehs, Otto	8/12/21 in Marienbad, CSR	*Obergefreiter*, 14./Gren.Rgt.55	10/11/43
Rinkowski, Leo	9/14/24 in Blumfelde, Poland	*Gefreiter*, 5./Gren.Rgt.670	9/21/44
Romm, Oskar	12/18/19 in Haindorf, CSR	*Oberfeldwebel*, I./JG 51	2/29/44
Rudler, Oskar	10/10/21 in Geishausen, France,	*Gefreiter*, 3./Jäg.Rgt.229	4/5/45
Ruppert, Hermann	8/8/15 in Irbit, Russia	*Oberleutnant*, 6./Stuka Geschw.77	11/23/41
Saürbruch, Peter	6/5/13 in Zürich, Switzerland	*Hauptmann*, K.Gr."Saürbruch"	1/4/43,
Sayn-Wittgenstein, Heinrich	8/14/16 in Copenhagen, Denmark	*Hauptmann*,9./NJG 2,	10/7/42,
		290th Oak Leaves, *Hauptmann*, IV./NJG5,	8/31/43
		44th Swords, Major, NJG 2	1/23/44
Schäfer, Oskar	1/16/21 in Nixdorf, CSR	*SS-Untersturmführer*,	4/29/45
		3./Schwere SS Panzer Abt.503	
Scherling, Ewald	9/26/21 in Dabrova, Poland	*Obergefreiter*, 9./Gren.Rgt.15	1/26/44
Schmitzer, Franz	9/9/20 in Bruex, CSR	*Obergefreiter*, 4./Art.Rgt.6	9/26/42
Schnaubelt, Alois	1/16/21 in Wachtel, CSR	*SS-Unterscharführer*, 3./SS FlakAbt.5	11/16/44
Schneider, Otto	9/28/31 in Schasslowitz, CSR	*SS-Obersturmführer*, 7./SS Panzer Rgt.5	5/4/44
Schön, Rudolf	11/6/21 in Grumberg, CSR	*Leutnant*, 3./Eng.Battalion 8	12/12/44
Schütt, Christian	2/3/17 in Terkellsbuell, Denmark	*Oberfeldwebel*, 1./Schlachtgeschw.1	11/18/44
Schultz, Harald	11/10/95 in Westerotten, Russia	*Generalmajor*, 24.Pz.Div.	4/5/45
Schultz, Heinrich	11/9/19 in Josefow, Poland	*Gefreiter*, 3./Eng.Btl.161	10/18/41
Semelka, Waldemar	1/8/20 in Domeschau, CSR	*Leutnant*, 4./JG 52	9/4/42
Siebenthaler, Richard	7/4/09 in Alexandrovka, Russia	*Oberfeldwebel*, 6./Pz.Rgt.2	4/14/45
Sonne, Heinrich	7/23/17 in Riga, Russia	*SS-Obersturmführer*, I. SS Infanterie-Brigade	12/10/43
Stahl, Hendrik	7.24.21 in Copenhagen, Denmark	*Leutnant*, III./StG.2	12/23/42
Strapatin, Stefan	10/15/22 in Ofzenitza, Romania	*SS-Rottenführer*, II./SS Frw. Panz.Gren.Rgt.49	11/16/44
Strehlau, Erwin	4/18/23 in Pultusk, Poland	*Gefreiter*, 2./Pz.Gren.Rgt.5	6/9/44
Syrowy, Jan	1/7/22 in Gniev, Poland	*Unteroffizier*, 3./Reiter Rgt.32	4/30/45
Tanzer, Kurt	11/1/20 in Moscow, USSR	*Oberfeldwebel*, 12./JG 51	12/5/43
Theissig, Franz	6/10/20 in Losdorf, CSR	*Unteroffizier*, 13./Gren.Rgt.32	4/14/45
Tichy, Ernst	8/26/22 in Mährisch-Ostrau, CSR	*Oberleutnant*, IV./JG 3	1/14/45
Tiesenhausen, Hans-Fr.	2/22/13 in Riga, Russia	*Kapitänleutnant*, U 331	1/27/42
Valtiner, Helmuth	10/7/19 in Lana, Italy	*Gefreiter*, 1./Geb.Jäg.Rgt.143	6/13/41
Weber, Franz	6/13/20 in Ober-Futok, Hungary	*Obergefreiter*, 8./Jäg.Rgt.28	10/28/44
Weichsel, August	10/7/25 in Minciuna, Romania	*Unteroffizier*, 6./Gren.Rgt.948	4/30/45
Wendrinsky, Gustav	1/24/23 in Bratislava, CSR	*SS-Oberscharführer*, 1./SS Pz.Jäg.Abt. 8	1/27/45
Wendt, Wolf	2/26/20 in Schrotthaus, Poland	*Hauptmann*, Gren.Rgt.88	8/12/44
Werra, Franz von	7/13/14 in Lenk, Switzerland	*Oberleutnant*, II./JG 3	12/14/40
Westberg, Günter	4/7/18 in Dorpat, Estonia	*Leutnant*, 1./Aufkl.Abt.8	1/31/45
Wittmer, Heinrich	2/28/10 in Bordeaux, France	*Hauptmann*, III./KG 55	11/12/41
Woidich, Franz	1/2/21 in Znoymo, CSR	*Leutnant*, 3./JG 52	6/11/44
Wolf, Karl	5/21/22 in Königshan, CSR	*Unteroffizier*, II./Gren.Rgt.432	2/28/45
Wolff, Hans von	3/19/03 in Lindenberg, Russia	*Hauptmann*, I./Schützen Rgt.8,	7/13/40
		Hauptmann, I./Schützen Rgt.28	1/16/42
		61st Oak Leaves,	
Wurdak, Franz	9/5/21 in Negranitz, CSR	*Feldwebel*, 4./Div. Füs.Btl.137	9/13/43
Zerth, Jakob	11/23/23 in Volka Tarnovska, Poland	*Gefreiter*, 3./Gren.Rgt.467	4/21/44
Zwesken, Rudi	8/13/19 in Marschendorf, CSR	*Oberfeldwebel*, 6./JG 300	3/21/45

Holders of the Close Combat Badge in Gold

The following ethnic Germans were decorated with the Close Combat Badge in Gold. Again, those so-called border and foreign Germans are listed who, at least at birth, had foreign nationality.

Name	Birth	Rank/Unit	Date
Bialetzki, Alfons	9/20/19 in Bogutschütz, Poland	*Oberleutnant*, Gren.Rgt.333,	11/17/44
Buck, Friedrich	1.30.22 in Friedensthal, Romania	*SS-Oberscharführer*, SS Kavallerie Regt.15	1/27/45
Christian, Arthur	8/4/22 in Ulmbach, Romania	*SS-Rottenführer*, 15./SS Pz.Gren.Rgt.4,	3/15/43
Homolka, Franz	12/21/21 in Glitt, Romania	*SS-Unterscharführer*, 1./SS Pz./Gren.Rgt.9	1/28/45
Lehmann, Waldemar	4/29/13 in Palatovka, Russia	*Hauptmann*, II./Gren.Rgt.3	5/15/44
Papp, Soltan	7/18/17 in Lasko, Hungary	*SS-Unterscharführer*, 1./SS Pz.Gren.Rgt. 9	1/28/45
Phoenix, Harry	1/13/19 in Szagarren, Latvia	*SS-Hauptsturmführer*, II./SS Artillerie Regiment 8	2/21/45
Seebach, Walter	11/5/21 in Heerlen, Netherlands	*SS-Obersturmführer*, 5./SS Pz.Gren.Rgt.24	3/16/44
Zakel, Johann	3/1/21 in Gross Basseln, Romania	*Obergefreiter*, Pz.Aufkl.Abt.11	10/30/43

BIBLIOGRAPHY

Bosse, Heinrich, *Der Führer ruft*, Berlin, 1941.

Christian, Dr. Ernst, *Europäische Armee im Zweiten Weltkrieg*, Nürnberg, 1985.
Christian, Dr. Ernst, *Volksdeutsche und der Zweite Weltkrieg*, Nürnberg, 1992.
Class, Heinrich, *Deutsche Geschichte*, Leipzig, 1919.

Dörr, F. & Kerl, W., *Ostdeutschland und die deutschen Siedlungsgebiete in Ost- und Südosteuropa*, Munich, 1987.

Henning, Emil, *Die Tausend-Mann-Aktion*, Farchant, 1994.
Herzog, Robert, *Die Volksdeutschen in der Waffen-SS*, Tübingen, 1955.

Janko, Dr. Josef, *Weg und Ende der deutschen Volksgruppe un Jugoslawien*, Graz, 1983.
Jost, Hanns, *Ruf des Reiches: Echo des Volkes*, Munich, 1942.

Michaelis, Rolf, *Die Waffen-SS: Mythos und Wirklichkeit*, Berlin, 2006.
Michaelis, Rolf, *Der Einsatz der Ordnungspolizei 1939-1945*, Berlin, 2008.

Neulen, Hans Werner, *Eurofaschismus und der Zweite Weltkrieg*, Munich, 1980.

Pencz, Rudolf, *Vor Haus und Hof und Kind und Weib*, Frankenstadt, 2010.

Reichenfelser, Heinz, *Sie folgten dem Ruf des Führers*, Graz, 1941.
Rumler, Gunther, & Otto Holzmann, *Freigemachtes Grenzland*, Berlin, 1942.

Scherzer, Veit, *Die Ritterkreuzträger*, Jena 2007.
Steenberg, Sven, *Sie nannten mich Gospodin…*, Munich, 1991.

Vegesack, Siegfried von, *Soldaten hinterm Pflug*, Berlin, 1944.
Voth, Berthold, *Das Pionier-Bataillon 114 der 114. Jäger-Division (vormals 714. Inf.Div.)*, Lahnstein, 1996.

Other Books by Rolf Michaelis

SS-Heimwehr Danzig in Poland 1939

SS-Fallschirmjäger-Bataillon 500/600

The 10th SS-Panzer-Division "Frundsberg"

The 11th SS-Freiwilligen-Panzer-Grenadier-Division "Nordland"

The 32nd SS-Freiwilligen-Grenadier-Division: "30.Januar"

Combat Operations of the German Ordnungspolizei,
1939-1945: Polizei-Bataillone • SS-Polizei-Regimenter

Cavalry Divisions of the Waffen-SS

Panzergrenadier Divisions of the Waffen-SS

The Kaminski Brigade

Belgians in the Waffen-SS

The German Sniper Badge 1944-1945

The German Tank Destruction Badge in World War II

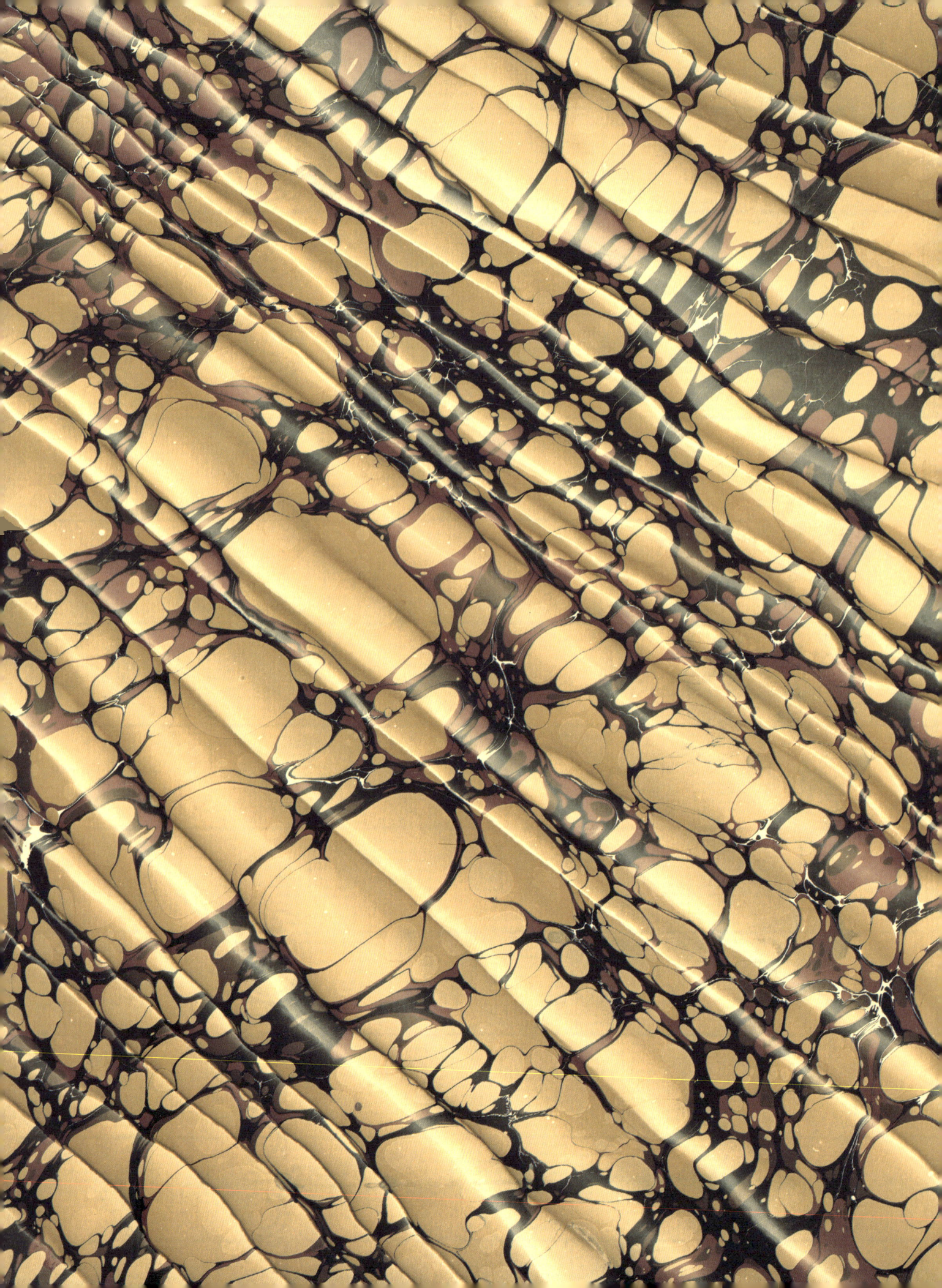